Harry Pearson was born and b̶... Teesside and is the author of ... His first book, *The Far Corner – A Mazy Dribble through North-East Football*, was shortlisted for the William Hill Prize and is still in print. He wrote a weekly sports column in the *Guardian* from 1996 to 2012, and has twice won the MCC/Cricket Society Prize for the Cricket Book of the Year. He lives in Northumberland.

Praise for *The Farther Corner*

'More than a quarter-century after *The Far Corner*, Pearson, older and perhaps a bit sadder, returns to grassroots north-eastern football and recaptures the qualities that made his earlier book a classic of football writing. Clear eyed about the economic challenges facing the region, he retains his trademark affectionate humour in depicting a world in which Easington Colliery v Ashington becomes "El Working Clasico" and there is a lingering "aroma of municipal biscuits". The index is a joy in itself.' *Guardian Books of the Year*

'Anyone missing the North East's trademark humour could do worse than checking out Harry Pearson's books on the region's football scene, *The Far Corner* and its sequel *The Farther Corner*. The latter contains a joke on page 17 that is alone worthy of a Nobel Prize.' *The Journal*

THE FARTHER CORNER

A SENTIMENTAL RETURN TO
NORTH-EAST FOOTBALL

HARRY PEARSON

SIMON &
SCHUSTER

London · New York · Sydney · Toronto · New Delhi

First published in Great Britain by Simon & Schuster UK Ltd, 2020
This edition published in Great Britain by Simon & Schuster UK Ltd, 2021

1 3 5 7 9 10 8 6 4 2

Simon & Schuster UK Ltd
1st Floor
222 Gray's Inn Road
London WC1X 8HB

www.simonandschuster.co.uk
www.simonandschuster.com.au
www.simonandschuster.co.in

Simon & Schuster Australia, Sydney
Simon & Schuster India, New Delhi

A CIP catalogue record for this book
is available from the British Library

Paperback ISBN: 978-1-4711-8091-0
eBook ISBN: 978-1-4711-8090-3

Typeset in Bembo by M Rules
Printed and bound by CPI Group (UK) Ltd, Croydon, CR0 4YY

MIX
Paper from
responsible sources
FSC® C020471

CONTENTS

Introduction

Raindrops the size of gooseberries pounded down on the Perspex roof of the bus shelter. A needling wind swerved in off the river and from a nearby industrial estate a burglar alarm mimicked the noise of a dying triffid. 'Still,' the bloke standing next to me said, 'not too bad for August, all in all.'

He was a gaunt man, in his sixties, wearing a grey tweed coat and an old knitted wool football scarf. The bus arrived, windows misted, wheezing exhaust. We got on. A chap in a replica shirt who was already seated greeted the scarf man warmly. 'What fettle, nowadays?' he asked.

The scarf man smiled. 'Much better, much better,' he said. 'I had the six-month check and I got the all-clear.'

The other man expressed happiness at the good news. 'Aye,' the scarf man said and fingered the coloured band of wool around his neck. 'Mind, I've still got the pitiful agony of watching these bastards.'

The other man grimaced like he'd barked his shin on

a firebucket. 'This year's been painful,' he said. 'Bloody diabolical.'

'If I hadn't been to the doctors that much recently,' the scarf man said, 'I'd be round there now begging some tablets for it. Something to wean me off them, like.'

The second man said, 'Boots the Chemist ought to make some patches.'

'They need to get shot of the bloody manager,' the scarf man said. 'As much use as an ashtray on a motorbike.'

'Aye, but who'd we bring in?'

The scarf man mentioned a shop-worn name, one of those plausibly suited managers who never seem to achieve much, yet somehow never lack for work. 'He's available and he's well respected.'

'If he's well respected why the hell would he come to us?'

The scarf man laughed mirthlessly. 'Aye, we don't want anyone that'd have us.'

The bus chugged on through the swirling rain, past a beauty salon with a banner yelping 'Brexit tan! No visa required!!', a shop offering 'balloons for all occasions' and a funeral home with a punning name and a row of football club-coloured coffins in the window.

The pair of fans tried to raise the mood by talking about the parlous state of local rivals, but it was plain their hearts weren't in it. The bus shunted to a halt by a viaduct, opposite a flat-roofed pub with a poster in the window for an upcoming performance by an Irish country and western singer ('The Next Daniel O'Donnell' it said, as if one wasn't enough).

'You getting off here?' the man in the scarf asked.

The other man shrugged, sighed and said, 'I was hoping not to. But aye, come on, let's go and take our punishment like men.'

It was early afternoon Saturday in North-East England. What team did these men support? It hardly mattered. The region's big three – Newcastle United, Middlesbrough and Sunderland – were all the source of bitterness and misery. Indeed, an outsider coming here might have formed the impression that the only time a local fan would happily get behind his or her team was if they were perched on the edge of a cliff and just needed a nudge to send them into the thrashing seas below. Yet still the supporters soldiered wearily onward, penitents bound for a floodlit reliquary.

Over the past twenty-five years, football had changed beyond all recognition. In 1992, the twenty-two clubs that comprised the old first division resigned from the Football League en masse and, with the connivance of the Football Association, a body so spineless it had to be carried round in a bucket, set up the Premier League. The first major TV deal this new, independent organisation struck with BSkyB was worth £191.5 million. Five years later it had risen to £670 million. The current deal with Sky Sports and BT brought in £4.4 billion. The FA Premier League was broadcast to 643 million homes across the globe, reaching an audience of 4.7 billion people.

Money had brought great changes. Before the Premier League and the implementation of the post-Hillsborough

Taylor Report, most clubs still played in the same rickety, unimproved grounds our grandfathers had watched in. You queued at the turnstiles, stood on crumbling concrete terraces crushed against rusting steel barriers, waded into the antediluvian toilets where the vandalised sinks offered as much hope of water as the Gobi Desert. The catering facilities were summarised by a friend's visit to the tea bar at Ayresome Park in the 1980s. Ahead of him a burly man in a donkey jacket asked for a black coffee. 'Can't do it,' the lad behind the counter replied. 'Got a new system. All the cups have coffee whitener put in them ready for the rush.'

The customer sniffed. 'Give me a black tea then,' he said.

The server shook his head. 'Same problem, pal, there's powdered milk in the cups, isn't there?'

The customer growled, 'Well, have you got owt that's black?'

The server thought for a second then said, 'The pies are the nearest, do you want one?'

Big television deals and Lord Justice Taylor had changed all that. New all-seater stadiums were built, old ones improved and expanded beyond recognition. Foreign stars flooded in. The quality of football improved as markedly as the grounds. Looking around Sunderland's freshly opened Stadium of Light, a friend breathed in the smell of fresh paint and mint plastic, grinned and said, 'It's like I went to bed with Thora Hird and woke up next to Uma Thurman.'

But, like A-list actresses, the new football was high maintenance. Games kicked off at whatever times the TV paymasters wanted, with no thought for how away fans might get home afterwards. Supporters were no longer the major source of a club's revenue, yet still ticket prices surged upwards like Wynn Davies with rocket boots. What had once cost the same as a trip to the pictures was now more like a night at the opera. People said the high cost had made football 'middle class'. That wasn't true – instead it had made the fanbase middle-aged, as only the well established could afford the prices. The average age of fans watching Premier League matches gradually nudged upwards until by 2018 it was close to fifty. Football – at the highest level – became another form of consumerism, the clubs and their multinational teams as dislocated from the everyday lives of their patrons as any Hollywood studio.

In the 1990s, North-Easterners like the Halls at Newcastle, Steve Gibson at Middlesbrough and Sunderland's Bob Murray had looked like exceedingly wealthy men. They spent heavily. Their teams did well. In 1996, Newcastle United came within a Graham Fenton goal of winning the Premier League title under Kevin Keegan (that Blackburn's Fenton was born and raised in North Shields was an irony so bitter you could strip the rust off gutters with it) and beat Barcelona in the Champions League with rubber-legged Colombian Faustino Asprilla scoring a hat-trick. Sunderland moved to the magnificent Stadium of Light and under Peter Reid, with Kevin Phillips finding the net with the alacrity of a suicidal haddock, finished seventh in the Premier League. Middlesbrough moved into a new stadium too, signed the Brazilian footballer of the year and an Italian who'd scored the winning goal in the previous season's Champions League final, claimed their first major trophy and played in European and domestic finals.

But the balance soon tilted. In 1997, Mohamed Al-Fayed acquired Fulham for £6.25 million, the first foreign billionaire to buy an English club. Six years later, Roman Abramovich bought Chelsea. Over the next decade and a half, he'd pump £900 million into the club. At Manchester City, owner Sheikh Mansour, deputy prime minister of the United Arab Emirates, spent £1.4 billion on new players. Transfer fees and wages soared. The old joke about a footballer breaking his foot by dropping his wage packet on it had to be abandoned. No envelope would hold it. He'd need a wheelbarrow or a shopping trolley.

On the bus through Ryton one morning in 2014, an elderly lady held up the back page of the *Daily Mirror* to show the pensioner sitting beside her. 'Have you seen this? Wayne Rooney is getting £300,000 a week.' Her friend sniffed, 'Aye, but he'll lose his child benefits, mind.' You had to laugh.

By 2010, club owners who'd once seemed super rich looked like they were barely scraping by. The pop-eyed, disbelieving excitement that had swirled around St James' Park, the Stadium of Light and the Riverside started to look like the product of some fervid dream.

'They think this is normal. They don't realise how lucky they are,' older fans chuntered, sounding like people who'd lived through wartime rationing did back in the 1970s if you said you didn't like mashed potato. And now the crazy days were over.

At Newcastle, the heady optimism drained slowly away like air from a punctured Frido. There were scandals, relegations, changes of managers and owners. Keegan left and came back. Alan Shearer retired as a player and returned briefly as manager. Joe Kinnear arrived and swore at a rate that amazed those parts of the world where the average schoolkid can't slip three expletives into the word hamburger. The soon to be reviled Mike Ashley bought the club and then tried to sell it again. Twice.

Sunderland were bought by a consortium of Irish millionaires and briefly looked like they might be on to something. Then the Irish economy collapsed. The millionaires sold out to a wealthy Texan oilman who knew nothing about the game beyond what others told him. When Paolo Di Canio arrived as boss in March 2013 amid protests about his fascist past, it was said it was on the advice of a waiter at the owner's favourite Italian restaurant. 'You want to have a say in how our team is run,' my old next-door neighbour who'd followed them since Raich Carter's days said with a scowl, 'you need to carry a giant peppermill.' Di Canio soon scuttled off. So did Gus Poyet, Dick Advocaat, Sam Allardyce, David Moyes, Simon Grayson and Chris Coleman. Sunderland went for over a year without winning a single home game and tumbled into the third tier, amid grim rumours of impending financial ruin.

Middlesbrough fell too, though not as melodramatically. They were now exactly where they'd been twenty-five years before – stable, safe and in the top half of the second flight. The past once again lent disenchantment. After a dismal 0-1 home defeat to Preston North End, a teenage fan raged, 'Bloody Boro are bloody shite,' only for an older fan to admonish him: 'If you think that was shite you should have seen us when Bobby Murdoch was manager.'

Lower down the league the story was much the same. Darlington had been taken over by former safe-cracker turned fitted-kitchen magnate, George Reynolds. Reynolds promised European football in five years, and moved the club from their charming Feethams home to a new out-of-town stadium with marble sinks and glass elevators. The 'Reynolds Arena' had 25,000 seats. Darlington had 4,000 fans. Reynolds was jailed for money laundering, Darlington went bust three times in six years and ended up homeless and playing in the Northern League.

Hartlepool United, subtly backed by Norwegian oil money, rose to the third tier and their highest-ever finish in 2005. They reached the play-offs for the Championship twice, the final once. Ten years later, with oil prices slashed and the Scandinavians gone they were relegated from the Football League for the first time in their 109-year history. Reportedly £1.8 million in debt, they stood on the brink of oblivion.

Everything had changed, but for the North East's

professional clubs, success still seemed as far away as it had done before the Premier League was formed.

At Middlesbrough's Riverside Stadium, Tony Pulis's grim reign ground remorselessly on, delivering a headbutt to hope and a dead leg to joy. Having a drink with a fellow sufferer, I fondly recalled the days when football fans threw toilet rolls on to the field. 'The Boro have been that bad this season, I've been tempted to throw the whole toilet,' my friend said in response, 'and I wouldn't flush it first, either.'

A Sunderland-supporting neighbour told me how he'd gone to the gents midway through second half of a match at the Stadium of Light during the final bug-eyed months of David Moyes. On seeing the exit door open, he went straight through it and into the night never to return. It was like escaping from a prison camp, he said. 'I don't regret it at all. I was like one of the zombies heading towards the shopping mall in *Day of the Dead*. I had no idea why I was doing it. All the shite we've put up with, I couldn't even get angry any more. It was like I could hear someone behind me saying, "Leave it, lad. It's not worth it," and when I listened closely the voice was mine.'

The pessimism had even begun to affect the Geordies. Optimism was generally so high in Newcastle it sometimes seemed like Prozac was being pumped into Tyneside's water supply, but eleven years of Mike Ashley had taken its toll. In late July, I stood at the bar of a pub drinking with a Newcastle United season ticket-holder. He was twiddling with the vintage black and white scarf around his neck.

'I thought you said you'd burned your scarf when Ashley forced Keegan out?' I said.

'I did,' he said.

'Where's that one from, then?'

'The bedroom cupboard,' he muttered. 'I've got twelve.' He bent down and pretended to tie his shoelace, embarrassed to be caught in the age-old conflict between patriotism and principle. 'Well, eleven now, obviously,' he said when he rose again.

'Why did you buy twelve scarves?'

'I was young and excitable. It was the 1983–84 promotion season. I wrote each of the regulars' names on them in magic marker.' He turned the scarf so I could see the faded legend 'David McCreery', the last three letters of the surname scrunched together to fit across the white bar.

'Who'd you burn?' I asked.

'John Ryan.'

The man stood along the bar from us who'd been staring at yesterday's results in the *Racing Post* with a reproachful expression that suggested he'd divined a coded message in them about his early death, grunted, 'Good choice, lad.'

'I don't know,' I said. 'I think if he'd really been vexed about Keegan going he'd have set a match to Kenny Wharton.'

The bloke grinned. 'Eh, remember when he sat on the ball against Luton, Kenny?' the bloke said, chuckling. 'Gazza did keepy-ups on the edge of the box. Christ, could do with a laugh like that nowadays.'

My friend shrugged. 'Seems like a bloody lifetime ago,' he said. 'I tell you, even with Rafa … In near half a century of following Newcastle, no matter how hopeless we've been the season before, when August starts approaching I've always felt sure we'd win something. But now, nah. The title is out of reach and when did we last even *try* and win a cup? It's just stay in the Premier League to scoop up the TV money so you stay in the Premier League. Football used to be an escape from grim economic reality, now it *is* grim economic reality.'

'Bring back Imre Banana,' the bloke down the bar said.

My friend laughed. 'Aye,' he said, 'that's where we are – pining for inflatable fruit.'

While the big clubs struggled, non-League football in the North East experienced an unexpected renaissance. The Northern League, in particular, was rejuvenated. While some of the clubs I had watched over the decades – Langley Park, Eppleton, Ferryhill Athletic, Horden, Evenwood Town and even the splendid Jarrow Roofing – had disappeared off the face of the earth, others such as Marske United, Sunderland RCA, Morpeth Town, Newcastle Benfield and Heaton Stannington (whose supporter of the year for 2017-18 was a chocolate cocker spaniel named Harry) had sprung up in their stead, while former greats such as North Shields and South Shields had been revived.

Northern League clubs had won the FA Vase final at Wembley nine times since 2006. Attendances over the past five years had risen by 20 per cent, year on year. South

Shields had exceeded even that, home crowds rocketing from under a hundred to over a thousand in the space of a couple of seasons. Buoyed up by new ownership and a return to their original stadium, the Mariners signed Argentinian Julio Arca. Not to be outdone, Washington – whose ground was a long walk up the drive to the Nissan car plant – brought in French World Cup player Pascal Chimbonda, while Morpeth fielded a Republic of Ireland international and Ashington were managed by England's Ashes-winning pace bowler Steve Harmison. Yet the Northern League remained far from the glamour of the Premiership, run by enthusiasts not oligarchs, the preserve of the committed, the wilful and the eccentric.

But there was change and uncertainty here, too. When the English Football Association had established the league pyramid as a means – lest we forget – of making the England international team stronger, the Northern League had decided not to be part of it, fearing that years of tradition would be sacrificed and the provincial integrity of the league compromised by unfamiliar interlopers from far-distant places like Lancaster and Harrogate. Instead, it existed out on its own, much as the Lancashire League and Bradford League did in cricket, or the Juniors did in Scotland.

In 1991, after much soul-searching, the Northern League reversed that decision and was slipped into the pyramid at what would become – after years of tinkering and restructuring – the ninth tier (confusingly also called Step 6). This meant that by 2018, to reach Football League Division Two, a club from the Northern League would have to win promotion five times.

With the move up into the tier above discretionary, this in truth made little difference to the integrity of the Northern League. Most clubs that won the title simply stayed put. Moving up was too expensive for many, and too disruptive for all.

The secretary of a Northern League club told me, 'In the Northern Premier League, with midweek games away in South Yorkshire, Merseyside, Lincolnshire and the like, the problem isn't the travel costs – you could scrabble around and find the extra £25,000 or so a season for that. No, the trouble is the players. They'd need to take days off work to get to these places and a lot of them aren't able to do that. Our centre-forward's a PE teacher. He can't just nick off at two o'clock to get a coach to Warrington. You'd likely lose half your team the minute you won the title.'

In 2016, however, the Football Association chose to ignore such fears and made promotion compulsory. Any club that refused to go up would instead be relegated a division. Clubs that didn't want the turmoil promotion brought would, of course, be able to avoid it, simply by not finishing in the top two – a situation that promised to see the Northern League season ending with the equivalent of the slow bicycle race. Perhaps the FA will one day take a leaf out of boxing's book and withhold payments if teams aren't aggressive enough.

However well or badly its big clubs were doing, the North East had always been able to pride itself on being a place that produced top-class footballers. It was – as one local journalist put it – 'Soccer's Golden Nursery'. The North East's status as a 'hotbed of soccer' had been well merited. (A hotbed, incidentally, is described by a gardening book I happen to have handy as 'a glass-covered bed heated by a layer of fermented manure'. Hardly the sort of slogan the Northumbrian Tourist Board is likely to find useful.)

The hotbed's heyday was between the wars. In 1933, for example, there were 341 players from County Durham alone registered with Football League clubs. Herbert Chapman's all-conquering Huddersfield team of the 1920s rarely fielded less than eight. After that, the sheer numbers tailed off somewhat, yet the presence of the North-East players continued to be felt. In 1967, there were only four clubs in the first division that didn't have a footballer from the region in their first team squad. Burnley had twelve. Through the '70s and '80s, the pits and the steelworks and the shipyards shut, but it seemed like the North East would churn out footballers for ever.

In the 1996 European Championship, Paul Gascoigne and Alan Shearer were the stars of the England team that reached the semi-finals, while Steve Howey and Steve Stone both sat on the bench. But something had happened since. Fabio Capello's 2010 provisional World Cup squad of thirty included just two men – Michael Carrick and the now disgraced Adam Johnson – born in the region. In

2006, Sven-Goran Eriksson's final twenty-three mustered only Carrick and Stewart Downing – who managed 150 minutes of football between them. In 1998, Glenn Hoddle's sole North-Easterner was Super Al. In Korea/Japan in 2002, there were none at all.

In the European Championship in 2016, there was not a single North-Easterner in England's starting XI – and only two in the squad (one of them, Fraser Forster, was the privately educated son of a high court judge). The fact the team went out abysmally, defeated by Iceland, was hardly a consolation. In the 2018 World Cup, Washington-born Jordan Pickford, who looked like a kid you'd see hanging around outside the SPAR asking grown-ups to buy him cider ('It's for me mam. She's sick in bed. Honest, mister'), had briefly become a national hero, and Jordan Henderson from Sunderland had performed tidily enough, but it was hardly the stuff of myth and cliché. Much has been written about Scotland's marked decline as a producer of great footballers – whatever the causes of that slump might be they seem to have drifted south.

One summer day, I sat watching cricket in Ashington with an old man who recalled being told that he should get along to see East Northumberland Boys in a match at Hirst playing fields in the dismal years of the early 1950s. 'The sky was dark, the pitch was solid mud and there was this little, thin blond lad floating over the field like an angel.' That was Bobby Charlton. Bobby might have gone to Newcastle, the team he supported, or Sunderland, where his idol Len Shackleton was the star. Instead, warned off St James' Park by his uncle, Jackie Milburn – who, despite being a Tyneside idol, took a dim view of the way the Magpies looked after youngsters – he crossed the Pennines for Old Trafford.

The old man was now involved with running Ashington Hirst's junior teams. The previous season he'd had to fold one of them. 'The kids didn't want to play on a Saturday morning. I asked why not. They said they liked to go to the Metrocentre with their mates.' He made a snorting noise that was a mixture of astonishment, disgust and derision, like a man who'd just learned his wife had run off with a circus clown. 'I never thought I'd see the day when a lad from Ashington'd rather go shopping than play football.'

It was not just football in the North East that had been through major upheavals. In the past twenty-five years, the last coal mines in Durham and Northumberland had shut down, and the final blast furnace on Teesside had gone, too. While the centres of Newcastle, Durham and Middlesbrough were thriving with micro-pubs, artisanal coffee shops and restaurants popping up faster than you could keep track of, outside, in football's old heartlands, things were on the darker side of grim. As post-industrialisation entered what seemed like nuclear winter, Durham and Teesside were consistently named the most deprived regions in Western Europe; within the EU only parts of Romania were considered worse. While politicians spoke blithely of the transformative effects of social media and the internet,

County Durham had the lowest computer ownership in Britain. Large communities in the old coalfields didn't even have broadband. People blamed Margaret Thatcher. But the truth was that despite the presence in government of Tony Blair (MP for Sedgefield), Peter Mandelson (Hartlepool), Alan Milburn (Darlington) and David Miliband (South Shields), little beyond the cosmetic was done by New Labour to address the problems afflicting the region.

On the way to a game between Easington Colliery and Ashington, which a mate had dubbed 'El Working Classico', I'd stopped in at the Co-op to buy chocolate. It was 2.30 in the afternoon and the only other customer was a teenage boy wearing a puce velour dressing gown as an overcoat. Across the street the Black Diamond pub was boarded up, the brickwork soot-stained from repeated arson attacks. A friend had been in there one time, post-match, and everyone was drinking 50p past-their-sell-by-date cans of Carling and chasers of the duty-free scotch you could buy for a fiver from an iron-shuttered semi-detached down the road locals called the Booze House. The man sitting next to him said to the barmaid, 'If I was reincarnated I'd like to come back as a giro. You know why? Because a giro makes everybody happy.'

Later I saw what I thought was a driverless car. It turned out to be a tiny teenage joy rider. Every few seconds his head would pop up above the steering wheel like a stoat stalking a rabbit in a field of long grass. The nearest police station was miles away and, the locals believed, so under-manned at night they couldn't answer calls.

This far corner of England had always seemed separate, now it felt increasingly abandoned. Disillusioned, the population of the region's most blighted areas turned increasingly rightwards. The Labour Party remained blithely complacent to the shift. When an Irish journalist I know asked the head of Sunderland Council (Labour-controlled since 1972) what he was doing to address the rise of UKIP he replied airily, 'People are angry, but they'll calm down.' As Peter Mandelson had reputedly once remarked, Labour did not need to worry about the working class because they had nowhere else to go. But now they did. UKIP was like some shitty political version of homeopathy – nothing they said had any basis in fact, but just by listening they made people feel a little better. And when the referendum came, the poorest parts of the North East voted overwhelmingly to leave the EU. Perhaps if their own lives were ruined, there was some solace in taking everyone else into oblivion with them.

The North East had changed, football had changed and my life had changed, too.

When I moved back here and wrote *The Far Corner*, I was living in a rented cottage in Northumberland and had no regular income. Twenty-five years later, I found myself in exactly the same position. The years that followed 2010 didn't quite go the way I planned. A twenty-five-year relationship ended when my partner ran off with one of my friends, I had to sell the house I'd lived in for twenty years and stopped writing a column for the *Guardian* after seventeen. Income streams slowed to a dribble. Debt piled up.

I was a fifty-year-old single parent bringing up a teenage girl. I had to learn a new set of life skills. Up until that point, like most men, I couldn't even pronounce 'menstruation'; now I found myself in supermarkets making price comparisons on branded sanitary towels. I looked after my daughter as everything else turned to mulch and I didn't mind, because I thought that if she was all right, then nothing else mattered. Sometimes at night I'd walk over the bridge across the Tyne opposite my house and it seemed like she was the only thing anchoring me to the ground, that without her I'd float away into the darkness.

And then she went off to university and the house was empty.

When things had fallen apart, I'd gone to my first Northern League game in many years. Out in the old coalfields. Hoping to relocate something in the wreckage, or find a place to hide. The surface was rutted mud, the players so vulnerable-looking that whenever the ball struck their pale thighs with a sound like an angry chef slapping an oven-ready chicken you felt the urge to call social services. And when the Tannoy announced that the sponsor had selected the big number six as the home side's man of the match, the bloke behind me bellowed, 'How can there be a man of the match when they've all been cack?'

It was a poor reward for his team's heroism. Though I'd have to say that the big number six would not have been my choice either. He was a singular figure who combined the lumpy torso of a grizzly bear with the slender, awkward legs of a young camel. I could only recall him touching the ball once. He had collected a hopeful through pass and humped it directly into touch and then, when one of his own midfielders protested, pointed to his right eye and barked: 'Anticipate, Dazza, son. Anticipate.'

My man of the match would have been the bloke behind me. He had bottle-top glasses, an elaborate macramé bonnet of lank grey hair and a shiny baseball jacket in a shade of blue so electric it might have powered the floodlights. The bloke behind me had played a blinder. All afternoon he'd been subtly prodding and probing from his position near the left touchline. It had begun in the first minute when he noticed that the linesman nearest us bore a passing resemblance to Aled Jones and signalled it by singing 'Walking in the Air' in a high-pitched whine every time the official was called into action. And it burst thrillingly into life with the lightning turn and finish on the half-hour mark that produced: 'Jesus Christ, referee, if you fell in a barrel of tits you'd come out sucking your thumb.'

With five minutes to go, the opposition broke away and the linesman failed to signal an obvious offside. 'Stop pissing about with that snowman and wave your bloody flag, you squeaky Welsh twat,' the bloke behind me cried. The onrushing forward collected the pass, rounded the keeper and popped the ball in the net.

It was too much for the man in a camel-hair car coat who

had been standing at an oblique angle to play for the entire match. He stalked off, pausing only to howl indignantly: 'The pitch is shite. The ground is shite and you lot are a fucking disgrace.' As he walked away, the bloke behind me yelled after him in the nasal-posh accent of a train customer service announcement: 'Thank you for choosing the Welfare Ground. We hope to welcome you again soon.'

And after that he and the rest of the spectators fell silent. A cold wind was blowing from the North Sea but I felt a warm tingle rising in my chest. It was a small sign of restored hope.

From that day on I went to a game every week, whether I wanted to or not.

One Wednesday night a friend from London phoned. He asked what I'd been doing. 'I went to a Northern League game last Friday night, a Northern League game on Saturday, another one on Bank Holiday Monday and a fourth on Tuesday evening,' I said.

My friend whistled. 'Boy, you really like the Northern League,' he said.

'Nah,' I replied. 'It's just the best place to meet women.' Which was by no means true.

Paul Gascoigne once said that a football pitch was the only place it felt safe. I had a similar feeling about non-League grounds.

The Saturday my daughter left for London, I went to watch Jarrow Roofing play Burscough in the FA Cup second qualifying round. Roofing's ground was next to the old pithead workings of Boldon Colliery, now a country park of sorts, scrubby woodland and muddy paths, the hedgerows decorated with discarded plastic bags blowing from the new-build estates to the west. The ground looked like it was assembled from old doors and scrap metal. The tea-bar was in a shipping container. The lady who served you also did the announcements, breaking off from reading out the teams to hand over a hot dog.

'My daughter went off to university today, so if I start weeping into my tea that'll be why,' I told my friends. And they responded as I knew they would by starting to talk about Bobby Mimms and which manager you'd least like to use the toilet before you if you were staying in a caravan (Sam Allardyce was the most popular choice, or the least). There are more ways to show kindness and concern than hugging.

Jarrow took an early lead, then got a second. Burscough were from higher up the league pyramid. They were stronger and fitter. They hit back and were leading 4-2 at half time. I bumped into a fan I knew. He was with his father, a retired pitman in his eighties who came from Boldon. He shook his head at the way the game had turned. 'At 2-0 up we were crooning,' he said.

I went back to football for that stability, warmth and companionship. To get back in touch with the familiar, to find part of me that seemed to have got lost, to remember a time when I was unambiguously happy.

Gradually I found it, in the washing flapping on lines at

Crook while snow swirled around the Millfield Ground, and a trip to the clubhouse was interrupted by a man in camo-pants shouting, 'How, Harry! You'll likely not remember me, but we had a bit of a chat in the Wembley toilets, Tow Law v Tiverton in 1998.' Or the bloke on the train between Sunderland and Hartlepool (the Durham Riviera Express) saying, 'Las Vegas? Man, it's just like Seaham seafront with more sand.' Or the world's slowest sending-off, at Benfield with the ref yelling like he was driving cattle. Or a young Penrith forward who'd scored a fantastic goal coming off the field at Sam Smith's Park to be greeted by the question: 'Eee, when did you get your braces took off, pet?'

My life has changed since I moved back to the North East. I had found a home and then I had lost it and then gradually I found my way back to it again. And slowly life got better. Football was no longer the only sanctuary I could find, but still I never saw the floodlights of some distant ground twinkling in the northern darkness without feeling a tingle of gratitude and moisture forming in my eyes.

Twenty-five years ago I would look around a ground – Ironworks Road, Croft Park, Brewery Fields, Kingsway, wherever – and wonder about the elderly fleece-clad folk in the unfashionable hats who leaned gingerly against the crash barriers, warming their hands on Styrofoam cups of turgid soup, wheezing condensation into the coal-scented air, chuckling throatily when the youthfulness of the match official prompted the bloke behind them to yell, 'Give it up, referee, and concentrate on your paper round.' I speculated on the circumstances that had brought them here, the drift of their lives, the joy, the love and the loneliness. I had never thought then that over time I would become one of them. What follows is an account of the 2018-19 season. It is an answer of sorts to the questions of a younger me.

1

NEWCASTLE BENFIELD V STOCKTON TOWN

The Emirates FA Cup Extra Preliminary Round

Saturday 11 August 2018

The football year had begun for me with a pre-season friendly. The day was hot and so humid even the cinders were sweating. The away team had come up from Teesside and one of the travelling fans boomed out that he felt like he was in Su-fucking-matra.

'You can't really enjoy football unless you've a coat on,' the bloke behind me said, a comment that made little sense in a region where the women wore crop tops and sling-backs when it was snowing, unless, perhaps, the coat was metaphorical.

The PA played 'Fly Like an Eagle' by the Steve Miller Band followed by a Rory Gallagher track. I recalled a previous visit to this ground, on a teeth-chattering winter's day, when, in the gathering darkness, the fourth official produced a weird disco-light effect in one of the dugouts with his flashing signals board while the speakers blasted out 'Wombling Merry Christmas'. That same afternoon a home player had been forced to remove his underpants by the ref, because they were long-legged trunks that didn't match his playing shorts. He took the whole lot off while standing on the touchline. Full frontal nudity in sub-zero temperatures – at the time I'd thought that might be a good advertising slogan for the Northern League.

There was nothing so exciting today. The game of football finds itself compared to many things: war, poetry, art and grand opera. In the buttery light of late summer, while hope still burns ('If we bring in a decent left back and an attacking midfielder I reckon we'll be fine'), anyone searching for similes for the sort of game I was watching might settle for something altogether less grandiose or bombastic. Familiar, free from alarms, cosy, comforting and smelling slightly of municipal biscuits, you sink into the ninety minutes as you would a warm bath, or a long-running midweek sitcom. Around you, fans-of-a-certain age chuckle wryly over fondly remembered things – Barry Siddall's waistline, Barry Venison's pink suit, a lyric by Half Man Half Biscuit. It is like a post-punk *Last of the Summer Wine* in which Nora Batty's stockings have been replaced by Dirk's white socks.

Nearby stood a fellow with bloodhound jowls and half-moon specs whose every dark prediction of cataclysmic disaster for his own side ('He's talking himself to a red card here, Smithy. We'll be lucky to get to half time with nine men') made the dull plop of failure that followed seem a victory of sorts.

It was an uneventful game. The teams played with all the urgency of a schoolboy walking to double physics. But that was fine. We had come not for wild entertainment, but mild diversion – we were standing around out of doors in the sunshine and society was allowing us to pass it off as doing something. It was like fishing without the maggots.

On the touchline, I bumped into the manager of a Northern League club I'd had a few chats with over the years. I asked him how the summer had gone. He let out a prodigious snort, like a blue whale clearing its blowhole after a long dive in icy waters. 'These fucking young play-ers,' he said. 'They've started coming in with agents. Agents! I had one in last week, he says, "What are you offering my client?" I says, "Fifty a week and fish and chips after home matches." He says, "We want seventy." I says, "He can have sixty but he's not getting curry sauce." Fuck's sake.'

On the bus back into town the blokes in front of me discussed a list of Newcastle's possible signings. Quite lit-erally – one of them had written them out on what looked like a serviette from the tea bar, along with the likely prices. I wasn't surprised. Several summers ago I had been in a Durham taxi. When talk turned to football, the cabbie started outlining which players Sunderland should retain and which they should sell. He delivered his speech with a fluency that was impressive until I noticed he was reading it from a card he'd Blu-Tacked to his dashboard.

Making a list of signings is a traditional summer activity for football supporters. The first thing to do is identify the areas in your side that desperately need improvement. Experience shows that nine times out of ten the players any team will be most in need of are: a high-quality attacking left-back, a box-to-box midfielder who can really play and a twenty-five-goal-a-season striker. Sadly, there are even fewer of these types of player in the world than there are un-tattooed women working in chip shops and by the end of August Manchester City, Manchester United and Liverpool will be linked with all of them. If you don't happen to support these three, then the only consolation is the remembrance of the time a big London club bumped Boro out of signing a top Dutch international. I can still recall vividly the sweet feeling of euphoria that engulfed me a few months later when I finally saw Glenn Helders play for Arsenal. I expect the Germans have a word for it.

The season proper began with what had become my traditional curtain raiser – the extra-preliminary round of the FA Cup. The teams that began at this stage of the competition would have to win more games to get the first round proper of the competition than any Premier League team would to actually get their hands on the trophy. But there was prize money for the winners of every round and a run of four or five victories could make a club enough cash to keep them going for an entire season. The FA Cup might have lost its lustre as far as the mega-teams were concerned, but down here it still meant something and, as I boarded the train into Newcastle, I felt a tingle of excitement in my chest that wasn't entirely down to the bacon sandwich I'd eaten before leaving the house.

In the carriages, hen parties from Cumbria cackled and yelped, and club-chart ringtones intermingled with the popping of prosecco corks, the bursting of balloons and the occasional scream from a middle-aged man who was trying to read an ex-library copy of Kevin Beattie's seminal autobiography *On the Beat*.

Boozing on the train was now quite a hobby in the North East. At one time, train drinking had been confined to the occasional morose squaddie returning home on compassionate leave and slowly working his way through a four-pack of McEwan's best scotch. But then, at the start of the new century, people determined rail travel existed in a separate dimension from ordinary life and normal social conventions about alcohol consumption were suspended as soon as you stepped aboard. 'Fancy a drink?' 'Well, I wouldn't normally at 7.15 on a Tuesday morning, but, since we are on the train, I'll have a gin and tonic and pour it on my Weetabix.'

The same rules did not apply to buses. Railways were the public transport equivalent of international waters – at some point I felt sure the Trans-Pennine Express would be hosting cockfights.

The train pulled out of Dunston and headed towards the

river. A couple of minutes later a group of Chinese tourists who'd been visiting Hadrian's Wall jumped from their seats and began pointing excitedly and videoing the view. It was a common reaction nowadays, but it still brought a smile to my face. The river Tyne had been cleaned up years before and gradually the banks had, too. Now from the Malmaison Hotel, where the barman once told me that Patrick Kluivert – the Magpies' ultimate trophy signing – could not walk 10 yards across the threshold before 'there are Gosforth wives stuck all over him like Elastoplast', you looked on a spectacle of sleek modernity. At night, pastel-coloured light melted across the black, glossy surface of the water. The rainbow arch of one great bridge was echoed downstream by the blue-green span of another, glass sparkled and the sound of celebration echoed downstream.

I'd gone down there twenty years before with a Tyneside restaurateur I knew. He was keen to buy a property on the Quayside and set up a business. 'You can't look at it as it is now, you have to imagine how it will be in the future,' he said as we inspected a grim-looking concrete building with slit windows of glass bricks and the whiff of an abandoned public convenience. 'This is all going to be transformed,' he said. I looked down the street of crumbling, abandoned warehouses, weeds poking out from busted gutters, an ancient piece of whitewash graffiti celebrating the wonder of Micky Burns and the pleasures of terrace violence, and thought, 'Yeah, of course it is.'

But the restaurateur had been right. It had taken decades,

but in my mind it seemed to have happened in a split second. It was like that moment in a corny Hollywood movie when the frumpy girl next door takes off her glasses and – aw gee! – it's Grace Kelly!

There had been hot weather and sunshine since the start of May. Hay had been harvested before the end of June, the grain cut by the time July was done. The port-a-loos of the fruit-pickers in the fields along the Tyne had long since been towed away. The land was parched and burned out – hungover after the festival of July. The air felt like a dry cough. Every so often there had been a half-hearted spasm of fine rain, which had landed on the earth like a chaste kiss and evaporated. Unsurprisingly, therefore, the pitch at Sam Smith's Park was hard as a North Shields doorman and just as unforgiving.

There had been extensive work at Sam Smith's since my last visit in April. A gym had appeared to the left of the clubhouse and there was a new shed for covered standing that sadly also covered the big banner along the far fence that advertised double-glazing with the baffling slogan 'Bang goes your mangos'.

The new buildings were all made of tongue-and-grooved wood which gave that corner of the ground a scent of larch and pine and a general air of Scandinavia that the presence of the obligatory angry bloke yelling, 'Get involved, liner, for fuck's sake' quickly dispelled. The game had not yet begun, I might add. But the experienced match official barracker knows that if you do not warm up your vocal cords properly, you are likely to damage them just at the point when a 'Where's your yellow card, wedged up your arse?' is most needed.

I went into the Snack Attack tea bar and got a tea and a KitKat. They had other types of chocolate too, but what I had thought was a witty and amusing request for the lady who ran the place to 'Give me a twirl' had not gone down well two seasons earlier and I felt as if I was still on probation. In front of me at the condiments table, a groundhopper who'd travelled from Merseyside to tick off another club from his list was pouring milk into his Bovril. When he saw me looking at him askance, he said, 'It makes it smoother,' and when he sensed I wasn't yet convinced added, 'You put a swirl of cream in consommé, don't you?'

Over in the regular seats, things had a thankfully less *Larousse Gastronomique* edge to them. Newcastle had just lost their opening fixture at home to Spurs, but most of the people I was sitting with thought they had been defeated by fewer goals than expected and took heart from that. The conversation turned back to Kevin Keegan – it always would. It was easy to see why people would get nostalgic.

On an August night in 1995, I'd gone to watch newly promoted Boro take on Keegan's Newcastle at St James' Park. It was an uneven contest. Peter Beardsley, Les Ferdinand and Keith Gillespie played brilliantly and David Ginola so bamboozled Neil Cox that by the final whistle the full-back was wandering round as if someone had put a tin bucket over his head and banged it with a hammer for ninety minutes. That it only finished 1-0 was a minor triumph. In the away section even die-hard Smoggies who despised the Magpies with bitter and unrequited passion had a sparkle in their eyes. Well, not all of them, obviously. A few yards from me, a bloke in a 1970s replica shirt with a stomach like a dumpy bag of gravel leaned on the fence separating us from the home fans and bellowed, 'Yees will win nowt.' 'Well, yees'll win nowt neither,' came the reply. The Middlesbrough fan puffed out his chest: 'We're the Boro, we don't expect to win owt.'

He was right, as it turned out. Keegan's Newcastle didn't win anything. Eighteen months later, after signing Alan Shearer and thrashing Manchester United 5-0, Special K had quit. Yet he lurked in the Geordie consciousness like King Arthur and his knights, slumbering until the hour of peril arrived. One fan, quoted in the *Daily Mirror* during one of many later crises at St James', raved, 'If Keegan came back tomorrow and wiped this shower of bastards away it would be like Christ throwing them crooks out of the temple.' If the biblical tone hardly seemed to fit the man himself ('Behold a pale horse: and his name that sits upon it shall be ... Mighty Mouse?'), it caught the mood on Tyneside perfectly.

Mike Ashley took total control of Newcastle United in the summer of 2007. At first, the Londoner was greeted as a hero. When he'd bought the club he'd been described as a recluse but now here he was downing pints with fans post-match in the Quayside bars where the waitresses wore bikinis and cowboy hats, and watching the football wearing a replica shirt and the sort of blank yet benign expression adopted by Her Majesty the Queen when attending a break-dancing display by disadvantaged youngsters.

In January of the following year, he sacked Sam Allardyce, a man whose pragmatic style of football, Sunderland playing career, and general air of someone who's bitten into a barbecue sausage only to discover it's actually a slug, had never endeared him to the Magpies' faithful. Wild rumours circulated about Fat Sam's successor. My milkman reported a definite sighting of José Mourinho outside a Chinese restaurant in Ponteland by a source close to his brother-in-law's best mate Liam; the postman confirmed reports from our Sandra's hairdresser that a suite has been booked at Malmaison in the name of Lippi; while the coalman whispered through the letterbox that this morning he took an order for ten sacks of best cobbles from 'a fella with a French accent in Ryton' and that I could draw my own conclusions from that 'because it stands to reason that if you've been living in Monaco you are going to find the weather up here a good bit chillier than what you're used to'. I finally learned the truth through the window cleaner. 'KEEGAN IS BACK,' he bellowed at me through the glass. 'THE MESSIAH RETURNS. AGAIN. IT'S THE THIRD COMING.' Football is a religion up here, you see.

Keegan was equally ecstatic about his new job, declaring that returning to St James' Park was like 'coming home' while more or less simultaneously proclaiming that he had 'never really left'. Ashley's decision was hailed by all. He was the toast of Tyneside. Then, just seven days after appointing Keegan, Newcastle's owner brought in ex-Wimbledon and Chelsea winger Dennis Wise as director of football. The Toon Army anticipated big-money signings comparable to the sort Keegan had pulled off in the past: David Ginola, Les Ferdinand, Alan Shearer. Instead, thanks to the efforts of Wise, they got half a dozen Spanish and South American players they had never heard of, and would come – in the case of Xisco – to wish the situation had stayed that way.

As the summer transfer window creaked shut, Newcastle sold one of their outstanding performers, James Milner, to Aston Villa. Talk was that money would be used to bring in exciting replacements, yet nothing happened. After six months of rumbling discontent, fan protests against the 'Cockney Mafia' and an eerie silence from within the club, it was finally confirmed that the Messiah had left the building. He remained in spirit – the source of misty water-coloured memories and vengeful dreams.

Luckily, before things could turn too wistful or vexatious at Sam Smith's Park, our attention was drawn to the field of play by the billowing cries of Benfield's long-serving and impressively acrobatic keeper, Andrew Grainger (an England beach football international), who had reacted to the visitors' early aerial assault by bellowing 'Big head! Big head! Big head!' at his defenders.

Benfield's opponents Stockton Town had reached the FA Vase final the season before, losing at Wembley by a single goal to Thatcham Town. They attracted decent crowds to their Bishopton Road West ground, a large number of them disgruntled Boro fans tired of the lumpy gruel served up at the Riverside by Aitor Karanka and his successor Tony Pulis. Town were not the original Stockton club; they hadn't been formed until 1979 and then only as a junior team. They'd grown rapidly after deciding to run senior football sides in 2008 and raced up from the Teesside and Wearside Leagues to join the Northern League in 2016. They'd won the Division Two title in their first season.

Their arrival had filled a void left in Stockton by the demise in 1975 of the town's original team, Stockton FC, who were known as 'The Ancients' and played in rather dashing red and black quartered shirts. The Ancients were formed back in the 1880s, were founder members of the Northern League, and won the title five times. They also won the FA Amateur Cup in 1899, 1903 and 1912 and were runners up four times. In a whimsical twist, the Ancients decided that any player who scored three goals in a match should not be given the traditional hat but an overcoat instead. Thus protected against the chill wind off the Tees, the Ancients moved into the semi-pro ranks just before the Second World War and were North Eastern League Champions in 1951.

One former Stockton player, Bob Chatt – from Barnard Castle – had moved to Aston Villa in the late Victorian era. His goal after just thirty seconds in the FA Cup final of 1895 would be fastest in the Cup final until Louis Saha netted in twenty-five seconds for Everton in 2009. Though Chatt had a place in football history, Stockton's greatest player was undoubtedly the legendary Ralph Smith, a short, stocky, beady-eyed striker who in photos appears so hawk-like you feel he might dart out and give you a nasty peck on the hand.

An engine-driver by trade, Smith's howitzer-like shooting earned him the nickname 'Bullet'. He won six amateur caps for England but truly earned national notoriety for his scandalous behaviour during and after the 1933 FA Amateur Cup final. The match was played at Ayresome Park; Stockton's opponents were Kingstonian, who by all accounts decided to play the match under Marquis of Queensbury rules. After a good deal of hacking and thwacking, Ancients' full-back Jack Thompson was carried off with a badly damaged knee. With no substitutions allowed, the southerners took full advantage of their numerical superiority overturning a one-goal deficit to win 4-1. Bullet was incandescent. He stormed off without collecting his loser's medal from FA President Sir Charles Clegg, and then got mortal at the post-match banquet and abused the dignitaries in terms so industrial it fair singed their eyebrows. The FA called an inquiry and suspended Bullet from all football for twelve months without appeal.

Back in the present day, Stockton applied most of the early pressure, but it was Benfield who scored first. Paul Brayson netting the rebound when his penalty kick was saved by Michael Arthur. Brayson had been one of

Keegan's first signings for Newcastle during the Geordie Messiah's debut resurrection. He'd never made a first-team appearance for the Magpies but he'd clocked up close to 200 League appearances for Swansea, Reading, Cardiff and Cheltenham. He was over forty, and spent more time running his taxi business than he did running about the pitch, but he still had the flicks and tricks along with the veteran pro's unfading ability to snipe at referees and point to where his team-mates *ought* to have passed the ball. His goal-scoring record in the Northern League was extraordinary – he'd hit close to forty every season.

The goal was celebrated mildly in the stand. But Stockton's full-back, James 'Munchie' Risbrough, who'd played for Ytterhogdals IK in the Swedish fourth division as well as in more exotic places such as Spennymoor, took it badly. 'Fuck off!' he shouted at nobody in particular.

'Mind your language,' someone shouted from the stand.

'Fuck off!' the defender answered.

'There are bairns here.'

'Fuck off!'

It wasn't P. G. Wodehouse, or even plain PG, but you had to admire his consistency. Later, when he struck a long-range shot that pinged off the bar, one of the blokes behind me called out, 'Oh I say, well played, James' in a mock posh voice. And the full-back looked in his direction and burst out laughing. He was a good player, quick and strong and seemed like a decent bloke, too.

Stockton levelled just before the interval, Nathan

Mulligan – who'd played for Darlington towards the end of their League days – striking a long-range curler over the leaping Grainger and into the top right-hand corner of the goal.

We repaired to the committee room for soup and scones. Phones bleeped with updates from games around the North East as racing from Wincanton went by silently on a wall-mounted TV. The Scouse groundhopper poked his head around the door and enquired if there might be anything for vegetarians. After a pause a white-haired bloke who was in charge of the tea urn shouted: 'You can crack the casing off a scotch egg, if you like.'

Just as Stockton Town had filled the vacuum left by the demise of Stockton FC, so Benfield had plugged a hole left in Tyneside non-League football by the implosion of Newcastle Blue Star. Blue Star had won the FA Vase in 1978 and the Northern League title in 2006, but an attempt to make it in the Northern Premier League backfired – as it did for a number of North-East clubs – and they went bust in 2009.

Formed in 1988, Benfield had performed decently in the Northern League top flight, winning the title in 2009, but crowds were modest, topping out at around 120. Back in 2016, when football at the lower end of the pyramid began to attain a certain craft-ale hipsterishness, the club briefly had its own band of ultras. Sadly, their attempt to create the atmosphere of Napoli's Curva Nord had foundered. Partly this was because Northern League fans are not as febrile as those in Campania, but mainly it was because the Benfield Ultras were only two in number and therefore couldn't bang their drum and hold up their banner at the same time.

At some point they had given up and disappeared. Now games at Sam Smith's were played out to the more traditional Northern League sounds of inventive swearing and the noisy sucking of boiled sweets. There was, I should say, generally a resistance to noise at Northern League games. Once, when travelling Ashington fans had been celebrating a goal rather too vociferously away at Northallerton, the steward had emerged from the clubhouse and asked them to pipe down because 'there are people in there trying to watch *Inspector Morse*'.

The second half meandered along in the sunlight, the chat on the terraces only disturbed by the defenders yelling 'Don't foul! Don't foul!' whenever an opposition player had the ball in the box. I'm not sure why defenders shout this. It seems a bit pointless, like fielders in cricket shouting 'Catch it!' when a batsman slaps one straight into the air. Though I guess it's possible that in the dressing rooms after every match, team-mates are being thanked for the reminder with the words, 'If you hadn't shouted that I'd likely have got him in a headlock and rammed him into the stanchion.'

The game went to a replay. Benfield won it 3-0.

I walked down and caught the Metro at Walkergate. In the city centre, crowds in replica shirts milled around the entrances to pubs blurred in the fog from e-fags. St James' Park towered over Newcastle as a cathedral must have done above a medieval city. Sitting in the upper tiers there was certainly a feeling of watching events from a bell tower. For away fans binoculars wouldn't be a bad idea. They were tucked away in the top corner of what used to be the ramshackle Leazes End, so high above the pitch low-lying clouds would interfere with their view of the action.

The giant Scottish and Newcastle brewery that stood opposite the stadium had been closed in 2004 and demolished a few years later – Sir Bobby Robson had pushed the detonator. This was no great loss to beer lovers, I should add. As my friend Steve's father – who'd spent his entire career there – once remarked, 'I started off as a brewer and ended up a chemical engineer.'

The area the brewery had once occupied had been rapidly filled with a flashy jumble of shiny buildings that seemed designed to impress on us that we were living somewhere bold, dynamic and global. To me it looked like a Poundland Rotterdam, not that I know anything about it, obviously.

On the westbound platform at Central station a middle-aged bloke with the long swinging hair of a '70s guitar hero walked towards me with the swaying, heavy-footed tread of the true metal fan, his hair flailing as if to the beat of a renegade drum. Another older man greeted him and asked what he was up to.

'I'm out on the drink the night.'

'Are you taking him with you?' the older man said, indicating the long-haired man's son, a ten-year-old with a round face and the saucer-like damp eyes of a child in a Woolworth's painting.

The boy shook his head then smiled, 'Not tonight but in ... eight years' time he will be.'

Ah, the crazy dreams of children.

2

DUNSTON UTS V
PONTEFRACT COLLIERIES

The Emirates FA Cup Preliminary Round

Saturday 25 August 2018

My daughter was home from London. At breakfast, I'd been telling her about the time back in 2002 I went to see Glenn Tilbrook from Squeeze play in a local pub and how, when he sang The Monkees' 'Daydream Believer', he gave up at the first chorus because the entire Mags-supporting crowd was singing the 'Cheer Up, Peter Reid' version and then they'd effortlessly segued from that into 'Peter Reid peels bananas with his feet' to the tune of 'Yellow Submarine'. When I'd finished laughing and wiping the tears from my eyes, my daughter looked at me sternly and said, 'I'm sorry, but I don't know who any of those people are.'

To avoid a further crushing, I got the train to Gateshead Metrocentre and walked along to UTS Park via Marks and

Spencer's food hall where I scoped the shelves for dramatic reductions. I'd got to a stage in my life when swooping on a stack of profiteroles that had just had a yellow label stuck on them slashing the price to £1.30 was the closest I'd ever get to picking up a winners' medal in the Champions League. Though, of course, you wouldn't be able to eat that for pudding with a few raspberries, so in many ways it was even better. Saturday lunchtime wasn't a good time for bargains, though – you really needed a midweek evening kick-off for them – so I contented myself with a Turkish delight bar and some cheese puffs.

At UTS Park I took up my regular seat next to Jimmy and Margaret. When I first met Jimmy and Margaret I was at a low point in my life. Admittedly the worst of those awful days – when I would occasionally curl up on cushions on the sitting-room floor and fall asleep next to the dog just for the comfort of living warmth – had passed, but every so often I'd open a drawer or a cupboard door and the past would leap out and stab a fork in my eye. That morning I'd been looking for a notebook with empty pages in it and the first one I'd picked up had fallen open on the words: 'I feel like I am staring at pictures of my own autopsy!' It was hard to know what was more painful – the reawakened memories of the dark, abysmal hours when I had written it, or the realisation that despair had driven me to using an exclamation mark.

I had arrived at UTS Park back then filled with a strange and chilling dread and was greeted by a jolly stranger with a big grin and a firm handshake, who said, 'Hey, Harry. Nice to meet you. You knew Kenny Twigg, did you?'

And that was Jimmy, a 75-year-old of such bubbling Geordie cheerfulness and enthusiasm that his smile alone could have heated an aircraft hangar. And in an instant I was back in the hazy world of two decades before when everything had seemed settled and yet filled with infinite possibility and I had imagined that around every corner was a glittering opportunity surrounded by an appreciative crowd rather than a bear trap: sharp, jagged teeth tipped with poison excreted by a venomous reptile.

I sat down with him and his wife Margaret offered me a paper bag filled with toffees. 'Aye, Kenny Twigg, he was a lovely fella,' Jimmy said.

Back in the 1960s my dad had worked at Dorman Long steelworks with Kenny Twigg. When I started writing about football, my dad had sent me to see him. 'If you want to know about football, you'll need to talk to Kenny,' he said. By then, Kenny was long retired. He lived in a neat bungalow in Hartburn, one of the leafier bits of Stockton-on-Tees. I got the train and then a bus. When I arrived, Kenny Twigg was sitting at the kitchen table, a stack of leather-bound scrapbooks piled in the centre. His wife brought tea and biscuits. 'Before we get started, I'll use the facilities,' Kenny Twigg said.

When he'd gone his wife patted me on the arm, nodded towards the books, 'I do hope he's not going to bore you too much, pet,' she said.

Kenny was born in Hetton-le-Hole. In 1939, he played right-wing in the Bishop Auckland team that won the FA Amateur Cup. One of his team-mates was Bob Paisley. Paisley came from Hetton, too. He was one of the stars of the team. 'Bishops used to send a car to pick him up and I'd be waiting at the bus stop,' Kenny said with a grin, 'Bob'd give me a little wave as he passed.'

Paisley wasn't the only great football manager to come from Hetton, I should add. Kenny Twigg had been at school with another of them, Harry Potts. Potts had turned Burnley into one of the greatest clubs in Europe. Potts was born a few doors up from his lifelong pal Paisley, a few streets away from a future Burnley and Spurs star, Ralph Coates. Burnley's attacking style of play and mastery of deadball routines had been established before Potts took charge, by the Northumbrian Alan Brown.

Potts's coaching style seems to have been less focused than that of his predecessor, one ex-player claiming that the only instruction the manager issued was that the wingers should use the Turf Moor advertising hoardings as a guide and 'never cross till you get to the "T" in Woolworth'. Despite, or maybe because of that, Burnley won the title in 1960 and came close to doing the Double a couple of years later.

Kenny Twigg told my dad all about Bob Paisley while they were working together on a site in Liverpool in the 1960s. My dad had no idea who Bob Paisley was. Few people did in those days. Paisley was Anfield backroom. He was invisible, standing in Bill Shankly's massive shadow – likely wearing a cardigan and carpet slippers.

When Shankly resigned and Liverpool gave his job to Bob Paisley, my dad phoned Kenny. He said, 'Is this new Liverpool manager the bloke you played with at Bishop Auckland?'

Kenny confirmed it was.

'It will be tough job, following Shankly,' my dad said.

'If anyone can do it, Bob can,' said Kenny Twigg.

Kenny had made his debut for Bishop Auckland when he was seventeen. 'There was a flu epidemic in Durham, half the team went down with it.' His first game was against Shildon. The Railwaymen were Bishops' biggest rivals in the Northern League; they had won the title four times in the previous five years. The game at Dean Street brought Kenny up against the legendary full-back Alf 'Whacker' Wild.

'People say Alf Wild was terrifying. And it's true that when he tackled you, you knew you'd been tackled. But I tell you something about him. I was pretty quick. First time I got the ball, I pushed it round him and I was away, got my cross in. He trotted over, "You're a young lad and you're new to this," he said. "So I'm going to let you off that one. Next time you do it, I'll break your bloody leg." So, you see, Alf Wild was rough, but he give you fair warning.'

Kenny Twigg poured tea. He asked after my father. He told me proudly of some complex engineering problem they'd overcome when building a bridge together in

Newport. I nodded wisely. Kenny Twigg took down the top scrapbook and opened it. The book was neat and tidy. The clippings straight and sharp. The captions, written in clear block capitals, gave the date, the place, the names. I recognised the style. My father's photo albums from his National Service days were just like this – the utilitarian aesthetic of the drawing office.

'Now,' Kenny Twigg said, tapping his finger on a faded postcard-sized team photo. 'This is the best side I ever played in – Willington Juniors.'

I peered at the picture. 'Five of these lads turned pro,' Kenny Twigg continued. The best known of them was George Storey, who played for Brentford several seasons, then returned to Durham when his playing days were over and went back down the pit.

'All the boys were good players, all of them,' Kenny Twigg said, 'but the star of the team was this boy, Billy Pears. Everybody called him "Biker". He was centre-forward. Strong. Quick. Fearless. Brilliant. He kept Tommy Lawton out of the England Schoolboys side. Newcastle had him on their books.'

'What happened?' I asked

'Accident at the pithead,' Kenny Twigg said. 'A steel joist fell on him, broke his spine. He had to wear a steel girdle after.'

We both grimaced. Heavy industry was like a warzone. The pit disasters lived in the public memory, but men were maimed every day. Steel erectors had the lowest life expectancy in Britain. In the big works, danger lurked round every corner. Men fell off buildings, were scalded by steam. Cranes toppled, boilers exploded, steel cables snapped, gas hissed, roofs collapsed. Limbs and lives were lost, promising sporting careers terminated.

The boys from Willington Juniors had all gone to work in mines, foundries, shipyards, steelworks and chemical plants. Several had suffered debilitating mishaps at work, a couple had not made it through the war.

'Aye,' Kenny Twigg said, looking at the youthful smiling face of Biker Pears, 'He was on the Magpies' books, Biker. If it hadn't been for the accident, I wonder if we'd ever have heard of Jackie Milburn.'

Kenny Twigg had died in 1998. He was ninety-two, but older people remembered him still. Jimmy's dad, like Kenny Twigg, came from Hetton-le-Hole and had played in the same junior team as Bob Paisley. 'He was a canny player, my dad,' Jimmy had said. 'Midfielder. Played with Carl Straughn and Kenny, too. Only problem was my father had trouble with his eyesight. He wore these thick, thick glasses. The lenses were like the bottom of pop bottles. When he put them on, his eyes looked the size of cooking apples. He couldn't play in them. Too dangerous. People who watched said he was brilliant when it was bright and sunny, but the minute the sky darkened he was instantly bewildered. Couldn't see owt. Just blundered about the field bumping into people.'

An obvious joke about several Newcastle players

suggested itself, but we left it alone. 'Nowadays he'd have worn contact lenses and who knows what he might have done then,' Jimmy said wistfully.

Jimmy had been involved with Dunston in one capacity or another since their early days playing out of the Mechanics Social Club. In 1986, the club – which had begun life as a works team for Her Majesty's Stationery Office – had signalled their growing ambition by leasing a ploughed field half a mile east of the Metrocentre and turning it into a ground. In 1987, they attracted sponsorship from the massive Federation Brewery – which overlooked the ground and produced millions of pints of fizzy beer for the local social clubs that owned it – and became Dunston Federation Brewery, entering the Northern League in 1991.

With manager Bobby Scaife, they won the League and Challenge Cup double in 2004 and 2005. Scaife, who came from Northallerton, had been signed by Middlesbrough as a boy and for a long while had held the distinction of being the only Middlesbrough player ever to get a winners' medal at Wembley – in the apprentices' race before the 1972 FA Cup final. He later played for Hartlepool and Rochdale. In Mark Hodkinson's wonderful book about Dale, *The Overcoat Men*, Scaife is described as having 'legs like dustbins, a big pirate face and straggly beard'.

In 2006, the Federation Brewery had withdrawn sponsorship. The brewery had been taken over by Scottish and Newcastle and became the place where Newcastle Brown Ale was made. Newcastle Brown Ale had a European demarcation order placed on it that meant it could only be brewed on Tyneside. In 2009, after a long legal battle, Scottish and Newcastle got the order repealed, moved production of Newcastle Brown to West Yorkshire and knocked the brewery down. It was hard to imagine the champagne producers of France fighting to have their appellation removed so they could centralise production in Chile, but in global capitalist Britain there was no room for such outdated parochial pride. Thank heavens.

Dunston found a new sponsor in pipeline company UTS. In their new guise as Dunston UTS, they won the FA Vase in 2012 with record scorer Andrew Bulford – a warder in a youth offenders' centre in Consett – getting a goal in every round and two in the final. Dunston had rarely finished outside the top six in the Northern League, but the previous season they'd struggled – an unlucky 2-3 defeat in the FA Vase quarter-final knocking the stuffing out of them. Results had gone haywire, they'd slumped down the table and fans drifted away until there was only about 140 in the ground for home matches. They were one of my favourite clubs and they needed a good season.

It was warm, sunny afternoon, shadows from the trees shading the touchline over by the Tommy Cooney Stand. Once again I had come prepared for winter, my bag stuffed with a fleece, gloves, hat and an extra pair of socks, when what I really needed was sunglasses and a bucket hat.

The game kicked off. Up behind me a man with amber-lensed sunglasses, wispy, saffron-tinged hair and the general look of an actor who'd have been cast as 'Continental Pornographer' in a 1970s' TV adaptation of a Len Deighton spy novel did what he did every match and bawled, 'Time! Time!' at any Dunston player who had the ball.

It was an acute case of Repetitive Saying Syndrome, the habit that some fans seem to pick up of yelling the same phrase over and over again during the course of a game, a season, a lifetime. The ginger-haired giant at the Riverside who would rise to his feet every five minutes to roar, 'Play like you mean it!' The lugubrious goon with the George Reynolds scrape-over who greeted any show of skill at St James' Park by groaning, 'Here we go, bloody Dickie Dancer.' The ubiquitous chap with the tartan blanket round his knees at Feethams who at some point could be guaranteed to wave a hand at the pitch and growl, 'Where's our width? Where's our bloody width?'

In the 1950s, my friend Roy stood on the South Bank at Molineux near a burly Black Country foundryman who at least once a match would point at Wolves' cultured midfield schemer Peter Broadbent and roar, 'Take him off, Mr Cullis, and put my granny on.' The foundryman would have got on well with my granddad who couldn't pass thirty minutes of a match in the late 1960s without barking 'Give him a jelly' at Eric McMordie – whose little flashes of elegance and guile having been enough to convince him that the Irish inside forward was a pampered lapdog begging for sweetmeats.

The 'Time! Time!' man lacked the linguistic invention of others I've encountered. The bloke in the pom-pom cap at Seaham who howled: 'We've lost our shape. We're like a bag of nuts,' seventy times per match, nor did he exude the air of tragedy of the man at Ironworks Road, Tow Law, who on icy days in the 1990s stood by the touchline looking as forlorn as a stork with chilblains and spent the entire ninety minutes calling out, 'Hell's bells, Lawyers, hell's bells!' in a voice so mournful he might have been auditioning for the title role in an amateur dramatic society production of *The Rime of the Ancient Mariner.*

'Time! Time!' the bloke yelled. Jimmy rolled his eyes. 'Time for him to ruddy pipe down,' he muttered, but without hope.

Pontefract's top scorer was the square-shouldered, rangy, pony-tailed Eli Hey, whose name suggested a character from a Mary Webb novel. He'd been signed from the equally evocatively named Campion in the summer and opened the scoring early, nipping onto an underhit back pass ('Time! Time!') and beating Karl Dryden with nonchalant ease. 'Sharpen yourselves up, Dunston. If you don't move faster than this, birds are going to nest in your hair,' a broad-waisted bloke along the barrier bellowed.

The rest of the half saw Dunston pressing and Pontefract engaging in what you might call 'game management', if you thought the phrase 'time wasting' was old fashioned and needed upcycling. Cries of 'Away, ref, he's never touched him, man' echoed around the ground as Colls' players plunged to the turf with a regularity that suggested some kind of addiction to feed and weed.

Despite Pontefract's attempts to fracture the rhythm, Dunston gradually worked up a head of steam. The skilful Liam 'Scrappy' Thear, a product of Gateshead's Academy, had a 1920s barnet and turkey-thighs. As Bob Paisley once said of a winger, 'He's not quick, but he's nippy.' Suddenly he was buzzing past Yorkshire defenders like a bluebottle round bullocks and little, gingery Jack Elliott, who had a Groucho Marx running style, was scurrying all over the pitch with the mad enthusiasm of a spaniel let loose on the beach.

The equaliser came from Mark Fitzpatrick. Fitzpatrick was Dunston's top scorer. He'd arrived from neighbouring Whickham in the summer. He didn't look like much of a player until he had a sniff of goal and then suddenly his shoulders hunched, his head went down and he was filled with the eager purpose of John Motson pursuing a statistic. Now he collected Scott Heslop's pass and took one touch before thrashing the ball past the burly Ryan Musselwhite.

Two minutes later the visitors were in front again. A long throw from the Dunston left was flicked on at the near post and the lurking Hey dived to head home, while the Dunston defence engaged in a game of musical statues for which nobody had brought a record player.

Thear responded by going on a slaloming run down the right that took him past three defenders. Eventually Jimmy Williams stopped him by the simple method of kicking his shin. Fitzpatrick took the penalty, strolling up to the ball as casually as Maurice Chevalier on the Corniche and stroking a shot gently down the middle while the keeper dived theatrically and pointlessly to his left.

Dunston took the lead five minutes later, Thear jigging into the box past the flailing feet of the Colliery backline. His knee-high cross was met by Heslop with a sidefoot volley.

In stoppage time, with anxiety cresting among the home support, Dunston broke out of their box and substitute Jordan Nellis benefited from a Thear flick to slot home the fourth and send Dunston through to the next round.

'If we're lucky, the prize money'll pay for a new perimeter fence,' one of the committeemen said merrily as he passed on his way back to the clubhouse.

3

RYTON AND CRAWCROOK ALBION V WASHINGTON

Ebac Northern League Division Two

Saturday 1 September 2018

I'd first met the taxi driver in the early years of the new century. He was a large man who spent so much time in his vehicle it appeared to have moulded itself around him. He was like some latter-day centaur – half bloke, half Nissan Primera. A plasterer's cap was permanently affixed to his head and from beneath it wild and wiry hair stuck out at all angles like stuffing escaped from a sofa. Mirrored shades, a Zapata moustache and a voice that had the wheezing rumble of ancient rolling stock were other characteristics.

The taxi driver lived in Annfield Plain in County Durham. He said Annfield Plain was a hard place. He said, 'You remember the boxer Glenn McCrory?' I did. McCrory was a cruiserweight from Annfield Plain who'd won the world title. He was a genial giant who looked like Terry Molloy from *On the Waterfront*. 'Aye, well,' the taxi driver said, 'after he beat Patrick Lumumba to take the title they put up a sign in Annfield Plain club. It said "Glenn McCrory Ranked Number One in the World", then underneath, "and Number Six in Annfield Plain".' He laughed so hard he started to choke and had to have a cigarette.

His working day was one long conversation that started the minute he turned the ignition and continued on through his shift regardless of the constant changes in the back of the vehicle. 'I mean, it's a tragedy when you think about it,' he was saying as I slid across the vinyl rear seat that first time and inhaled that unmistakable minicab smell of fresh mountain pine, king size, curry and vomit. 'A hundred years-plus of football ended at the flick of a lighter.' I judged from this that he was speaking of the recent demise of a non-League club, forced to fold after an arson attack on its clubhouse.

'It was vandals, was it?' I asked him, because that is what I had read in the local papers. The taxi driver let out a world-weary sigh. 'Mebbes, though I heard a few weeks before she went up they'd got notice of an Inland Revenue audit. And there's nowt more likely to spark a blaze in a North-East club than a letter from the Revenue.'

The taxi driver was a Sunderland fan. He was jointly obsessed by Niall Quinn and Alan Shearer who to him represented the yin and yang of North-East football. As other men have had 'love' and 'hate' tattooed on their fists, so might he have had 'Quinn' and 'Shearer' etched on his. Although, obviously to do so he'd have to have five fingers on one hand and seven on the other, which as my old next-door neighbour – who had known the taxi driver back when he'd been on the force and the taxi driver had been young and scampish – pointed out is an unlikely configuration, 'even for someone who was born in Murton, like he was'.

I should say that, in my view, this is a slight on Murton, though I have visited the Durham village only once, admittedly. That was back in the days when they still had a team in the Northern League. My friends and I had got off the bus from Durham and were struggling to locate a pub, the International, which also served as a clubhouse. It was raining. The afternoon was so dark that even if the workers' flag was flying you wouldn't have been able to see it from a distance of more than 6ft.

The streets of Murton were deserted. The chip shop on the corner with the sign in the window proclaiming the availability of something called a 'Donna Kebab' (whether a misspelling or an unfortunate fate for some poor woman, I cannot say) was shut.

As we began to despair, and consider suicide, or a trip to Spennymoor, a bloke lurched into view from a side street. He was walking in the classic manner of the daytime drunk, with his feet planted far apart as if to brace himself against the swell of the pavement, a grin on his face proclaiming: 'I'm palatic, but I'm getting away with it.'

We stopped him and asked the way. He gave us directions and as we walked off bawled after us: 'The beer's piss, mind, lads.' Kirstie Allsopp would doubtless get all prissy about the lack of hand-crafted almond croissants but I found it impossible not to warm to the place.

Murton FC, I should say, had some claim to being the unluckiest club in the North East. They'd finished the 1999–2000 bottom of the Northern League having conceded 133 goals and scored just twenty-five. Then, after the summer recess, officials arrived at the club's ground, Murton Park, to find a thirty-metre crater had opened up in the middle of the pitch. They had to play at Peterlee.

Help was swiftly offered from the unlikely quarter of the BBC who decided to use Murton as the subject of a reality TV science show fronted by Sophie Raworth. Psychologists, physiotherapists, nutritionists, balance and vision coaches descended on east Durham for three months. The players were kitted out in lightweight boots, given state-of-the-art training kit and sent on bonding weekends that didn't involve drinking lager and throwing pies at each other. They rose from second bottom to eleventh and by November had exceeded the previous season's goal tally.

Alas, it didn't last. In 2005, Murton were expelled from the Northern League for consistent failure to meet ground standards. They bumped down the lower steps of the league pyramid and flopped into the Durham Alliance. The ground suffered horribly from vandalism. The main stand – which was once shifted 80 yards by volunteers using ropes and block and tackles – and floodlights had now all but disappeared, the remains too worthless to be carried off by scavengers, even here where it seemed desperate people would take a chainsaw to a live cable if they thought they'd get something for the copper wire.

I had seen the taxi driver on Wednesday. 'You know what they're saying,' the taxi driver said when I got in and nestled down on the blue velour tiger-stripe seat-covers he'd just installed. He didn't wait for an answer. 'That [he named the spokesperson for one of the Newcastle fan groups campaigning against Mike Ashley] goes into a pub and orders 50,000 pints of ale. "That's a lot of beer," says the bar man. "Ah yes," comes the reply, "But I am ordering on behalf of all Newcastle supporters."' The taxi driver let out a wheezing laugh that sounded like the squeak of a rusting mattress, 'On the telly again this lunchtime, did you see him?'

I said I hadn't. I said, 'I preferred your joke about Kenny Dalglish.' The taxi driver chuckled. 'Bloody Dalglish. Second in the Premier League and still looked like he'd just licked piss off a thistle. He goes in a bar. Says, "Why's it so busy in here?" Barman says, "It's happy hour." Dalglish says, "I better leave then."'

'Yes, that one,' I said.

'But see,' the taxi driver said. 'These Mags. They're always saying there's going to be some protest, aren't they? They're going to walk out, or turn their backs, or stop in the pub. But it never, ever happens. I tell you, they're that full of hot air if you pushed them off a roof they'd not hit the ground. And believe me,' he added pointlessly, 'I would push them off a roof.'

It was true the protests against the Ashley regime had been going on for a long time, or hadn't. Part of the problem was that there were so many different anti-owner groups. There was the Magpie Group, NUFC360, If Rafa Goes We Go, Ashley Out, Mike Ashley Out, the Newcastle Supporters Group, the Newcastle Independent Supporters Group . . . It all had a *Life of Brian* quality about it.

There was nothing new about fan protests at St James' Park either. I started going to St James' Park with my friend Steve when Gordon McKeag was running things. Back then the chants of 'Sack the Board' were to the Gallowgate End what Hail Marys are to St Peter's – it was an act of both faith and atonement. Much has changed at St James' in the thirty years since then, but the relationship between Newcastle supporters and the club's owners has remained more or less constant throughout.

The last time I saw Steve was shortly after the announcement that Ashley's weirdest managerial appointee, Joe Kinnear, had left Newcastle. I quoted Dorothy Parker's response to the news that Calvin Coolidge had died: how could they tell? Steve chuckled. 'Some things in life you can always rely on: the sun rises in the east and sets in the west, and Newcastle United is run by bastards.'

'To be honest, mind,' the taxi driver said, 'It's the same everywhere. Fans used to get really mad back in the 1970s, 1980s. They'd be running on the field with banners made out of old bedsheets daubed with paint left over from doing the spare room. "Sack the board." Nowadays all they do is go on bloody Twitter. And that's your problem right there, to my mind – social media. First thing that happens they're straight on it shouting the odds, then it all fizzles out. Never gets a chance to build up steam. Not like it used to. Rage, you ask me, is something needs to simmer a long while, like an ox tongue.'

I'd been intending to go the Billingham derby – Town v Synthonia – but when I arrived at the station there were signs up everywhere announcing a strike by Northern Rail staff and limited services. The last train back from Newcastle was a little after five. Any trip to north Teesside by public transport that didn't involve an overnight stay in Seaton Carew was off. I walked up to the bus station muttering to myself and caught the westbound service to Ryton and Kingsley Park.

Ryton and Crawcrook Albion's encounter with Washington had a certain sentimental value to me as it was at this same fixture seven years before that I'd been reunited with my friend Ian. Ian was a Newcastle fan. He and I had met at the high point of Keegan mania, when the Magpies were top of the Premier League and main rivals Manchester United's Eric Cantona was still serving his ban for the kung fu kick at Selhurst Park (the following day I'd been on a phone-in panel show on BBC Newcastle and after I and the other panellists had all decried the Frenchman's actions – while acknowledging the provocation – an old lady from Scotswood had rung in and said, 'I hear what yees is all saying and I cannot for the life of me understand it. When I was a lass and two big strapping young fellas wanted to have a bit of a set-to people just said, "Let 'em get on with it and may the best man win."' Cantona's two-footed lunge, I feel compelled to say, followed his sending off by Alan Wilkie of Chester-le-Street).

I asked Ian if he thought Newcastle would win the title. 'If they don't do it this season, they never will,' he said.

We went to Filtrona Park South Shields that day. On the way back, Ian told me that he played in goal in a Tyneside six-a-side league. He said that a few nights earlier he'd rushed out to collect a through pass and stepped outside the D-shaped area keepers were not allowed to leave. 'One of their players shouted at the ref, "The fat twat's out of his box!" I said, "Thanks, I'll use that as the title of my autobiography."'

After that game we took to roaming about together watching football all over the old Durham and Northumberland coalfields, visiting new venues once a month while always strenuously denying to anyone who asked that we were groundhoppers.

Then Ian's life hit a bump and by the time he'd got over his troubles I'd got problems of my own. Half a dozen years elapsed, likely more. Then in 2011 he'd got in touch and said he was going to RACA v Washington if I fancied it and soon after we'd commenced our Northern League wanderings again, still fending off suggestions we were groundhoppers.

One early summer Saturday in 2016 – the English season long since over – Ian and I had travelled up to Scotland to watch the Ayrshire Weekly Press Cup quarter-final between Beith Juniors and Auchinleck Talbot. Bellsdale Park was the home of a legendary chicken and haggis pie and my main recollection of the match is a Talbot fan responding to a mate's enquiry on its quality by growling, 'Way, it's no fucking ambrosia, is it?'

On the train back (Beith won 5-4 on penalties after a 1-1 draw, if you're bothered), somewhere between Kilmarnock and New Cumnock Ian said, 'What you doing tomorrow, then?'

'Going to see the Sugarhill Gang,' I said.

'I hope you don't hurt yourself doing the worm,' Ian said. 'Who you going to see them with?'

I thought for a moment before answering. 'A woman,' I said.

Ian grinned. 'Is it a date?'

'I don't think so,' I said.

Ian scratched his head. 'Well,' he said, 'is anyone else coming?'

'No.'

'Are you meeting her there, or going in to town with her?'

'With her.'

'Are you having a drink before?'

'Yes.'

Ian slapped his hand on the table. 'Well, that, mate,' he said, 'is a date.'

I denied it. I told him it showed what an utter shambles my life was that I was taking advice on romance from a man who looked like some wild Irish folk singer and wore pink plastic sunglasses on his head. And he laughed and offered me one of the cupcakes his girlfriend Laura had baked us for the trip.

The following afternoon he put up a Tweet that said, 'Best of luck tonight to the Fresh Prince of Teesside.'

As it turned out, that first time I went out with the woman Ian took to referring to as 'the Flame-haired Hip Hop Lady' wasn't a date. But the next time was and slowly, in a miracle that seemed as inexplicable to me as the Holy Trinity and more profound, I found that I was in love with someone who loved me back.

Just before midnight that New Year's Eve I had a text from Ian. It was the last hour of 2016, the year the UK voted to leave Europe, the US elected Donald Trump and Newcastle United were relegated to the Championship. 'The only good thing that happened this year is you and D getting together,' it said.

I took the phone outside into the garden and reread the text. It was a clear night, the Northumbrian sky striped with stars, and the air so icily cold the tears froze on my cheeks.

Now two and a half years had passed and I was on my way to Ryton again. It was a warm day and the westbound Tyne Valley bus was filled with the usual collection of Metrocentre-bound teens shouting about fights they had witnessed out of the bathroom window while sitting on the toilet. 'There's fists flying, boots flying. Man, it was proper abombable,' a boy with a face so barnacled with acne he looked like a seaside souvenir exclaimed.

The route took us along the south bank of the river, through the upmarket suburban sprawl of Riding Mill and Stocksfield and on into Mickley and Prudhoe. There had once been coal pits all along this stretch of the valley – in Crawcrook, Clara Vale, Stargate, West Wylam and Greenside – but football never seemed to have had such a great hold on the population as it did to the south and east. The area had produced notable players – Bob Stokoe, Howard Kendall and Joe Tulip, who'd been one of the first Englishmen to play in the Scottish top flight, banging in over forty goals for Queen of the South when they were one of the best teams north of the border. But the area's football clubs had never risen to any great heights and many – including one from Prudhoe that had played in the Northern League – had disappeared without any of the locals noticing.

Kendall, I should add, had played in the same school team as another famous North Easterner, Bryan Ferry. Ferry was not the only junior rock star footballer from the region. A friend of mine played age-group school matches in Newcastle twice a season for five years against a winger he would later realise had been Sting: 'And if I'd had the faintest inkling, I'd have kicked him a fuck of a sight harder.'

I got off by Crawcrook Co-op and walked down the hill towards the ground. Two men were farting around with the engine of a car. A lad of about seventeen emerged from a nearby house and shouted across to them, 'Dad, Dad, that massive spider's back in the kitchen.'

'Well, stamp on it then,' one of the men said, looking up from beneath the bonnet.

'I can't,' the lad replied, 'I haven't got any shoes on.'

I had a soft spot for Ryton and Crawcrook Albion because several years before I'd accompanied Northern League chairman Mike Amos and a couple of others on a sponsored walk from Hexham to Ryton. One of the party was Stevie Carter, Ryton's secretary, laundryman, electrician and grass-cutter. It was a horrible day, slanting winter rain the thickness of dog slather slapping into our faces for the entire 10 miles. Stevie – who spent a good deal of time in the Faroe Islands and was therefore used to this sort of weather – kept our spirits up with a series of bizarre tales, one involving comedian Bernie Clifton at a Skegness holiday camp that is sadly too libellous to be repeated.

When we finally arrived – wet and frozen – at Ryton we found the game we had been supposed to watch had been postponed because of the weather, but Stevie rustled up big plates of sausage sandwiches and then drove everybody home. When he dropped me off I was still so cold I had to thaw out by making a mug of soup and then getting in the bath to drink it.

RACA had been created in the first years of the 1970s using a loan of £12 from Ryton Social Club. The players changed at Crookhill Labour Rooms. They'd moved to Kingsley Park in 1998. They were promoted to the Northern League in 2005. They made it into the top division in 2008 by which time they had a covered standing area sufficient to meet ground standards – it was made up of a row of seven plastic bus shelters. In 2011, the club finished bottom of Division One and with a lack of sponsorship and players almost went out of business. They battled on, changed their name to Ryton and Crawcrook Albion, built up a decent cluster of youth sides and a ladies' team, and were kept alive – like so many grassroots clubs – by the energy and enthusiasm of men like Stevie Carter.

I bought a ticket and a programme, got a cup of tea from the snack bar and said hello to Stevie who was busy trying to locate a new bulb for one of the floodlights. Kingsley Park would never win any architectural awards (unless there was one for the vernacular use of ancient netting) and the main seating area behind the goal appeared to be more ornamental than practical, but it was a pleasant place to spend a sunny afternoon. There were fine views to the north across the Tyne and, every once in a while, on the bumpy strip of brown-and-green that constituted the pitch, a bit of football would break out.

RACA had got off to what, for them, was a blistering start to the season, losing just once in the opening five matches. Visitors Washington were currently second bottom, having lost four matches and shipped a dozen goals.

Whereas Stevenage and Milton Keynes both boasted league teams (controversially in the latter case), the

North-East's new towns had not fared well when it came to football. Only Newton Aycliffe had really managed to establish themselves, drawing in a couple of hundred fans. In County Durham, attracting residents of Peterlee and Washington to watch Northern League had proved about as easy as selling matches to the Human Torch. Peterlee had a population of 23,000, but Peterlee Town had regularly performed in front of crowds that were outnumbered by the playing staff and had finally given up trying in 2013. Washington was close to three times the size of Peterlee and had older roots, but here too football clubs had struggled to drum up local support. The town's original team, Washington Colliery, had played in the North Eastern League.

One of Colliery's former players was Jimmy Hagan who, after a long pro career with Sheffield United, went on to manage Benfica to three successive Portuguese titles in the early 1970s. The Washington-born Hagan was an old-school drill sergeant-style manager who seems to have terrorised the Portuguese players. The training regime he implemented at Benfica was so punishing Eusébio recalled players throwing up during sessions. In the first weeks of Hagan's reign, the squad came close to mutiny, but once the season started and Benfica's players saw how much fitter they were than their opponents they began to warm to the Englishman. They won the 1973 title without losing a game all season. Hagan would go on to take charge of Sporting Lisbon, Boavista and Vitória de Setúbal.

He was one of a number of North-East managers who'd succeeded outside the UK, including Reg Mountford from Darlington who'd led the Danish national team to an Olympic bronze medal in 1948, Walker-born Eric Keen who'd coached Egypt and Besiktas in the decade after the Second World War, Randolph Galloway who started his career with Sunderland Tramways and coached Valencia before the Second World War and Uruguayan giants Peñarol after it, Teessider Ken Furphy who took charge of New York Cosmos during their Studio 54 heyday, Tynesider Keith Armstrong who was voted manager of the year three times in Finland (and once turned up on BBC national news defending the cuisine of his adopted homeland after Silvio Berlusconi and Jacques Chirac had said Finnish food was shit) and the amazing Jack Greenwell (we'll get to him later).

Washington Colliery folded before the Second World War and the current club, nicknamed the Mechanics, had been formed at Washington F Pit in 1946. The club had begun by playing at Spout Lane around the same time Hagan was winning his first Portuguese title. They were forced to leave Spout Lane after the council allowed a road to be built through the middle of it – an indication that football was not a top priority among local town planners.

Washington FC had joined the Northern League in 1989. They now played at the sports ground attached to the giant Nissan plant. The Japanese car makers had arrived in the North East in 1984, shortly after the brutal wave of steelwork closures presided over by Scots-American hatchetman Ian MacGregor, who was by then swinging his tomahawk at the coal industry. They'd been the region's biggest business for close to a decade. Seven and a half thousand people worked at the plant. Against the advice of their employers the majority of them had, reportedly, voted to leave the EU, casting doubt on the future of the works plant. 'Do turkeys vote for Christmas?' Geordies – who'd mainly supported Remain – joked, 'They do if they're Mackems.'

Washington had brought barely a handful of supporters with them and when the ref blew the opening whistle there were only sixty people in the ground. That number soon rose to sixty-one, kind of, because one of the singular features at Kingsley Park was the neighbour with the ladder. He lived in a house on the other side of a larch lap fence on the north-east corner of the ground. When the game kicked off he came out of his house, raised his ladder to the fence and watched the match from it. Since he was evidently retired, this saved him the OAP admission of £2.50. 'I can't believe that bloke watches the game like that,' I said to the man standing next to me. He shrugged. 'I can. He used to be a referee.'

The ladderman was by no means the oddest person I'd come across at non-League football. Several times I'd sat in front of a bloke who described and explained every incident as if to a blind man or somebody who has never attended a football match before. 'The referee had to reach for a yellow card there,' he said in the hearty tone of a fellow at ease with his subject, 'because though there was no malice in the tackle it was plainly a cynical attempt to thwart a potential breakaway.'

He was like those members of the crowd in a *Roy of the Rovers* comic strip who bring us up to date with events via flurries of exposition. I half expected that at some point he would say, 'And at 3-0 down with just five minutes to play in this vital relegation clash, Melchester need a miracle . . . and Roy Race is just the man to provide it.' Instead he said, 'Ridley's initial touch was good, but his cross failed to beat the first man, which, you have to say, is unforgivable at any level.'

When it got to the interval the first time I encountered him, I looked around and was surprised to find he was sitting all on his own. Though looking back now, I realise there was probably a very good reason for that.

As it transpired, the opening period of today's encounter was so soporific the neighbour and his ladder was gone after fifteen minutes, during which time so little had happened it was like a football version of *Last Year in Marienbad*. Both keepers could have slung a hammock in the goal and reposed undisturbed as the ball bounced around the halfway line as if sucked towards it by a centre circle vortex.

In the twentieth minute, pulses were briefly raised when Washington's Craig Hennis fired in a booming shot which streaked past the shaggily bearded Stefan Holden and smashed into the stanchion with a sound like a steam hammer striking a rivet.

Things returned to normal straight afterwards and half time came without anything further to disturb the bloke behind me's description of his recent colonoscopy.

Five minutes into the second period, Washington looked to have won the game when the unmarked Dan Robinson headed in from near the penalty spot.

At that stage Ryton had not mounted a meaningless attack never mind a meaningful one.

With sixty minutes gone, however, the home players seemed finally to notice they were playing a football match. With a fresh burst of energy like cows released onto a spring pasture they were soon cavorting about the place creating havoc. Jamie Dunn collected the ball 30 yards from goal and galloped 10 yards before walloping a curving shot that left Craig Williams in the Washington goal flapping at thin air like a man shooing midges from a picnic.

Inspired by that spectacular effort, RACA began thumping the ball into the visitors' box high and low and from all angles however improbable. In the seventy-third minute after a goalmouth scramble on the edge of the six-yard box that saw the ball ricocheting about from one shin to another for what seemed like five minutes, RACA's top goal scorer Scott Jasper, a signing from Whitley Bay whose dark stubble and glowering demeanour was suggestive of a Spaghetti Western shoot-out, toe-poked the ball into the net.

The game ended 2-2. RACA were now on an unbeaten five-game run, which for a team that prided itself on being home-spun was more or less the equivalent of winning the treble.

I caught the bus home. There was nothing much to report on the number 10 so I may as well tell you about Jack Greenwell.

Catalan journalists who watched the team from England demolish Barcelona 4-2, were in no doubt they were witnessing something special. 'This is the best side seen here since football has been played,' wrote one. The team in question? Crook Town, naturally.

That was in 1913. The man responsible for organising Crook's trip to the Iberian Peninsula was Jack Greenwell. A miner's son from Peases West, Greenwell had debuted for Crook as a teenager, had an excursion to Turin with West Auckland when they won 'the first World Cup' in 1909, and three years later – at a time when most North-Easterners regarded a trip to London as a dark and fearful journey into the unknown – left for Spain to play professionally at the newly formed Barcelona. A skilful midfielder, Greenwell made eighty-eight appearances for Barca, hit ten goals and picked up two Campionat de Catalunya medals. Photos show a rugged, stocky man with the sort of tightly crinkled hair – running like plough furrows across his pate – that nobody seems to have had since 1960.

Crook's trip to Spain was part of Barcelona-founder Hans-Max Gamper's efforts to increase football's popularity in the city. The Swiss merchant's efforts – and those of his English partners the Witty brothers – didn't go down well with the local middle class, however. The Catalan bour-geoisie found the sight of men running around in shorts 'morally reprehensible' and supported only those sports such as riding, fencing and tennis that were performed in long trousers. Enraged by the menace to Catalonian youth posed by the fruity Anglo-Saxon game, they reacted violently to the news that King Afonso XIII planned to come and watch the English visitors at the Camp del Carrer Indústria. Death threats were issued. The king was a big fan and patron of the game (all those Reals in La Liga were named in his honour), but having already dodged several anarchist bombs, he decided to stay in Madrid. The game went on without him.

The Crook players remained stoic throughout the furore. When the game kicked off, one thing perplexed them though: Barcelona's habit of swapping one player for another in the middle of a game. Substitutions, already a feature in Spain, would not become the norm in England for over fifty years. Following the opening 4-2 win, Crook played Barcelona twice more: drawing 1-1 and 2-2. They left with happy memories and a historic pennant that hangs in the Millfield clubhouse.

The Black and Ambers returned to Barcelona twice more, in 1921 and 1922. By then Spanish football had improved and the moral panic had ended. The side from Millfield played Barca seven times more: losing four, drawing two and winning the final encounter 3-1. It is rumoured that in one of the games the great Spanish goalkeeper, chain-smoking dandy Ricardo Zamora, guested in goal for the visitors. If the results didn't mimic the triumph of the first trip, for a team of amateurs from a town with a population of fewer than 10,000 it's still not a bad record against the four-time European club champions.

The remarkable Jack Greenwell was coach of Barca for both the latter series of matches. He'd taken charge in 1917 and remained for seven seasons, longer than anyone in the club's history apart from Johan Cruyff. In that time, he won two Copa del Rey and five Catalan championships. He returned for a second spell in the 1930s and won another Catalan title, but his last season in charge was so poor he wrote to the club president asking that his annual bonus and that of his players be reduced. I expect Jose Mourinho did the same at Old Trafford.

Greenwell also helped prepare the Spain national team for the 1920 Olympics and coached Sporting Gijón, Espanyol and Valencia. The outbreak of the Spanish Civil War saw him depart for Turkey. From Istanbul, Greenwell somehow found his way to Lima. He won the Peruvian title with Universitario, was assistant manager to the Peruvian national team at the Berlin Olympics (the South Americans were disqualified after refusing to replay a controversial match with Nazi-favoured Austria) and then took charge of them for the 1939 South American Championships, which they won for the first time (they've only won it once since, in 1975). Following that triumph Greenwell took up a post in Barranquilla, Colombia. Sadly, his wife Doris refused to travel with him, staying put with their children in Lima.

Separated from his family, Greenwell died of a heart attack in Bogota aged fifty-eight, a few days after the team he was coaching at the time, Santa Fe, had won a league match 10-3. One of the most successful and influential of all expatriate North-East coaches, Greenwell is buried in the Colombian capital, though no one seems quite to know where.

4

DUNSTON UTS v NORTH FERRIBY UNITED

The Emirates FA Cup First Round Qualifying

Saturday 8 September 2018

The Northern Rail strike continued. I stood on the platform waiting for one of the intermittent eastbound trains while a stodgy little bloke with a briefcase on wheels said repeatedly into his mobile, 'I know. A strike. It's *obsurd*. Absolutely *obsurd*. Well, what can I do? It's *obsurd*.'

I had to walk away so I couldn't hear him any more. It was hard to know what was more annoying – the fact an industrial dispute was interfering with my football season or that this pudgy shortarse couldn't pronounce the word 'absurd' properly. That, I realised, was one of the problems of being a middle-aged man – you constantly found yourself unable to choose which of a multitude of trivial matters you should be getting angry about. It made my blood boil, I can tell you.

North Ferriby were playing in the Evo-Stik Northern Premier League Premier Division having been relegated the previous summer from National League North. The Villagers had won the FA Trophy in 2015 and came close to promotion to the National League the following year. Earlier in the season they'd thrashed the apparently invincible South Shields. 'Might just be damage limitation today,' Jimmy said gloomily, before his natural sunny optimism kicked in and he added, 'but you never know.'

North Ferriby wore green-and-white striped shirts and green shorts, their keeper a vogueish pink. Like many higher level sides, they were big, wide and uniform in size, like a Playmobil set that had spent weeks in the weight room. Just getting around the two centre-backs looked like it would require a route map. Another sign of the higher level they played at was that they'd brought so many coaching staff they couldn't all fit in the dugout and blew along the touchline like crisps from a burst bag. A management posse this size is like the A-Team – every member has a narrowly defined task.

The man with the breezeblock face and the bus driver haircut's is to yell 'How many more times, ref?' whenever one of his players is fouled. Or an offside decision goes against them. Or a throw-in is given the other way. Or he's bored. Another in trainers the size of kipper boxes is purely there to turn to the closest cluster of supporters and give a rueful what-can-you-do? shrug whenever one of his players slices a cross into the distant trees. A third, small and bustling, applauds every mis-hit pass ('Right idea, Nutsy') as if potty training a toddler; a fourth in a floor-length warm-up coat that conceals his feet and makes him waddle like a penguin hurls abuse at his midfield even as the ball bulges the back of the opposition net ('Get fucking tighter!'); while another, older than the rest, leans back against the perimeter fence and allows himself one single, repeated comment on the action: 'Shitting pitch.' This is the way of the modern game. You need specialists in all positions.

Against all expectation Dunston took the lead with their first attack, the 6ft 5 Liam Brooks rising above two defenders to loop in a header from 15 yards.

Far from calming the home support this only stirred fears that the visitors would now be provoked into a fury.

'It's come too soon, way too soon,' Jimmy groaned.

A bloke sitting to our left, who wore a waxed jacket and had sideburns so luxurious it looked like a couple of badgers were setting up house in his ears soon revealed himself to be that lamentably rare species of English terrace beast, the Long-Winded Barracker. 'Come on, Dunston,' he called after five minutes as attacking menace drifted towards melancholy, 'if you'd only pass the ball more accurately to one another and get the occasional shot on target you'd likely find yourself further in front at this juncture.' His voice was as mellifluous and devoid of rage as that of a parson outlining plans for Harvest Festival.

When Liam Thear and the North Ferriby left-back, a man with a shaved-head-and-beard combination and the vague look of someone who'd lead a mutiny on a pirate ship, got involved in a bit of sea elephant-style chest bumping following a foul, the Long-Winded Barracker turned his verbose disapproval upon the match official: 'Referee, I think you'll find that as the Laws of the Game currently stand, a player may challenge an opponent with his feet or his shoulder but never by placing two hands on his back and forcibly pushing him as occurred in the previous challenge but three ... four ... er, five.'

The referee must have been able to hear but he chose to ignore it. That was not always the case. In non-League football you can't afford to equivocate. The slightest hesitation is the cue for a white-haired old lady stood by the corner flag to cry, in a voice like Edith Piaf gargling gravel, 'If you're not sure, ref, ask your bloody guide dog.'

The match officials may see themselves as facilitators, people who help create an environment in which football can flourish, but what happens the moment they make a decision? A fifty-year-old bloke standing on the touchline, an oily, nicotine-tinged quiff curled upon his head like an Ottoman's turban, bellows, 'How referee, what happened there, did one of your glass eyes mist up?'

As a result of this constant barrage of insults, old-school non-League match officials tended to take on the air of frontier marshals in a hostile saloon. As a refereeing friend of mine who'd once mistakenly sent off a spectator in a Northern Alliance game ('He was stood by the dugout wearing a tracksuit. I thought he was a sub') remarked, 'It's like dogs: if you show any sign of fear, you're dinner.' This seemed a little unfair on dogs, but his point was well made.

At the Doctor Pit Welfare Ground in Bedlington many years back, I saw a salutary example of the sort of attitude that prevailed. As a Terriers' player ran on to a long through ball the linesman raised his flag. Incensed, a home supporter who was a few yards away from him, leaning on the perimeter fence, yelled, 'Away, man! That was never offside.'

The linesman, an individual so large his parents must have needed planning permission for him, turned round, fixed the complainant with a gunslinger glare and barked, 'You're talking rubbish, sunshine.' After that, criticism of the linesman's decisions was confined to mild nose wrinkling and the occasional short burst of eye-rolling, though only when his back was fully turned.

Never apologise, never explain was the credo back then. Lately that had changed. The Northern League had introduced a no-swearing rule for players and spectators. Some will feel that this was all for the good. They will say that a football ground is not a fit place for calling people names; that if you want to hurl abuse at someone anonymously you should do so in a proper environment – the internet. For some, however, the hi-tech excitement of being able to insult people on five continents without ever leaving your mum's house is just not authentic. They still like their slagging live and unplugged. But, though the swearing ban had never been fully embraced by either teams or fans and you could still hear quite a bit of industrial language (including the linesman being denounced as a 'total Bessemer converter'), it was fair to say the abuse, which was once as blue and salty as the little paper bags you got in crisp packets, was no longer as prolific.

As a consequence, perhaps, the liners in particular seem to have softened. The previous season an assistant-referee responded to a similar cry to the one I'd heard at Bedlington not with an admonition, but with a long and patient explanation of the reasoning behind his raised flag. He delivered it without ever taking his eyes off the pitch, like a parent driving a car while telling a story to a toddler and trying to avoid smashing head on into the lorry in front. After he'd finished, a supporter of the rival team who was wearing a wool cap with the words 'Lawn Ranger' embroidered on it, yelled, 'You don't have to explain yourself to anyone, liner,' only to demand clarification for a non-given foul thirty seconds later.

It went on like that for most of the match. It was edifying, in a way. Though I confess that by the third time I'd heard the words 'active' and 'inactive' I found myself pining for the old days of gun law.

At UTS Park the referee awarded Dunston a free kick ('About time you set about rectifying the imbalance left by your previous decisions ...') on the North Ferriby left. It was whipped in with pace and curve. On the edge of the six-yard box the Villagers' midfielder Danny Norton inexplicably dived and headed spectacularly into his own net.

Two minutes later, Thear went on a run into the

opposition box so meandering he might have stopped halfway through for a picnic. Instead he fell over. The ref pointed to the spot. Mark Fitzpatrick scored.

Even at 3-0 it didn't feel as if Dunston were safe. In the second half, North Ferriby seemed bound to wake up. Sure enough, after the interval they began to pile forward. Shots and crosses splotted in like a winter shower.

Around me, supporters shuffled their feet, rubbed their hands together and checked the time. 'They want to watch themselves here, if these get one goal . . .'

'There hasn't been many stoppages has there?'

'Referee, even allowing for five substitutions and a minor injury to the visitors' bustling number eight jersey there should be no more than the almost generally approved allotment of four minutes' additional time.'

With four minutes left, Thear put an end to the anxiety, latching on to a long through ball and beating the onrushing keeper for Dunston's fourth.

Over on the far touchline, Jordan Nellis and a Ferriby player tangled and tussled over a loose ball until both fell over and sent the linesman sprawling. The sight of a match official falling over is one of the great joys of all football fans. On the first Saturday of the season three years before at Sam Smith's Park, Benfield versus Shildon, the linesman on the touchline nearest us had set off on a trot, slipped and fell flat on his face, provoking the following:

First fan: 'Sniper!'

Second fan: 'Cheat!'

Third fan: 'He never touched him, ref.'

Fourth fan: 'There's no one near him.'

Fifth fan: 'Diving is the scourge of the modern game.'

There was a pause. The linesman picked himself up. Thirty seconds went by. Then a Shildon fan shouted, 'Don't worry, lino – nobody noticed.'

To spare his colleague a similar dose of ridicule, the ref at UTS Park blew for full time before the linesman was back on his feet.

5

Dunston UTS v Irlam

The Emirates FA Cup Second Round Qualifying

Saturday 22 September 2018

I walked up to UTS Park with an elderly fan. He'd grown up in the Durham coalfields and, though he'd been a handy footballer and cricketer, his father had not encouraged him in either pursuit. Not every man in the North East in those days was sport crazy, he said, but this was more than mere indifference. 'My dad was a committed socialist, big on workers' education programmes,' he said. 'He thought that sport – like religion – had been created by the ruling classes to hold the proletariat back, to divert them from the politics of self-improvement. He believed that once ordinary people had access to higher education all sport would disappear. "Instead of bothering himself with football," my father used to say, "the pitman of the future will come home from his shift and listen to Beethoven on the Third Programme."'

I thought of an old school friend of mine whose grandfather had been a Durham pitman and hard-line communist. He refused to have the BBC on in the house, believing it broadcast only the propaganda of the ruling class. If he'd wanted to listen to Beethoven he'd have had to wait till the launch of Classic FM.

'Aye tuning in for the Moonlight Sonata, that's what he thought,' the elderly fan said. He looked at the rows and rows of cars heading past us towards the packed Metrocentre car parks and sighed.

It was another brightly sunny day. Sitting in the north stand and looking south made me squint like Clint Eastwood in a Sergio Leone movie. Meanwhile, those in the north-facing Tommy Cooney Stand were in dark shadow, many of them wearing parkas.

Irlam, from near Salford, played at the same level as Dunston, in the North West Counties Premier Division. They were having a good season, but the home support were relatively confident. The Northern League was generally a higher standard than most others at Step 6.

Part of the reason for that was the North East's compactness and geographical isolation. Players who were good had far fewer options than their counterparts in Lancashire and West Yorkshire where there were dozens more clubs at higher levels they could move to without having to relocate. In the North East for most of the past couple of decades there was only Gateshead and Blyth Spartans. Latterly they'd been joined by Darlington, Spennymoor and, most recently, South Shields, but the Northern League still felt a bit like an island, connected to the mainland by a causeway that was covered over at high tide.

A small cluster of those pale-skinned, thin-armed, big-nosed teenage boys who traditionally gather at non-League football had assembled by the side of the stand. They'd travelled up from Lancashire that morning. One of them, a tall boy whose heavily rimmed glasses were held together with Elastoplast said, 'Locked in for three and a half hours and forced to listen to bloody Elvis. Talk about child abuse.'

He was clearly the leader of the group, a position achieved by the sheer force of his knowledge. When one of his pals ventured the opinion that a schoolmate might be a good footballer because 'his brother's dead brilliant, like', the spectacled boy cocked his head to one side and said, with the careful deliberation of someone attempting to explain the concept of time to a sheepdog, 'Doesn't work like that. Doesn't work like that, does it? Listen – Mario Balotelli, right? Mario *Balotelli*, City *legend* and *striker for Italy*. His brother, Enoch Barwuah, signed by Salford City in Evo-Stik Northern Premier. And you know what? He were useless. Couldn't have found back of net if you fired him at it with a cannon. And that were when Salford were a sack of shite. So you see, doesn't follow, that. Not at all.'

Irlam wore red shirts and black shorts in the manner of Ron Atkinson-era Man United. Their goalkeeper Lee White was surprisingly short and slight by modern standards, conjuring memories of the diminutive keepers of the '60s such as Bill Glazier and Ronnie Simpson. John Burridge, who'd played for Newcastle (and pretty much everyone else), had once been described to me as being 'a couple of inches too short to be a top-flight keeper'. Not that Budgie hadn't worked at growing taller, dangling for hours by his ankles from balconies. He'd tried to improve his reaction speed in a similarly singular manner. During his days at Aston Villa he'd tasked his housemate with throwing pieces of fruit at him when he least expected it.

After retiring from playing, Burridge became manager of Blyth Spartans. He set up his own company selling designer gear from what might be described as a mobile retail outlet, though 'the back of a van' is the cruder term employed by some people. Soon he was kitting out the Northern Premier League side from top to toe in the latest clobber. Unfortunately, the team made the mistake of appearing on a Tyne Tees TV to show off their new look.

The next day trading standards requested a copy of tapes as evidence in a criminal prosecution. The clothes were designer all right, but the designers weren't the ones it said on the labels. Burridge protested that he had not realised what was going on and that a supermarket chain had also been selling stuff from the same supplier. It was to no avail. He was fined £16,000.

The opening quarter of the game was as disjointed as a bowl of spaghetti. The ball, bouncing around apparently at random, cannoning off bellies and knees, was sliced, shanked, ballooned and generally treated with a lack of care that bordered on cruelty.

One Dunston effort from outside the box was sliced so badly the spectacle boy started to offer his opinion on how far off target a shot could be for Opta's stat-bots to still count it as a 'shot off target'. 'It's got to at least cross the by-line, hasn't it? Otherwise it'd be a farce.'

Eventually Liam Thear managed to momentarily take charge of the ball, ran forward a few yards and slid a pass into the penalty area. White was first to it, but his clearance thwacked off a defender's backside straight to Liam Brooks, who directed it back across the goalkeeper and just inside the left-hand post.

The spectacle boy was called into action again moments later when an Irlam midfielder crunched into Thear with all the finesse of a drunken clog dancer with a dead leg. 'Referee,' he squeaked, 'You can't give that, he's got a bit of the ball.'

At the sound of these words, Jimmy looked at me and rolled his eyes. I understood where he was coming from. This phrase was repeated so often that it was hard to avoid the conclusion that if some football fans had their way the He Got a Bit of the Ball Principle would replace presumption of innocence as the cornerstone of the English legal system. A defence attorney would then address the jury: 'While it is true that my client murdered Mr Smith in cold blood, cut his body into pieces using a chainsaw and then buried it at various locations across the Home Counties I would remind you that *he did get a bit of the ball.*' The judge would bring an end to the consequent wild hullabaloo in court only by rapping his gavel and croaking, 'Case dismissed. Release the accused.'

A few minutes after the tackle from behind, Dunston were two goals in front, Brooks tucking away Fitzpatrick's cross.

Two-nil, the pundits often assure us, can be a dangerous lead (and as a Middlesbrough fan I'd say I feel the same way about 3-0, 4-0 and 5-0, though at 6-0 I have been known to stop biting my nails) and so it proved. On the twenty-seventh minute, Irlam were awarded a free kick a few yards outside the D. There are some words you only ever really hear in connection with football. Two of them are 'sumptuous' and 'aplomb'. Both applied to Matty Boland's free kick. Two-one.

The game returned to its previous turmoil. A man standing a few yards along the perimeter fence now introduced himself as one of those foghorn-voiced blokes who watch football as if coaching their local junior side. 'Wake up, forwards,' he bellowed as a lofted pass over the Dunston defence went to waste, 'we need to be looking for those.' As the home side passed the ball through the visitors' midfield: 'Come on, boys, who's picking up their number 7?' And when an Irlam midfielder got the ball he invariably called out, 'Get your head up, son, and look for the runners.'

I wondered for whose benefit he was doing it? The players didn't appear to hear him, and even if they did, would they actually take instruction from some random voice in the crowd? The more the bloke roared out his directions – 'Look wide and spread it!' 'Watch for the ball through the channels, lads!' – the more I started to feel that maybe he was hoping to be spotted by a scout. I imagined that he envisaged a situation in which an eccentric club owner would say to his assistant, 'Things are not working out with the manager. But I'm getting good reports on a fellow who leans against the fence at Irlam. Apparently he knows quite a lot of likely sounding phrases and has a very loud voice, which basically is all you need at our level.'

As the match went on a feeling of impending doom gripped the home support. 'Keep going, man, Dunston!' a lady with a Tibetan terrier on her lap yelled every minute or so, her voice rising each time as the tension mounted until by the end she sounded like Flipper the dolphin signalling impending danger.

Fitzpatrick missed a penalty. Irlam pressed. Dunston defended. Bodies flew into the box. Keeper White came up to join the attack. 'Away, ref, has your watch packed up?' Dunston fans bawled as stoppage time trickled by as slowly as treacle on a freezing day. Eventually he put his whistle to his lips and blew.

'If we want to move to the next level we need to show some ambition,' the spectacle boy lectured as the home support streamed past. 'Dump this manager and get in someone else. You know who I'd appoint? Big Sam Allardyce. Currently seeking work and Lancashire through and through.'

'Aye, like tripe,' a Dunston fan said as he walked past.

I headed back to the station, past the site of an engineering works that had once stood behind Dunston's clubhouse. The land it had stood on was now covered – like so many former industrial sites across the region – with the blue steel containers of a self-store unit, filled – if my own was anything to go on – with the overflow of furniture, crockery, glasses, clothes, bedding and, well, *stuff* from people's homes. If North-Easterners didn't produce as much as we once did, we certainly bought more.

On the Wednesday following UTS's victory I went to see a Durham Senior Cup tie.

The Durham Senior Cup had once been one of the hardest trophies in all of football to win. 'People forget,' Kenny Twigg had told me, 'that in the 1938-39 season Bishops not only won the Amateur Cup and the Northern League title, we also won the Durham Challenge Cup. In my book that last one was the greater achievement. The Durham Challenge Cup was harder to win than the Amateur Cup. The standard of football in County Durham was tremendous. There were hundreds and hundreds of sides from pit villages, collieries, factories, foundries. Everyone was desperate to do well – especially against the big clubs like us. It was fierce.'

Sometimes literally.

'We played a tie one time up by Stanley. Middle of winter. Ruddy freezing. Wind going right through you. The ground was packed. There was two or three thousand in there. The home side scored early. From then on we were all over them. Chance after chance. You could feel the tension rising. Five minutes from time Matty Slee goes down in their penalty area. The ref points to the spot. Straight away the crowd comes hurtling onto the pitch, screaming blue murder. We ran for our lives. The officials came charging off with us. We piled into the dressing room, barricaded the door. They were trying to kick it down. Took an hour for the police to calm things. Our team coach had to have an escort out of town. There was a replay. The police told us to have it on the morning and not publicise it in the newspapers. We played the match virtually in secret, beat them in front of two sets of committee men and the tea ladies.'

I said I thought crowd trouble was something that only started in the 1970s.

'Oh, you'd be surprised what went on back then,' Kenny Twigg said with a chuckle, 'especially out there. In Wild West Durham in the 1930s anything could happen.'

The match I saw conjured up little of this raw excitement, but I found myself sitting close by an elderly fellow with a face as creased and weatherbeaten as an abandoned boot. I'd sat near him a few times before across a band of venues that stretched from Ryhope to the 'Scotch Estate'. Peering out from the swaddled depths of a calf-length warm-up coat that reached to the tops of his ears, the man shouted comments that were utterly unrelated to anything happening on the pitch. As the visiting team lined up a free kick, he'd call out, 'If this goes in it's curtains' even though they were trailing 0-3. At others he'd bellow, 'Has the ref lost his whistle, or what?' after a series of challenges so innocuous even Pippo Inzaghi would have greeted them with a disdainful waft of his silk foulard.

Laughing scornfully at the least contentious decisions, chortling with boyish excitement at the award of a throw-in, or yelling something that sounded as if it might have been the catchphrase from a long-forgotten wartime radio comedy ('You want to tie a knot in that, Mr Butler!'), the old boy passed matches in a mixture of glee and exasperation while all around him people glanced at one another in puzzlement, like an audience seeking explanation of the jokes in a Shakespeare comedy.

At first I assumed the old man was listening to a match on an earpiece and responding to that. How else to explain the shout of 'You might get away with that in Spain, sunny Jim' evidently directed at a centre-back whose football career has taken him nowhere nearer to the Iberian peninsula than Northallerton? After a while, though, it became clear the veteran fan wasn't listening to anything – he was simply watching a totally different game in his head. And I confess there have been times when the howling wind has sent the ball scuttering across the turf like an escaped hen, and the bulldog-chopped man by the sign that says 'No Standing in the Seated Area' has just cleared his throat with a noise like a shovel scraping slush off gravel, and gobbed out a lump of spit the size and texture of a spinach tortilla, when I wished I was watching it with him.

6

DUNSTON UTS V CHESTER CITY

The Emirates FA Cup Third Round Qualifying

Saturday 6 October 2018

I'd been down to visit my parents in the middle of the week. My dad said, 'I met one of the old platers in Darlo last week. We were talking about Duffy. He was a real rough bugger, worked in the stockyard. Fight anyone. The only bloke he wouldn't take on was an erector, Davy Walker – ex-para. I said, "You've never had a go at Walker." He said, "I'm waiting till he's past it . . . And he's almost past it now." Duffy, he'd have six, seven pints and his fingers would start flexing. People saw him doing that, the pub cleared out. This old plater said, "His wife was the only one who could control him. When she was with him everyone could relax. After she died, he went berserk." Good job he was in his seventies by then, or somebody could really've got hurt.'

He said: 'It's lucky the stockyard never got to play in that bloody inter-departmental football league.'

The inter-departmental football league at the steelworks only lasted one match. It was the brainchild of a new personnel manager who'd arrived from the south. He had a lot of clever ideas about bonding and team-building between the different skill bases in the works. He said, 'If your defence doesn't know who your attack is, then how can you expect to win the game?'

The first and only match in the inter-departmental football league was between one of the welding bays and accounts.

My dad said: 'It was abandoned midway through the second half when the accounts team was reduced to six men by injuries. Three of them were hospitalised. A big gangly welder that everybody called the Praying Mantis did most of the damage. The Praying Mantis had double-jointed elbows, and he wasn't particular about where he stuck them.

'I went down to the welding bay next day. I saw one of the foremen. I said, "What was all that about yesterday, then?" He said, "I don't rightly know. But I tell you what, I bet it's the last time they bugger up our overtime payments."'

That was more than twenty years ago, but my dad still chuckles every time he thinks of it.

When I decided to become a writer, my dad was worried. He'd worked all his life in the steel business. So had his father. The world of the writer was precarious and unstable – the steel industry was invincible. When a son got an apprenticeship at Dorman Long, Cargo Fleet, South Bank Steel or any of the other yards that lined the Tees, they felt pleasure and relief. 'Our Micky's set for life, now,' they smiled and pictured grandkids. Then in the 1970s and 1980s the steelworks and the blast furnaces began to disappear one by one like co-eds in a slasher horror and for a decade or more my career choice seemed prescient and wise. It didn't last. Nowadays I can list the newspapers and magazines I've worked for that have disappeared – the *Sunday Correspondent*, the *Independent on Sunday*, the *Listener*, *Punch*, the *News of the World* . . . just as my father can the steelworks. But then, as my dad is fond of remarking, 'When one door closes, another one slams in your face.'

There were over 800 in UTS Park and the club had even got the Manhattan Grill burger van in to deal with food demand. I stood in the queue at the tea bar. The elderly bloke standing next to me at the condiments table waiting for use of a teaspoon said he'd grown up in Ashington in the 1950s and been a decent player. He'd started out at Port Vale when Stanley Matthews was the manager. After that he'd spent most of his career in North-East non-League football. Over the years he said he'd played for many different managers, but one in particular stuck in his mind.

'I joined a Northern League club not far from here,' he said, 'I'll never forget the first game. The manager's pre-match team talk goes like this. He takes an egg and he holds it up in front of us. He says, "This here, this is the opposition." He put the egg down on the floor of the dressing room. Then he goes outside. He come back in a few seconds later with this bloody great slab of slate. He says, "And this here, this is you." And he lifts this bloody slate up above his head and slams it down on top of the egg. "Now," he shouts, "I want you to go out there and splatter the fuckers."' He raised his eyebrows and shrugged his shoulders. 'I didn't stop there long,' he said.

A healthy contingent of Chester fans had arrived by coach. They were a cheerful bunch, happily proud of the fan-owned club they'd dragged from the brink of oblivion. They'd just gone fully professional and had to part company with stalwart manager Marcus Bignot. Now they had Anthony Johnson and Bernard Morley in the dugout. These were the shouty duo who'd come to public prominence when Salford City was taken over by a group of former Manchester United players and featured in a BBC TV documentary series. The series seemed to delight just about everybody except the fans of other non-League clubs. 'Yeah, it's the fairy tale of five millionaires and a billionaire from the Far East spending their way to success,' a Darlington supporter scoffed to me one afternoon, 'It's just like Cinderella, isn't it? I fair choked up when they won promotion.'

Johnson and Morley were, I suspected, of the egg-splattering school of management. Chester City were now in National League North, but they'd been a football league club until their financial implosion in 2010. Nobody was anticipating a home victory. Most fans were hoping for a good show, a decent performance, the avoidance of a humiliation. The more optimistic voiced thoughts of a money-spinning replay.

As it was, after barely two minutes Brooks latched on to a knockdown from Fitzpatrick on the edge of the box and struck a shot that bobbed and hopped all along the ground, but somehow evaded Chester's keeper. 'Well, at least we've done summat,' the old man behind me said.

'This'll sting them,' Jimmy said grimly. 'They'll not like that.'

The idea that Dunston had been foolish to make Chester angry looked to be a shrewd assessment when they equalised through a Deane Smalley header, then shortly afterwards took the lead, winger Dan Mooney cutting inside from the right and smashing the ball past Karl Dryden, turning away before it struck the net like a man who'd conclusively won an argument.

When the ref blew to end the half, people around me shrugged and sighed. 'Well,' they said, 'that's that then. But we held our own for forty minutes.'

Fitzpatrick had spent the first half battering the visiting defenders like a Japanese salaryman attacking an inflatable model of his boss and he was the rumbustious centre of everything in the second period. A few minutes in, he stepped up to take a penalty after Jack Elliott – as persistent as a winter cold – had been hauled down in the box. 'He missed the last one, mind,' someone said. We held our breath. The striker struck it hard and straight. The keeper dived. The ball hit the centre of the net, halfway up.

A few minutes later Fitzpatrick shrugged off his marker and hurtled towards goal. He was wrestled to the ground by Danny Livesey on the edge of the box. The referee pulled out a red. The resulting free kick was cleared, but when it was banged back in again Andrew Grant-Soulsby, diving so low his chin was scraping the ground, headed home.

Reduced to ten men and a goal down, Chester surprisingly began to dominate and Mooney got a second wonderful goal to level it.

'Aye well, cash from a replay would be very handy,' the old man opined.

The visitors seemed intent on finishing things in ninety minutes, however. They attacked remorselessly. It seemed only a matter of time. And then something extraordinary happened. Thear won the ball in his own penalty area, advanced five yards and struck a long ball downfield. Fitzpatrick was closely marked on the halfway line, but a cunning nudge in defender Matty Thomson's back sent him off balance. Fitzpatrick span away and raced after the ball, collecting it thirty yards from the Chester goal. He shuttled it towards to the on-rushing Grant Shenton, pursued by defenders gaining on him by the yard. He'll never score, I thought, he'll never do it. But then he did, striking the ball hard with the outside of his right foot, curling it round the keeper. When the shot struck the netting, people who'd previously sat through games as silently as Trappists yelled at the heavens in delight.

The last fifteen minutes seemed to go on longer than the Brexit negotiations. Dryden denied Mooney a brilliant hat-trick, dived full length to parry a long-range free kick from Craig Mahon and watched the ball flash just over his bar from a Steve Howson header.

When the final whistle blew, old blokes jumped to their feet, roared and punched the air in a manner that suggested back spasms later. I was one of them. I had to have a hot water bottle pressed to my spine for the next three days.

On my visit to my mum and dad's as I was about to leave my mother thrust a big orange carrier bag into my hands. 'There's a few things in there of yours I kept,' she said. Among the contents was Bobby Charlton's 1968 autobiography *This Game of Soccer*, which I ordered with my seventh birthday money. It was the first grown-up book I ever read. Not that I confined myself to simply reading it. Dissatisfied with the oblique style of the author's captions I filled in missing information, so that the photo showing the England number nine about to unleash one of his thundering shots titled simply 'The famous left foot in action' has 'Bobby Charlton (man utb)' written next to it in pencil. The photos throughout the book are in black and white except for the ones that have been 'hand-tinted' using crayons (a lack of a light blue surely the only explanation for Manchester City's mint green shirts).

It wasn't just me who made reading the book an inter-active experience either. On the diagram showing the team formation for the World Cup final, for example, somebody – probably my friend Deano who was a year older than me and had the burgeoning self-confidence that comes with being eight – has written 'is pumpy' next to the name 'Hunt'.

As well as *This Game of Soccer*, the bag also contained my primary school news book from the same period. Alongside accounts of a trip to town during which I 'nearly got an anorak', a visit to the cinema to see '*Plant of the Apes*' and a thrilling retelling of the night water got in through the garage roof, the news book contains my first match report: 'Yersterday I went to a football match at Midlsboro it was between Deaby County and Midlsboro'. My teacher, Mrs Welch, has corrected Middlesbrough and Yesterday, but left Deaby untouched, suggesting that her knowledge of football clubs of the East Midlands was not as great as that of the story of Jonah and the Whale and what things Stephen Humphrey shouldn't on any account be sticking up his nose. (The game incidentally was a 0-0 draw, which perhaps explains my reticence on the details.)

Football features gratifyingly frequently in the news book. At one point, for example, I have to replace my football after it 'get bursted on thorns'.

I remember that bursted football with great affection. It was a white vinyl 'Ayresome Angel' ball, the name stencilled on it in red, and it lasted for what seemed like years despite frequent attacks by the neighbours' Aberdeen terrier and getting run over by the coalman's wagon. When my dad announced that its condition was terminal, despite his best efforts to revive it using rubber solution glue and swatches from a bicycle repair kit, I wept more keenly than when the family dog passed away and kept its lifeless carcass on top of my wardrobe for years (the football's not the dog's).

When I went to buy another one, I found the Ayresome Angel had been discontinued. Instead I came away with a bright orange Frido, its surface covered in blisters that made it easier to grip in the days when the only goalkeeping gloves available had been knitted by Aunt Bertha from wool left over from doing a balaclava for her Bobby to wear on his moped.

The orange Frido didn't match the Ayresome Angel, but it was far superior to the balls you could buy in the local newsagents. A lot of these cheaper, lighter footballs weren't even spherical – when kicked through the air they wobbled around like a wounded duck. Before every World Cup in living memory, the goalkeepers have complained that the new Fifa ball (inevitably given some name that makes it sound like a blood-sucking anthropoid from a sci-fi movie) moves too much. Imagine if they had to play with the sort that, in the faintest puff of headwind, is likely to loop directly back at them like a boomerang.

Also in the newsbook is mention of another disappointing football-related outing: 'On saterday I will go to buy some football boots and the type of boots I am getting is stylo.'

I went with my grandfather to get the football boots and I knew exactly the pair I wanted. To this day, I can still recall the tingle of excitement that ran down my spine when I opened *Jimmy Hill's Football Weekly* and gazed upon the advert for George Best-endorsed Stylo Matchmakers. These were a kind of Regency buck football boot that came in a dandyish shade of burgundy and had the laces down the side. Paired with a pair of mauve Crimplene bell-bottoms, the Matchmakers might have been just the thing for impressing chicks at a groovy nitespot, but for actually playing football in they were – I later discovered – more or less useless, the fashionable chisel-toe causing every kick to loft into the air like a balloon struck with a hockey stick. The fact that Best could dribble round defenders in them is greater testament to his skills than a thousand hours of personal tributes from red-faced old blokes who can't help tittering when they think of how often the Irishman 'did it' with Miss World.

Matchmakers were what I had my heart set on. I'm sure they would have been disappointing. I didn't get to find that out, though. And this was all thanks to Jack Hatfield's Sports Shop. Jack Hatfield was a great swimmer and one of Teesside's first sporting heroes. He won two Olympic silver medals at the 1912 Stockholm Olympics. His rivals, Americans and Australians, trained in the warm, azure blue waters of the Pacific. Hatfield trained in the River Tees at Smith's Dock, South Bank. 'Two silver medals,' my grand-dad used to say, 'and they'd both have been golds if only the Olympic swimming pool had been freezing cold with dead dogs floating in it.'

Jack Hatfield had opened his sports shop in Newton

Street just after his Olympic adventures. It had been there until 1970, when it moved to bigger premises round the corner in Borough Road. In 2018, it finally closed down, causing a tidal wave of nostalgia among the thousands of Teessiders who'd shopped there.

The atmosphere in Hatfield's was always frenzied. By the time I went, Jack had retired and left the running of the shop to various sons and in-laws. The Hatfield brothers were fantastic salesmen. They shouted and yelled and rushed about, scaling ladders and rugby-passing shoeboxes, Subbuteo sets and badminton racquets to one another over the heads of customers, speaking all the while in rapid-fire Teesside double-speak. To shop there was like being in a Marx Brothers movie, or an episode of *Top Cat* voiced by Tony Mowbray and Chris Kamara.

Back in the 1960s, shopkeepers in Britain took a particular delight in telling you they didn't have what you wanted. You'd ask them for something and they'd shake their heads, all the while giving you the affronted yet superior look of a Calvinist preacher refusing gin from a drunk Catholic. 'Oh no, sir,' they'd say, 'I'm afraid not. There's no *demand* for them.'

Jack Hatfield's was different. In Hatfield's they didn't have what you wanted, they had something far better than that: they had what you needed. But you didn't know what that was until they told you.

My attempts to buy a pair of Matchmakers therefore came to nought. The Hatfield who served us instead brought forth something far, far better – a pair of ankle-high boots the colour of baked brick and the weight of a Cromwell tank.

'Now, looker,' he said to my grandfather, indicating the side of the boots on which an ancient spidery scrawl could vaguely be made out. My grandfather looked. His eyes widened. He cackled with glee. To this day I have no idea whose signature it was, but since my grandfather regarded every footballer who'd played the game since the General Strike as a workshy shitehawk, I imagine it must have been Andrew 'Wingy' Wilson or Steve Bloomer.

My frenzied attempts to turn my grandfather's mind back to the Matchmakers were utterly futile. The mighty boots were purchased and for good measure a pair of shinpads thrown in. These were stitched and stuffed with coarse fur that may well have been shaved from a woolly mammoth. When I wore them they made my socks so thick I had to run with my feet wide apart, like Frankenstein's monster. Not that I could run anywhere in those boots.

7

DUNSTON UTS v GATESHEAD

The Emirates FA Cup Third Round Qualifying

Saturday 20 October 2018

The game was a midday kick-off and was featuring on some far distant BBC channel that you could access via a coloured button. Jimmy and Margaret, who'd bought my ticket, had got to UTS Park at ten o'clock to secure our seats. I turned up forty-five minutes later and the ground was already full. 'There's been people here having their breakfasts,' Jimmy said.

The last time there'd been quite so much FA Cup excitement in the Northern League had been twenty years before when Bedlington Terriers had run amok. Shortly after the Terriers' 4–1 hammering of Colchester United of what is now League One in front of 2,400 fans at Doctor Pit Welfare Ground, I'd got a bus up to see the team one Wednesday evening. When I asked for directions to the ground the man in the chip shop had pointed eastward to a patch of pale, glimmering blue that broke the darkness above the slate roofs of distant terraced houses. 'See them bright lights?' he asked. 'Well, that's it.'

The players were training for the second-round tie away at Scunthorpe United; a league fixture with South Shields had been postponed and a media event arranged instead. The original FA Cup was on display, committee-men delivered china mugs of tea to assembled hacks and photographers and three separate camera crews filmed the team jogging in front of the pitch-side advertising hoard-ing, giving unexpected national exposure for H. Ternent, Family Butcher.

In the clubhouse, where the older locals' distinctive, phlegmy rolling Rs mingled with the RP sound of a PR woman fretting over misdirected press releases and the dulcet tones of Gerald Sinstadt, the Christmas decorations were up beside the pennants of visiting teams and the framed signed shirts from Spurs and Forest. The tape deck was rolling out 'Hark the Herald Angels Sing'.

Things had not looked quite so festive when then man-ager Keith Perry had arrived at Doctor Pit Welfare Park five years before, and not just because it was March. 'We were bottom of the second division of the Northern League, struggling to put together a committee or a side or to drum up support, on the verge of going under,' he'd said.

In 1993, however, the threatened disappearance of the town's football team had finally shaken local people from their apathy. Relegation and oblivion were avoided. That summer the newly appointed committee set about rebuilding the club. Literally. Keith Perry, who ran a construction company (brother Dave, the chairman, was in demolition), dug the holes for the floodlight pylons himself.

The following year, beneath their new lights, Terriers took the second division title at a trot. In 1997, they repeated the feat in the first, finishing twelve points clear of their nearest rivals and completing a double by defeating neighbouring non-League giants Blyth Spartans in the Northumberland Senior Cup final at St James' Park. They were regularly watched by crowds nudging 300.

When Colchester United had arrived in the Northumberland pit village even the most optimistic (or pessimistic if they had travelled from Essex) fan would not have anticipated seeing the home side triumph so brilliantly. They did so courtesy of a couple of goals by John Milner, Terriers' all-time top scorer, a masterful display at right-back by John Sokoluk, a Scot with a Ukrainian father and experience with East Fife and Berwick Rangers, and the visitors' ill-disciplined collapse when things didn't go their way.

The game against Scunthorpe proved more difficult. It was away, for starters, and Bedlington's hammering of Colchester had sent up a warning flare against complacency. Meanwhile, Scunny's manager, ex-Middlesbrough midfielder Brian Laws (born in Wallsend), had an impeccable source of local information: his brother John lived a hundred yards down the road from Doctor Pit Welfare Park and had been a regular visitor. The home side won 2-0.

It wasn't the end of Bedlington, though. They won the Northern League again that season and for three more seasons after that, too. They also reached the final of the FA Vase, losing 0-1 to Tiverton at Wembley. During the 2005-06 season there had been trouble in the boardroom that left the club in financial peril. They were saved from disaster by the unlikely intervention of one of the world's 500 richest men, US frozen food magnate Robert Rich. Rich had traced his ancestry to the area around Bedlington. This, apparently coupled with his wife's fondness for dogs, led him to sponsor the club. He also flew the squad out to the States to play FC Buffalo for the Lord Bedlington Cup and sent them an impressive gift – a massive electric scoreboard, which allegedly fused the electrics when it was switched on. Like many of the wealthy benefactors of non-League football, Rich's involvement was brief and the club has struggled to survive ever since, but mention of the FA Cup game against Colchester still lit up the sky above Bedlington.

There had been a fear before the Dunston–Chester match that a thrashing loomed. Gateshead were in the National League, so much further up the league ladder than Dunston their heels were barely visible through the clouds. But the result didn't really matter. Dunston's progress had secured them £35,000 in prize money, BBC coverage had netted them an additional £2,000 and the bumper crowd against

Chester – about 600 more than usual – and today had poured more money into the club coffers. 'They'll be able to replace all of this perimeter fence with what they've made so far,' someone said. It was a far cry from Premier League fans whining on phone-ins about a meagre £50 million transfer budget, but all things are relative.

The visit of Gateshead had attracted a club record attendance of 2,500. TV cameras were mounted on a gantry above the Tommy Cooney Stand, and groups of foreign students milled around taking selfies and basking in the Magic of the Cup.

To be honest, I have mixed feelings about times such as these. That's because the person who took me to football when I was a kid, my grandfather, used to react to success by stopping going to matches. You could guarantee that as soon as Boro got beyond the fourth round of any cup competition, or started to look like Division Two title candidates, he'd point-blank refuse to get his Morris Minor out of the garage on Saturday lunchtimes. He felt the same way about friendly matches featuring foreign clubs and the Anglo-Italian Cup competition, too. Watching Eusébio playing pre-season for Benfica or the *La Dolce Vita* playboys of Roma was glamorous. My granddad did not go to football for glamour. He went to see the latter-day equivalent of one of his youthful idols, Willie 'Pudden' Carr, get carried off on a stretcher with blood coming out of his ears.

He didn't like anybody he perceived as a 'fancy Dan'. Since this category included anyone with long hair, side-parted hair, dark hair, thick hair, or – now I come to think of it – any hair at all, there were not that many players in the 1960s that my grandfather did care for. He also disliked defenders with the temerity to hold onto the ball for longer than it took to launch it over the roof of the grandstand. Players who combined this – to his mind – unwarranted affectation with lustrous hair were a particular vexation. The Middlesbrough captain in the 1960s was Gordon Jones. Jones slotted into both categories of irritant. 'Look at him,' my granddad would say, whenever the skipper took possession and didn't immediately whack it down the field, 'auditioning for Hollywood. Why don't you blow us all a kiss, little Shirley Temple?'

My grandfather had grown up in hard times. Youthful poverty had affected him deeply. In his house you could have bread and butter, or bread and jam, never butter *and* jam. He took a similar attitude when it came to football. You could watch an unsuccessful team, or you could *not* watch a successful one. There was no wonder I always felt funny on days like these. I was betraying his ideals.

Not that anyone else around me felt that way. There was a Christmas morning excitement about UTS Park coupled with nerve-jangling anxiety. In the latter case, this had been exacerbated by the news that Dunston's consistently excellent Liam Marrs would be missing due to best man duties at a friend's wedding. He'd choked up on local TV talking about it. Scott Heslop too was not in the starting line-up, replaced by a rangy youngster with an angular face and a high ponytail that gave him the look of a character from a manga comic.

Gateshead were wearing mint green shirts with two diagonal stripes. They looked like they'd been modelled on a 1970s menthol cigarette packet. The players wearing them had the sleek physiques of people for whom taking care of themselves is a professional duty. Mike Williamson, the captain, a centre-back, had played 150 games for Newcastle. Heed's players controlled the ball effortlessly, their movements precisely rehearsed. They created space as if by sorcery – vast pockets opening up all over the field. And when they lost the ball they seemed to spring back into formation as if someone had clicked a reset button.

Watching them reminded me of something Kenny Twigg had said to me all those years before, sitting at his kitchen table in Hartburn. After the war, Kenny had left Bishop Auckland. He'd been offered terms by various league clubs, including Chester City, but 'I had a good job and in those days, with the maximum wage, you could earn a better living working and playing part-time than you could as a full-time pro.' So he went to play for Spennymoor United. Spennymoor played in the North Eastern League. While the Northern League was – ostensibly at least – amateur, the North Eastern League was professional. Founded in 1906, it lasted until the mid-1960s when the abolition of the amateur status effectively rendered it obsolete. In the 1940s, Blyth Spartans, North Shields, South Shields, Consett, Stockton, Ashington and Horden played in the

North Eastern League. So did Workington and the reserve teams of football league clubs Sunderland, Middlesbrough, Hartlepool, Darlington, Gateshead and Carlisle.

'The first year I was at Brewery Field we won the title,' Kenny Twigg said. 'That was remarkable really, when you see the teams we were up against.'

I asked him how the standards compared with the Northern League. His reply has stuck with me ever since. 'There was no comparison,' Kenny Twigg said. 'The North Eastern League was so much better – it was professional! Now, a professional – I don't care what job he does – he always knows more about his trade than any amateur. He lives his work.'

He continued: 'I'll give you an example. Spennymoor had this veteran centre-forward, Alf White – he'd been born in the town. He was knocking on forty by then, but he'd spent four seasons at Derby County, played 150-odd games for Bournemouth in Division Three (South), been at Wrexham. He was still a hell of a player. The first game I played for Moors, I got the ball on the touchline, in our half, facing towards our goal. There was an opponent on my back, so I did what I'd have done at Bishops in the same situation: I played safe, kicked the ball into touch. Next second there's Alf White yelling in my face, what the ruddy hell was I playing at giving possession away?

'"Why didn't you pass to me?" he said.

'I said, "I had my back turned. I didn't know where you were."

'He said, "If you were me, where would you have been?"'

'I said, "I don't know, I suppose on this same touchline looking for a pass up the line."'

'Alf White scowled. He said, "There you bloody go, then. Next time, play the ball where you think I'll be, because that's where you'll bloody well find me."'

'That was the difference,' Ken Twigg said. 'The pros understood the game. The amateurs, the amateurs just played it.'

There was plenty of evidence of that at UTS Park. In the fourth minute, Gateshead worked the ball rapidly down their left, Scott Barrow's cross found ex-Carlisle United forward Steven Rigg. He slipped it on to Greg Olley whose shot was deflected into the net. A few minutes later a move of half a dozen passes culminated in Olley feeding Rigg who dinked a shot over the sprawling Dryden. A minute before the interval, the visitors established what was clearly an unassailable lead, Scott Boden tapping in a cross from Rigg.

In the second half, Gateshead played at little more than training pace, yet still dominated.

Autumn leaves had fluttered down and now marked the far touchline. 'Let's have a one Dunston' the big blokes along the touchline bellowed. It would have been nice: a consolation, at least. But it was Gateshead who scored. In the final minutes a smoke bomb exploded and a streaker ran across the field. Even so, after the rip-roaring excitement of the Chester game it was an anti-climax.

I walked through the trees that flanked the north-west corner of the ground. What had once been the Federation Brewery was now a flat waste ground dotted with the Portakabins of businesses that sold used cars, rented out vans and repaired cherrypickers. It was an attempt to fashion something new in the demolished shell of the old, but it felt temporary and makeshift, as if confidence had been too shattered by the past events to believe that anything would last. And I knew how that felt.

Just beyond a pizza takeaway I fell in alongside a tall, round-faced man I'd often nodded a greeting to at games but never actually had a conversation with. He was in his eighties and spoke in the stop-start machine-gun-rattle style of many Durham pitmen of his vintage, as if his jaw was constantly catching up with his thoughts, then over-taking them.

He said he'd played trumpet in a silver band since he was fourteen and started at Chopwell Colliery. He still did competitions. 'It's changed now, mind,' he said. 'These days we've solicitors, accountants, everything. There's only about two of us without university degrees. Back when I was at Chopwell in the '50s it was all pitmen. There was some of them older ones; I'm not being disrespectful, they could barely read a newspaper. But you put a sheet of music in front of them and [he snapped his fingers] they could play it just like that.'

He said he'd never been much of a footballer, but his brother had been. He'd played centre-forward for Heworth

Colliery back in the '50s. His brother was fearless, he said, and tough. He'd got all his teeth knocked out by eighteen from the football. When you went in a penalty box out at Willington Quay or Bebside in those days, he said, it was bloody mayhem.

'He had a full set of dentures, our kid. Used to put them in a glass by the side of his bed at night. We lived in a miner's cottage. No heating. In winter he'd wake up of a morning and the glass would be frozen solid. He'd have to boil a kettle and defrost his teeth before he could chew his toast.'

I chuckled at the image. It reminded me of the stories about Big Billy Cruddas. Cruddas had been an old school Northern League targetman with Newcastle Blue Star. He had an attitude so combative he made Tyson Fury look like blancmange. He didn't have any teeth either. When he quit playing, Cruddas moved into management with Durham City, striding about the touchline berating everybody in earshot (which was most of the North-East and the parts of Cumbria) and generally getting so hot under the collar he needed an asbestos shirt. Managing Durham in a game at Chester-le-Street, Cruddas castigated the referee in such fulsomely colourful terms he was sent not just off the field, but out of the ground as well. Undeterred, he climbed up a tree that overlooked the pitch and carried on his onslaught from the upper branches. 'People say referees were scared of me, but I've never hit anyone in my life,' he'd once commented reassuringly.

Cruddas was notorious for half-time rants at his team to which his dentures added an element of danger. As one City player later recalled, 'When he started shouting you had to be careful where he was pointing. Because the first time he said "Fuck" his teeth'd come flying out and if they caught you wrong they'd give you a nasty bite.'

The trumpeter and I got to the stairway that led up into the station and parted company – he was getting a bus up to Clara Vale. Just before he left me, he chuckled and shook his head, 'Thawing out his teeth to eat his breakfast, you cannot picture Cristiano Ronaldo doing that, can you now?'

8

RYTON AND CRAWCROOK ALBION V BRANDON UNITED

Ebac Northern League Division Two

Saturday 10 November 2018

The train strike dragged on like a Garth Crooks question, so on Saturday I caught the bus and went to Ryton again. It wasn't such a hardship. The buses that ran from Hexham to Newcastle were a good deal more luxurious than the trains. Northern Rail still used ancient Pacers with tartan benches and whiff of Stalinism about them. The buses had leatherette seats with headrests, Wi-Fi and plug sockets. The bloke three rows along was taking advantage of the latter to charge up a cordless power drill. I wasn't surprised. One of my daughter's friends said that when they were getting the number ten to school in Blaydon, he and his mates would take a toaster and a kettle with them and make their breakfast on it.

The visitors at RACA this time were Brandon United. Brandon was a pit village just to the west of Durham, and the club's ground, on a hill facing east, had spectacular views of the cathedral and castle from which the home side's football rarely distracted you.

United were founded in the 1960s as the works team for a wastepaper company. In 2002–03, they'd surprised everybody by ending Bedlington's record run of five consecutive titles by winning away at Doctor Pit Welfare on the final day of the season to grab the title. Despite a string of managers that included ex-Newcastle players Alan Shoulder and Steve Howey and a scientific Dutchman B. J. Heijmans, success thereafter had been as rare My Little Pony manure.

The last time I'd been to Brandon had been three years before. I'd gone there for their game with South Shields. The Mariners had just created a minor sensation by signing former Sunderland and Middlesbrough midfielder, Julio Arca.

'Julio Arca playing for South Shields and Lee Cattermole playing for Sunderland – the world's turned upside down,' a bloke outside Ivy's Tea Bar at Jarrow Roofing had snorted on the Saturday the Argentinian made his home debut for Shields in the Northern League second division. The remark was greeted with the kind of knowing laughter that generally follows a joke containing a bitter truth.

South Shields have just moved back to their own ground after a couple of years playing home fixtures in Washington.

The return to base, and a wealthy new backer, has sparked a revival of interest in the Mariners. Six hundred turned up to watch their opening game. Yet still, the signing of a player who made close to 400 appearances for Sunderland and Middlesbrough was a thing of wonder.

South Shields' opponents in Arca's debut were Stokesley, a team from North Yorkshire so inept that – despite the presence of former Premier League referee Jeff Winter's predictably vast son Craig in the dug-out – they had lost all of their matches and had a goal difference of minus thirty-six.

The crowd for Arca's first appearance was swelled to 800 (the visitors' average home attendance was twenty-seven). At full time we learned that Arca had grabbed a goal, but that Stokesley had forced an unlikely 1-1 draw. 'I wonder if the former captain of a Fifa Under-20s World Cup-winning team has ever previously scored against Stokesley,' I said.

'And not finished on the winning side,' came the caveat. A quiz question for the future, surely.

For Arca's next game, I caught the 49 from Durham bus station to Brandon Turning Circle via Sawmills Estate. My companions for the trip were two old ladies who had bought a plastic mop bucket and – because it is more or less the law round the Durham coalfields – a shaven-headed youth with one of his limbs in plaster.

There was a rare crackle of excitement at the Welfare Ground and the pies had long sold out. Unbidden, the gateman showed me his copy of the programme, autographed by the former Premier League midfielder. 'That's his motor over there,' he said, pointing across the car park. 'He's a lovely fella, mind.'

At one time, top players often dropped down in to non-League football as their careers wound down. These days it was not so common, though. The players simply don't need to. You wouldn't expect Michael Carrick to end his career playing midfield for Willington any more than you'd imagine him using his savings from the game to buy a milk round. Arca joined a small band who carry on because, well, they just like playing – men such as Chris Waddle, who began his career on the icy plateau of Ironworks Road, Tow Law, and continued turning out for Hallam in the Northern Counties East well into his forties.

If it's tough to step up to a higher level in football, sometimes it's equally hard to step down. As Kenny Twigg had said, the pro operates on a different wavelength; his expectation of others is higher. As a friend of mine remarked of Peter Beardsley's struggles with Hartlepool in the twilight of his career: 'It's like Albert Einstein walked into the local pub and started explaining the theory of relativity – the fact no one understands what he's on about doesn't make him stupid.'

At the Stadium of Light and the Riverside, Arca showed for the ball, got it, gave it and moved on again. He was a player keen to dictate the pace of play. Often, though, it seemed the sharp Tito Puentes rhythms he favoured were out of time with the bass drum thud of the English game.

At Brandon it wasn't so very different. The little Argentinian flitted about in midfield, but was quite often bypassed by a long punt out to the wings. There was appreciative applause from the crowd – it was hard to calculate the number but certainly at least 500 more than the thirty-three that had witnessed the visit of Billingham Town – for a neat twenty-yard pass and couple of free kicks that went close.

Arca didn't return for the second period, and was later to be found sitting on the terrace behind the goal chatting about motors with an injured team-mate.

The 49 bus back to Durham after the match stopped just outside Langley Moor to admit an elderly man dressed in full pirate costume: velvet coat, lace shirt and thigh boots. As the pirate walked down the bus, he nodded a greeting to two old blokes sitting near the front. One of then raised a hand and said, 'All right, Tommy.'

I imagined that later in the evening his mate would ask him: 'Who was the fella on the bus earlier?' and he'd reply, 'Tommy Robson. He's a buccaneer. Well, he used to be. Got made redundant a few years back, but he still does a bit of consultancy work.'

I paid at the gate at Kingsley Park and walked into the ground. Stevie Carter and a gnarled gaggle of committee-men were gathered by the teams' whiteboard discussing what to serve the match officials for tea. One of that afternoon's linesmen had a reputation for Saturday nights on the beer and there was a widespread belief that he refused to flag for offside for fear of tiring his drinking arm. 'Have we got any of them rock-hard Jaffa cakes left over from the last home match?' one of the committeemen said.

'Aye,' another replied. 'The birds wouldn't eat them.'

The first speaker looked up at me and winked, 'Even the rats bring a packed lunch round here,' he said. 'D'you want a ticket for the half-time draw? Pound a strip.'

I bought one, more out of charity than in anticipation of victory. In twenty-five years of attending non-League football, I've not won a single raffle prize. A conservative reckoning of the number of tickets I've bought over that period would be 2,000. Given that attendances rarely top 250, are quite often down in double digits and at places like Shotton Comrades in the late '90s struggled even to make that, the odds against anyone pulling off quite such a phenomenal run of failure must be astronomical. When I thought about it, I felt my chest swell with what I took to be pride, though on reconsideration it may just have been the fried eggs I'd had before I set off.

Back when I'd first started buying non-League raffle tickets, the job of informing the crowd of the winning number was generally entrusted to one of the pre-teen urchins who used to flock to grounds in those days. The urchins took on many important duties including scaling the goalnetting as if it were the rigging of Captain Hook's galleon, making coffee in the tea bar using so many spoonfuls of instant granules it had the texture of porridge, breaking into a chorus of 'We Are the Champions' for no apparent reason, or standing behind the goal and yelling, 'We saw your bum, mister' at the opposition goalie every time he dived to make a save.

The latter is not quite the cakewalk it might appear. Once at Shildon, the goalkeeper became so incensed he booted the ball down the field and chased the urchins. They jumped over a fence and into a neighbouring garden. The game continued until, a few minutes later, a large man came storming through the main entrance, pushing up his shirt-sleeves, with a look of grim violence on his face. Behind were the two boys, each of them eagerly pointing at the goalie and yelling, 'That's him, Dad. That's the one who said he'd kill us.' Players from both sides had to intervene to prevent a fracas. Later the referee called the two teams together and reminded them of their duties. It was in those years when Uefa were considering allowing English clubs to play in European competition again. 'If word of this reaches Lausanne it could jeopardise the chances of that happening,' the ref warned.

Amazingly, despite all this, one kid would still find the energy to carry around the blackboard with the winning raffle ticket number chalked on it. This was a character-forming exercise since it inevitably involved the kid being subjected to disgruntled punters bellowing, 'There's only sixty-four folk in the ground, how come I'm 757 out, you little bastard, eh?'

I can't say I haven't wondered at that myself on occasion. I've never pursued it, though. Non-League football needs my quid more than I do, and to be honest, not winning is a relief given the nature of some of the prizes.

Once over in east Durham at a ground whose clubhouse was a windowless bunker and served lager so bubbling with chemicals it practically glowed, Ian and I asked what the raffle prize was and were told, 'A fiver. It was going to be a bottle of brandy but when we looked at it just now it had floaters in it.'

On another occasion it was a small box of groceries on the table. 'It's all good stuff, lad,' the ticket seller said in a plangent tone, wafting a blotchy hand gently over several packets of instant mash potato, a tin of pease pudding and a pine-scented air freshener in a manner that filled me with a terrible melancholy.

At Evenwood Town, during the managerial reign of madcap metallurgist Dr Graeme Forster, the first prize had been a greyhound.

Traditionally, though, the prize was a meat packet. The meat packet was a great box loaded with sausages, chops, liver and whatever else could be packed in. The grandest looked like an autopsy, the smallest like one of those drawings of the digestive system on the side of a bottle of constipation medicine. The meat packet was generally proudly displayed at the entrance to the ground as if to attract terriers and repel vegetarians.

Then, a few years back, the meat draw was gradually withdrawn. 'Can't do it any more,' one ticket seller at Shildon explained when I asked why we were being offered a case of lager instead. 'You see, trouble is people sometimes take days to collect the prize. You can't have a bag of kidneys kicking around all week, goes off.'

A little while later I went to see North Shields against Ashington. I followed an old bloke in through the turnstiles and waited as he bought his raffle tickets. He was a small man with the piercing dark eyes of a pole cat. 'Prize always used to be a meat packet,' he said to me as we walked off past the tea bar.

'Ah well,' I said. 'You see it's because ...' And I outlined what had been told to me earlier in the season.

The old man eyed me for a while after I had finished, cocking his head to one side like a terrier hearing a high-pitched whistle. 'Is that right?' he said. I confirmed that it was, adding, 'You know, pork and that.'

The old man shook his head and spat vehemently on the grass. 'It's political correctness gone fucking daft,' he said.

Brandon were rooted to the foot of the table. The RACA had achieved the sort of mid-table security that was their ambition. Home manager Tony Fawcett had been forced to make some late team changes when he received word that the car carrying midfielder Lewis Shorrock had broken down on the way to the ground. The last-minute reshuffle did not seem to hinder the home side too much and they were on top from the kick-off. Despite RACA's pressure it was over half an hour before Brandon's creaking defence finally gave way. Scott Jasper's header was cleared out of the six-yard box but fell at the feet of Callum

Turnbull and gave him the sort of come-hither look that begged him to shoot.

The home side continued to press. The visitors meanwhile treated the Ryton penalty box as if it were the boundary to some dark hell they chose not to explore. To make up for it, defender Chris Spence sent in a series of shots from an increasingly crazy series of distances and angles. 'If he carries on like this he'll be launching one from behind the clubhouse bar,' someone observed as a forty-yard effort sailed into the hedges behind the goal.

In the second period, Brandon – perhaps fortified by the brick-like biscuits on offer – became more adventurous. The Ryton penalty box no longer seemed to hold the same terror, possibly because they were familiar with it from the first half. After a series of attacks, they finally bundled the ball into the net in the fifty-fifth minute. However, the penalty area before the goal had been like a PTA rummage sale in a rough school and instead of pointing to the centre spot, the ref awarded a free kick to the home side.

Ryton doubled their lead shortly afterwards, Jasper beating Carl Robinson to a through ball and nudging it past him. There were still over twenty minutes left, but both teams were drained and the game faded away with the sunlight as the blokes around me checked their phones for scores. Newcastle United had finally got their first victory of the season – a 1-0 win over Watford – the Saturday before and now they were beating Bournemouth. 'How many matches do you have to win to make a streak?' one bloke asked his mate.

The following week it was announced that police had charged Paul Gascoigne with sexual assault following an incident on the York to Durham train the previous August, for which he was subsequently cleared. Gascoigne had once told reporters, 'I don't make predictions, and I never will.' Sadly, there was something all too foreseeable about the noxious path his life had taken over the previous decade.

To my mind, Gascoigne is the best player England has produced since Bobby Charlton. The sudden shuffling of the ball from foot to foot was incredible, the pedantic accuracy and delicate weighting of his through passes a wonder and he struck a free kick as well as anybody. And yet ... When talking of the midfielder Brian Glanville was fond of paraphrasing Sainte-Beuve: 'When asked to name the greatest writer of the present day, I reply, "Victor Hugo, alas!"'

It is hard to think of a figure in English sporting history who has pissed away as much public goodwill as Paul Gascoigne. Whenever things seemed to be going swimmingly for him, something always turned up and burst his waterwings. At first it seemed like misfortune, but after a while you began to wonder. People in football are fond of remarking that 'you make your own luck in this game'. As someone once observed of the equally self-destructive Scott Fitzgerald, there were times when you suspected a fear of disaster had become a longing for it.

Back in the late 1990s, I spent a happy Sunday afternoon

with Evan Bryson who ran Redheugh Boys Club. It was here that Gascoigne's erratic career began. Redheugh Boys had produced dozens of top footballers, including Don Hutchison, David Hodgson, Joe Laidlaw, Billy Woof and most recently Andy Carroll. Like all of the Tyneside Boys clubs, they did their work with minimum help from the professional game. As Sid Sharp, secretary of Wallsend Boys, had once told me, 'If we got just 1 per cent of the transfer fees our ex-players generate, we'd be in clover.' If such a system were in place, Redheugh Boys Club would, for example, have pocketed close to £700,000 from Andy Carroll alone. But it isn't. Because, while Premier League clubs are apparently happy to hand over millions to agents, they steadfastly refuse to put more than the bare minimum back into the grassroots game. As the secretary of Cleveland Hall Boys once said to me, 'Usually, when they take a lad from you, the League club will send you an autographed football. I knew Steve Stone must be a good player because when he went to Nottingham Forest they give us two.'

Bryson was a lovely man. Retired after years working in a factory, he'd devoted himself to helping the community he'd grown up in. I asked if he'd known Gazza well. 'I got to know him a bit, aye,' he said. 'He'd started coming here when he was about nine years old. He was too young to play, but he was so keen you felt you had to include him. His father would bring him along for the evening training sessions. Then he'd go off down to the club and quite often he'd forget to come back and get him. Paul was a little lad, it was dark and it was a long walk back to his house, so after I'd finished up I'd give him a lift home in the car.'

That was Gascoigne, right there. Mercurial, vulnerable, brilliant and reliant on the kindness of strangers, the Blanche DuBois of English football.

9

NEWCASTLE BENFIELD V
SEAHAM RED STAR

Ebac Northern League Division One

Saturday 24 November 2018

The train strike was still on and in protest against Northern Rail and all it stood for I took the express bus into Newcastle. It clicked through Corbridge in whose long since vanished maternity hospital Steve Bruce had uttered his first cries. Bruce had been one of the most successful North-East-born players of recent times, but for all his rugged centre-back physique there was something about his backcombed hair and broad, benign face that always put me in mind of an old-fashioned Northern dinner-lady. (Don't believe me? Then picture him in a nylon tabard and a hairnet, a massive stainless steel bowl of lumpy mashed potato in one hand, a slotted spoon in the other and the orange glow of the heat lamps playing across his jaw. See, frightening, isn't it?)

The X85 cut along the north bank of the Tyne through Heddon and Throckley. The latter had once had a team, Throckley Welfare, that played in the North Eastern League, though in my mind its strongest link with football history had been established by an old fellow I used to meet when out walking my dog back in the 1990s. The old fellow was a Sunderland fan and at the mention of any Newcastle United great would purse his lips, close one eye and appraise me through the other as if watching through a telescope, before saying, 'Aye well, you know he was knocking off a lassie worked the petrol pump in Throckley?' When he'd first said it – about Hughie Gallacher – I'd thought it was an insight into local life. However, by the third time – Frank Brennan – I'd started to severely doubt his reliability and when he got to the seventh – a leading member of the 1983–84 promotion team – it seemed the lassie who worked the petrol pump's use of experience to overcome a lack of mobility in the manner of late era Chris Waddle had stretched credulity beyond breaking point.

The bus rattled on through Blucher village (named after the Prussian field marshal) and Walbottle, birthplace of Tommy 'Boy' Browell who'd hit 139 goals for Man City and helped them reach the 1926 FA Cup final.

In Newcastle city centre, gangs of blokes were wearing T-shirts emblazoned with their nicknames – 'Cidergut', 'Sumo', 'Nobby' – and an announcement of whose stag do they were on. It's as if they needed a constant reminder of who they were and the mayhem they were bent on.

Without the shirt you suspected they would totally lose focus, start calling each other Orlando, sipping mint tea and discussing French symbolist poetry.

I walked over to the Metro only to find all lines running eastward were shut due to a computer failure, so I had to go to Manors to catch the bus along to Walker. I waited among a large mob of people with their Saturday shopping as traffic rumbled past. An old bloke next to me, who had more hair in his ears than seemed feasible, appeared to be counting very slowly: 'Ten . . . eleven . . . twelve.' It took me a while to work out he was tallying the buses going in the opposite direction while he waited for one going in ours. He'd got to seventeen before he had to stop and manoeuvre his tartan shopping trolley on board.

Given that two of the top three biggest North-East firms in terms of turnover – DB Arriva and Go-Ahead – were public transport companies, the continual shambles of the region's network was either darkly ironic or indicative of some grimmer truth of life in provincial England in the second decade of the twenty-first century. 'You're not in London now,' was pretty much the catchphrase of any parent whose kids had gone off to college in the capital and returned to moan about the earliness of the last train home or the way the four buses that ran per hour were all timetabled to depart in the same fifteen-minute slot. Between them, DB Arriva and Go-Ahead employed over 80,000 people. And as you watched the station noticeboard flashing up news of another cancelled train ('Due to more locomotives needing repair than usual'), or stood in the rain waiting for a bus replacement service at a Metro station because of problems with overhead lines, you might have been forgiven for wondering what the fuck they were all doing.

I took a seat on the top deck, so I could scope out the stop I needed. The mobile of the woman in front of me rang. She answered, groaned, said, 'I'm not fucking David Attenborough, am I?' and rang off. It was hard to tell if she was unable to answer a question about the natural world or was simply denying an evil rumour.

The bus took us through the backways of Byker, where rows of big initialised warehouse stores – WH Smith, B&M, B&Q – butted up against bonsai modern housing estates, Victorian terraces and abandoned engine sheds. It looked like the result of a reality show where a dozen people with radically different ideas had been tasked with giving the place a cut-price makeover.

Nearby Shields Road had just been declared the worst high street in Britain twice on the trot. The locals protested about southern bias (of the twenty best high streets in Britain only one – in Edinburgh – was further north than Cambridge), but if there were worse places it was hard to picture them without the aid of hallucinogens.

Shields Road was barely two miles from the Quayside and the bars and restaurants of what readers of the glossy Condé Nast *Traveller* magazine declared to be Britain's number one party city. In the past it was common for people who had visited South America or India to remark on the vivid contrast between rich and poor. Increasingly in the North East you could see that divide too. Tank-sized SUVs and growling Italian sports cars cruised back to their security-gated estates along streets of boarded-up shops, past pawnbrokers, cash4clothes warehouses, betting shops, loan sharks, pubs with frazzled Christmas decorations in the upper windows twelve months of the year and second-hand shops whose stock rekindled memories of a Lithuanian fleamarket in the immediate aftermath of the collapse of the Soviet Union.

You didn't have to step far from the multi-million-pound showcase regeneration projects to find feral kids dealing drugs in burned-out basement doorways, or toothless madmen on mobility scooters fighting with coat hangers. And the certainty was that if you wrote anything about it, described what you saw, as you saw it, you would receive a letter of complaint from somebody on the local council berating your negativity for jeopardising potential invest-ment and putting livelihoods at risk. And maybe they were right to do so. It's hard to determine the truth in a world where perception is more important than reality.

I got off by Walkergate, near a martial arts supplies store and a bridalwear boutique. On the flat roof of the local Food N Booze a giant dog barked at the sun.

Seaham Red Star had been founded as pub team in 1973. They'd produced a few notable players over the years including Nigel Cleghorn (who won the League Cup with

Birmingham City), Newcastle United goalkeeper Steve Harper and Bobby Davison. South Shields-born Davison made over 200 appearances for Derby County and close to 100 for Leeds, and is probably the only former Northern League player to manage a side in the Hungarian top division. He took charge of second division Ferencvárosi in 2008 and led them to promotion the following season.

The game kicked off to the sound of Seaham's manager bellowing, 'Get tighter! Get tighter!' Seaham's manager worked during the week as an announcer at Newcastle Central Station. He didn't really need a PA.

Mark 'Sparky' Turnbull, the Benfield skipper, was such a consistent presence in the defence you barely noticed him. Whether at full-back or in the middle he seemed the very model of reliability. There was nothing fancy about him. He did his job. So it was quite a surprise when the Seaham number ten crossed low and hard from the left and Turnbull slid in towards his own goal and hammered the ball into the roof of the net.

The North East tends naturally to drift towards nostalgia – it's pretty much the premise of *Whatever Happened to the Likely Lads?* (and they don't make sitcoms like that any more . . .) and so it was no surprise that Sparky's aberration caused the bloke behind me to sigh and say, 'Whatever happened to the teleprinter?'

There was a collective chuckle and somebody added, 'I liked it when a team scored eight and it used to type out the number in words in brackets after in case anybody thought it had made a mistake' and we all laughed some more.

It's a sure sign you are middle-aged when the second most common question you ask – after 'Why don't these trousers fit any more?' – is 'Whatever happened to . . .?' 'Whatever happened to the half-time scores being put up on the touchline using a code printed in the programme?' you find yourself muttering to nobody in particular. Or 'Whatever happened to football managers taking the first team down a coalmine to "give them a sense of perspective"?' Or 'Whatever happened to footballers being photographed with their dogs?' Or 'Whatever happened to playing with an orange ball when it was snowing?' Or 'Whatever happened to goalkeepers wearing polo-neck sweaters? Or those sweatshirts with the quilted fronts?'

Nobody ever gives you an answer to these questions, though quite often a loved one will volunteer the information that 'If you say "Whatever happened to . . .?" one more time, I'm leaving and I'm not coming back.' Which hardly helps.

Although, to be honest, I don't think that was the main reason.

The other odd thing about reaching your fifties is that you start getting nostalgic even for things you didn't like from the past. Like the Simod Cup, for instance, or hot Oxo and Wagon Wheels, or Steve Watson's somersault throw-ins, or PA systems so primitive and feeble that even if they'd played 'The Power' by Snap at top volume it would still have sounded like an elderly pug whimpering through an upside-down megaphone. Back in the 1980s I used to get incensed watching *Saint and Greavesie*, but these days I find myself thinking wistfully of their lazy jokes about efficient Germans and Russians who parked their tanks on the goal line and wondering why Dan Walker and Gabby Logan can't do a bit of amusing banter about how crap Scottish goalkeepers are.

Benfield levelled through a Dennis Knight penalty. A few minutes later a cross was slung in from the left by Jake Orrell and Turnbull popped up to head it firmly into the Seaham goal. 'Away Sparky, you're on a hat-trick,' someone cried.

He didn't get it but Knight added another before the end.

The next day I went down to Bishop Auckland to visit the newly opened Gallery of Mining Art. Unlike a lot of social realist paintings, they were devoid of sentimentality. In the Pays Noir, the Belgian equivalent of County Durham, artists such as Constantin Meunier had painted the mineworkers with a kind of saintly glow – as if suffering brought with it redemption. In these paintings, working down a pit didn't look heroic or purifying. It looked grim and claustrophobic, a thing worth avoiding. Perhaps that was why the coalfields had produced so many footballers.

Ashington (population 27,000) alone had churned out hundreds. Indeed, three English Footballers of the Year – Bobby and Jack Charlton and Jimmy Adamson – had been born in the same street, Laburnum Terrace. The Charltons' uncle, Jackie Milburn, was also from Ashington. Winger

Billy Gray was another lad with ties to Ashington. He started his pro career at Gateshead just after the Second World War, was transferred to Leyton Orient, then moved across London to play nearly 150 games for Chelsea. In 1953, Gray joined Adamson at Burnley, establishing an uncanny understanding with Jimmy McIlroy.

Thickening around the waistband and heavier in the legs, Gray was shifted on to Nottingham Forest. Here he gained a new lease of life when manager Billy Walker switched him to inside-right with Roy Dwight (Elton John's uncle, I feel compelled to say, even though I know you already knew that) on the wing outside him. In Forest's run to the FA Cup final of 1959, Gray hit five goals, including one direct from a corner. In the final he set up Forest's second for Tommy Wilson as the Tricky Trees ran out comfortable winners. After retiring as a player, Gray managed Millwall to back-to-back promotions before ending his working life tending the pitch at the City Ground during the glory days of Brian Clough. Gray's had been a remarkable career. Anywhere else it might have marked him out as a local celebrity. Yet so rich was Ashington in football lore that few in the town today had heard of him.

The same held true in the old Durham coalfields, though extensive work was being done here to preserve the heritage of football in the region. The last time I'd been in Bishop Auckland it had been to give a talk at Auckland Castle, a tie-in with the excellent exhibition on Bishop Auckland FC, 'Birth of the Blues'. Afterwards, members of the audience came up to chat. Many had brought mementos of North-East non-League football: winners' medals from long-forgotten local cup competitions, faded velvet England amateur caps, photographs in ageing frames. All the items had tales attached, a memory trail to long-dead relatives, to pit villages once lived in, some of them now abandoned forever.

Shortly after I'd learned, with some relief, that Kenny Twigg's carefully compiled and labelled scrapbooks were being held in safe keeping, a lady in her mid-seventies opened her handbag and pulled from it an autograph album covered in tartan cloth. Her parents, she said, had been involved with Stanley United back in the 1950s. 'When I was a teenager,' she said, 'I served the players their post-match teas, and I got them all to sign my book.'

Stanley United was one of the oldest clubs in Durham. They won the Northern League title three times. Stanley played at Mount Pleasant. Like many places in the North East, it seemed to have been named by someone of ironic bent. Mount Pleasant was on a freezing hill above Crook, so isolated the white-washed two-storey clubhouse, where the players changed and ate, and the spectators defrosted at half time in front of a blazing fire, was nicknamed 'The Little House on the Prairie'.

The lady opened the tartan-covered book. 'Here, look,' she said, 'the Bishops team, 1955.' She ran a finger under the signatures, the well-practised autographs of men who were the superstars of the amateur game: Corbett Cresswell, eccentric 'keeper Harry Sharratt who was once booked for building a snowman on his goal line. I pointed at one which had an extra flourish: Seamus O'Connell.

Seamus O'Connell was Bishops' wealthy and glamorous inside-forward. His tailoring was Savile Row and he arrived by Jaguar. Even photos of him give off the whiff of Floris cologne, single malt and Cuban cigars. He left Bishops to play as an amateur for Chelsea, helped the team from Stamford Bridge win their first League title in 1955, then quit saying that football was no kind of life for a man. An infamous womaniser, O'Connell was allegedly so well-endowed that, after catching a glimpse of him naked in the shower, one London society hostess remarked, 'Built like that he really ought to trot.'

The woman with the tartan autograph book grinned at the recollection of him. 'Eee, aye,' she said. 'Seamus O'Connell. He once give me a lift home over the moor top in his sports car,' and she shivered at the thought of it.

'So you must have known Geoff Strong, then,' I said.

Geoff Strong was the centre-forward at Stanley in 1957. Between the start of the season and Christmas he scored thirty-one goals. Arsenal came looking to sign him. They offered Strong £13 a week. It was a tougher decision than you might think. The amateurs of Stanley were paying him £10 a week 'boot money' and he picked up another £4 as an apprentice fitter. In the end, he decided to take the pay cut and move to Highbury. He scored sixty-nine goals for the Gunners, then Bill Shankly bought him for Liverpool. He died two years ago.

The woman's eyes twinkled when I said the name. 'Ooh, Geoff Strong,' she said, and she placed the autograph book down on the table we were standing beside and ran her hands back and forwards across it. 'I used to iron his number nine shirt every week,' she said, looking at the tartan book as if it was the targetman's red-and-white striped jersey, 'and, you know, I always ironed that shirt with love.'

Stanley United folded in 2003. The Little House on the Prairie was burned down by arsonists. Only the goalposts and the memories remain.

Among the exhibits in the Birth of the Blues exhibition was a programme from the 1954 FA Amateur Cup final between Bishops and Crook Town. It was a remarkable match that in many ways encapsulates North-East non-League football during its glittering years. The two sides battled each other for five and a half hours, at three different stadiums and in front of an aggregate crowd of close to 200,000 – almost ten times the combined populations of the two towns. Those indeed were the days.

The struggle began at Wembley. Bishops were runaway favourites. They'd played Crook twice in the Northern League that season, beating them 4-1 at home and 3-1 away. The men from Kingsway were on a roll. They'd spent the late-summer on a three-week tour of Rhodesia, guests of the local FA, then returned to the North East and embarked on an incredible goal-scoring spree that would see them net over 200 goals that season. In the five games they'd played to get to Wembley, Bishops had scored twenty-six times, including five in a semi-final win over Briggs Sports from Essex that drew 54,000 fans to St James' Park.

Captained by Londoner Jack 'The Galloping' Major, Bishop Auckland were the Real Madrid of amateur football and the 1950s were their glory years. They took the Northern League title six times, appeared in five Wembley finals, won the Northern League Cup three times and the Durham Challenge Cup twice.

Bishops' best players were household names, not just in the North East, but across the whole of England. This, after all, was the only amateur side to have its own Subbuteo team. Wing-half Bob Hardisty (his given names were John Roderick – he'd been nicknamed 'Bob' by a midwife at the hospital and it stuck) was considered by many the greatest amateur footballer of his generation (one man who didn't join the chorus of adulation was Kenny Twigg, who considered Hardisty amateurish and lacking in positional sense).

A midfielder who liked to roam forward, Hardisty had captained the Great Britain side – managed by Matt Busby – that reached the semi-finals in the 1948 Olympics. He was tall, elegant, and prematurely bald due to an illness contracted in India during World War Two. A PE instructor at a local teacher training college, Hardisty, was, according to Reverend John Marshall, 'a man who unified the town, a story that folk lore is made of'. Despite the veneration, Hardisty was no saint. He had a roving eye when it came to women and a reputation as a reckless gambler. 'There was bookies chasing him all over Durham,' a resident of

the town once told me. And bookmakers in those days –
operating illegally off track – were not gentle when it came
to debt collection. 'The club had to bail him out for fear
they'd break his legs,' my informant said.

That the club would do such a thing was an underlying
truth of 'amateur' football: gate receipts were high and the
players were valuable assets. As a consequence, it wasn't just
Geoff Strong who earned more as an amateur than a League
professional. Sometimes payment came through services in
kind. 'Every Saturday your wife or mother could pick up
the Sunday roast at a local butchers and the bill went to the
club,' Kenny Twigg said, 'and a couple of times a year you
could go and get a suit made, stuff like that. I never took
cash, though I could have, if I'd needed it.'

Compared to Bishops' swaggering *galácticos*, Crook
Town (or 'The Crooks' as the Pathé News commentator
would insist on calling them) appeared modest and home-
spun. The Black and Ambers' best-known player was
winger Jimmy McMillan. McMillan was quick and skilful
and he'd finish his career with a record four Amateur Cup
winners' medals, but he was no glamour boy. He'd turned
down the chance of playing for Newcastle United and
Chelsea to train as a local government planning officer.
Sensible, decent, honest. The same might be said of the
entire Crook squad. Coached by the young Joe Harvey –
who'd later lead Newcastle to their Fairs Cup victory – and
skippered by former Bishop Auckland centre-half Bobby
Davison, the side from Millfield was greater than the sum

of its parts. To borrow a phrase from Franz Beckenbauer: the star was the team.

The game was given an extra edge by the two clubs' slightly bitter rivalry. It all went back to the infamous Crook Town Affair of 1928, an investigation into illegal payments in the Northern League that had ended with 341 players suspended and Crook hoofed out altogether (they were nailed-on certainties to be champions, too). The club that had secretly brought the matter to the attention of the FA – Bishop Auckland.

Supporters from the two Durham towns travelled down to London on twenty special trains and 250 coaches. Wembley was a sell-out. Bishops' preparation for the game had already been disrupted, Scottish international full-back Tommy Stewart going down with jaundice. Worse now followed. Half-back Jimmy Nimmins slid into a tackle and didn't get up. He'd broken his right leg. With no substitutions allowed, they were going to have to play the rest of the game with ten men. Their supporters looked on grimly. Bishops had played three finals at Wembley and lost them all. Fans muttered of a curse.

The mood brightened when Les Dixon opened the scoring, slashing the ball past the rangy Fred Jarrie in the Crook goal.

Crook were a fine attacking side too. The season before they'd won the Northern League, scoring an average four goals per game, and they'd gubbed Hitchin 10-1 on the way to Wembley. They responded almost immediately, Ronnie

Thompson planting a low shot into the left-hand corner of Sharratt's goal.

With their one-man advantage Crook might have expected to take control, but Ken Williamson soon pulled up with an ankle injury and spent the rest of the game hobbling up and down the wing.

Bishops took advantage of the disruption. Railway worker Bob Watson found Ray Oliver on the edge of the box. The big centre-forward accelerated past a couple of opponents and blasted the ball into the top corner from 18 yards.

The second half saw Crook on top and they equalised when Bill Jeffs, a summer signing from Whitby, crossed for winger Eddie Appleby to hammer home.

The replay, ten days later at St James' Park, drew a crowd of 56,008 – the highest ever for an amateur match outside the capital.

Things began badly again for Bishops. Within four minutes they were 2-0 down, both goals scored by the prolific Ken Harrison, a schoolmaster from the rugged Annfield Plain who'd bagged a hat-trick in the semi-final win over Walthamstow. Bishops refused to panic. Gradually they took control, stringing passes together in the smooth-flowing style that had had BBC commentator Kenneth Wolstenholme purring with delight during the first encounter. After sixty-nine minutes Oliver pulled one back and in the eighty-first he got a second. Extra-time brought no more goals. By the final whistle the players looked ready to collapse.

With league fixtures piling up, the second replay was

hastily arranged at Ayresome Park three days later. This time it would be settled in ninety minutes. If it was a draw at the final whistle the two teams would share the trophy. Despite the short notice and the difficulty of getting off work in time for the 6 p.m. kick-off, 36,727 turned up on a blustery Teesside night.

The first two matches had been marked by excitement, goals and free-flowing football. This one turned into a trial of strength and stamina. Midway through the first half, Bishops had the ball in the net, Oliver rising to head home Major's corner. The jubilant players had danced all the way back to the centre circle before they realised one-armed referee Alf Bond – inevitably dubbed 'the one-armed bandit' by aggrieved Bishops fans – had disallowed it. In the end, one goal settled the match. It went to the Black and Ambers, Harrison inevitably the scorer.

Joe Harvey's team returned immediately to Crook aboard a special train, skipper Davison waving the silver trophy from the window at the supporters who lined up beside the tracks at pit villages along the way. When they got home 15,000 people and a silver band greeted them despite the fact it was going on midnight. There was to be no all-night partying for the Crook players, mind. They had work the next day, and in the evening there was a Northern League fixture at West Auckland to play.

10

WHICKHAM V NEWTON AYCLIFFE

Ebac Northern League, Division One

Saturday 8 December 2018

It was the second Saturday of December. If my gran had still been around she'd likely have put the sprouts on today so they were ready for Christmas dinner. Modern chefs think veg should be crisp, but my gran held to old tried and true northern methods, boiling them until all the dangerous nutrients were dead. When she scooped a sprout onto your plate it gradually collapsed until it lay there flat, green and gelatinous as a Vulcan's snot.

I took the train to the Metrocentre. The strike was still on but the trains were being staffed by management who carried out all their duties with studious and exaggerated efficiency as if to prove a point.

At every station the acting conductor did that thing of opening one of the rear doors and sticking his head out

150

quickly, then ducking back in again before opening the rest. Why do they do that? What are they looking for? Every time I watched them, I thought: this time they'll yell, 'Zulus! Thousands of 'em!' and we'll speed out of Prudhoe with assegai points clattering off the windows ... But for some reason it never happened.

The Metrocentre bus station was the usual scene of pre-pubescent mayhem as boys and girls went through the traditional mating rituals of kicking each other and running away. Thankfully the 97 Green Arrow arrived quickly and we were soon heading to the calm uplands of Lobley Hill.

'We're going out for brunch with them tomorrow,' the woman in front of me told her friend and then laughed and said, 'When you think about it, us Geordies should call it "brinner".'

Whickham was a relatively prosperous suburb of Newcastle with a high street lined with café bars and craft ale pubs. It looked like the sort of place where 'brinner' would involve toasted sourdough and mashed avocado, rather than a big fry-up and a left-over Yorkshire pudding with jam and Carnation.

I walked up the road to the Glebe Sports Ground. The football club had been formed during the Second World War by members of the Home Guard and were originally called Axwell Park Colliery Welfare. Thankfully for the people who have to type out the football results, they changed to Whickham in 1962. They'd originally been nicknamed the Home Guard, but these days they preferred the Lang Jacks. Lang Jack was Georgian giant John English, aka the 'Tyneside Samson', who stood 6ft 4, could lift stones that defied four ordinary men and reputedly made a habit of leaping in the air to headbutt pub ceilings. It was before TV or the internet and you had to make your own entertainment. Lang Jack lived in Whickham in a cottage he built himself with stone he'd carried all the way from Blaydon. There was a statue of him in the town and a nightclub had been named in his honour, though it seemed to have closed down when I walked past it.

The Lang Jacks won the FA Vase in 1981 and had been beaten semi-finalists in 1979 and 1984. Since joining the Northern League in 1988, they'd spent most of their time in the second division, but a new chairman and the arrival of Andrew Bulford, Dunston's all-time record goal scorer, had seen them promoted to the top flight in 2018.

The clubhouse was busy when I arrived, with horse racing blaring from the TV, so I took my drink round into the function room bar where tinsel hung above a drum kit and assorted club officials in badged warm-up coats and blazers had gathered to swap team sheets.

Newton Aycliffe was a new town a few miles north of Darlington. It was built just after the Second World War. William Beveridge, architect of the welfare state and a key figure in the government's new town policy, owned a house in Pease Way and wanted Newton Aycliffe to be a shining example of the bright, modern, carefully planned Britain of the future.

Alongside the housing estates was a large complex of factories and industrial units. Living in the new, futuristic Britain would mean working at Great Lake Chemicals, Union Carbide or Eaton Axles. Though the consolation would be that when you got home a robot butler would have got a dinner of pills ready for you and washed all your Crimplene jumpsuits.

Nowadays, Newton Aycliffe was home to Ebac – a British manufacturer of fridges and washing machines – who sponsored the Northern League; Ineos, who sponsored the road race cycling squad that used to be Team Sky; as well as Hitachi's rolling stock factory, which as far as I could tell had avoided getting caught up in sport.

The football team had grown from a side formed at a Methodist youth club. Their most notable former player was Ferryhill-born Mr Punch look-alike Eric Gates, who'd left to join Ipswich in 1972. The Blues manager, Bobby Robson, sent the club a cheque for £25 as a donation. Gates went on to play just shy of 300 games for the East Anglian club, scoring seventy-three goals and helping them win the Uefa Cup. In 1985 he was sold to Sunderland for £150,000. After retirement he picked up a sackful of coins every Sunday playing pub football around Staindrop and Barnard Castle. These days he has a pig farm. Eric Gates was just 5ft 6 and weighed under 10 stone. His brother Bill was considerably larger. He spent a dozen years kicking lumps out of opponents as centre-half for Middlesbrough, had his jaw broken by an outraged Brian Kidd, made a small fortune from a sports shop business and now lives in the Cayman Islands. It's fair to say they are an interesting pair.

The quiet of the function room I was sitting in was soon disturbed by a sudden influx of Aycliffe fans: big, raw-boned Teessiders with voices that reverberated like underground explosions. There are lots of men on Teesside who sound as if they've just come off shift from modelling in a foghorn factory. I had an uncle who was the same. People said it was from the effort of shouting over the roar of heavy machinery, though after a while listening to him you started to think maybe his co-workers had invented heavy machinery expressly to drown out what he was saying. When he came in my gran's house and began talking, the windows rattled and the tea tray shuddered. Sometimes by the time he'd finished an anecdote the milk in the jug would have turned to butter.

'Now, here's a thing,' my uncle would boom. 'The other day I was sat in the Commercial having a quiet pint. I've just finished saying to our lass how these steel workers who're out on strike are a bunch of lazy, workshy shirkers, when suddenly this barstool comes flying out of nowhere and hits me on the head.'

'Were you hurt?' we'd ask.

'No,' he'd roar back. 'Luckily for me it clipped our lass on the way through and that drew the sting out of it.' One of the Newton Aycliffe fans was talking about his elderly mother. 'She's gone totally fucking Louis, hasn't she? Sent us a Christmas card and when I opened it a fucking Yorkshire pudden fell out.'

They bought pints and sat down. The men were Boro fans and they were unhappy. I have to say that this is pretty much the general state of Middlesbrough fans of a certain age. 'This is the last season, for me, for sure. Deffo,' one of them said in a voice that set the windows rattling. His friends laughed. They had heard this before. We all had.

I cast my mind back to another winter Saturday afternoon. Four more burly men with voices that rumbled like cement mixers and made eavesdropping compulsory even for those several streets away, stepped out of the concrete bunker that houses Potter's Sporting Club in the Dundas Arcade. The weather seemed to be working overtime to confirm Mrs Emerson's notorious description of Teesside as 'a dark and terrible place'. Sharp rain fell from a sky the colour of tarmac and the wind whistled death ballads.

I was a few yards behind them. The collective mood matched the elements. The previous week Peter Taylor's Leicester City had slaughtered Boro at the Riverside. The home team's performance was so hopelessly shambolic that even a language as rich and diverse as English could not fully do justice to it, though the bloke behind me tried, yelling so hard and ceaselessly at the back of my head that when I got home I looked like I'd been in a wind tunnel. Around me fans vented their fury. Beside me, a young woman with a voice that would have stripped barnacles off a ship's keel used so many expletives she must have been swearing for two. Her partner was plainly an educated man, because at one point he berated the referee using the word 'pedantic', alongside several other more Anglo-Saxon verbs and nouns. In front of me, a fellow with a plaster on the end of his nose masking what looked like a bite mark, filled the air with predictions of the team's future fate so dire they made the Book of Ezekiel look like a magazine horoscope page.

At one point in the second period, the visitors had strung together close to a dozen passes in Middlesbrough's half.

'Fuckyerbastardshitfuckinchristonafuckinstickborojesus,' the bloke behind me howled.

Even that was more coherent than Bryan Robson's tactics.

The memory of the crushing defeat lingered like a garlic fart. Today's visitors were Bradford City, a team who hadn't won away from home since the last days of Byzantium. That fact only made home fans more apprehensive. If you were looking to end a losing streak, Boro were the team to play. Always. Or so it seemed.

As we crossed the road one of the men said, 'If we get beat off Bradford today and Robson doesn't resign, I'm going straight to the Transporter and chucking myself off.'

'You'll have to get in a queue,' his mate said.

'Aye,' another added. 'They'll have a ticketing machine like the DSS.' He adopted the nasal tone of all bureaucracy: 'Number 976, a position is now available to deal with your suicide claim.'

And on we had walked into the darkness of the afternoon.

'I'm fucking serious,' the bloke in Whickham's clubhouse said. 'I can't take it any more. Not with that fella in charge.' Ah yes, Boro boss, Tony Pulis.

When mother was a young infant school teacher in Redcar she played a recording of the Overture from *Swan Lake* to a class of six-year-olds and invited them to close their eyes and let their imaginations roam. When the record had finished, she asked what pictures Tchaikovsky's music had conjured in their minds. 'My dad's garage,' one of the boys said.

I thought of this down-to-earth lad whenever I saw Tony Pulis. The Welshman appears the sort of man whose romantic yearnings would be stirred by creosote and cans of WD40. Though Pulis began his managerial career in the 1990s, he seemed to belong to a much earlier age. Even his photo gives off the National Service odour of carbolic soap, wintergreen and yesterday's swede. If the former Stoke boss wears aftershave, you know it will not be some unisex *eau de parfum*, but something with an unambiguously masculine name like Grip or Roofbar that comes in a bottle shaped like a locknut and stings so badly it makes you wince.

He calls to mind gaffers of earlier times, such as Newcastle's Gordon Lee who, with his dark, flapping trench-coat and gaunt, pallid and expressionless face, gave the impression that he slept upside down, suspended from the ceiling in a hammock formed by his own membranous wings (this sense of something crepuscular was enhanced by the Newcastle boss's celebrated comment that 'just because you are dead doesn't mean you have to lie down and be buried'), or one of Lee's successors, Bill McGarry, who wouldn't let his players eat prawns (bawling at one of them, 'What do think this is, a fucking holiday camp? You eat what I eat, and I don't eat that!') and rationed bread rolls for fear they would weaken core strength.

Pulis has garnered an old-fashioned reputation too, rejecting intricate patterns of passing in favour of advancing up the touchline, throw-in by throw-in. To some his approach is anathema. It is wrong. It is not the game *the way it is supposed to be played*. Pulis might have taken Stoke into Europe with less than 40 per cent possession, or finished higher up the table than any team with the fewest goals in the division really ought, or beaten Arsène Wenger's stylish Arsenal more times than seemed polite, but this is not the era for such Jack Charltonesque pragmatism. At Middlesbrough, Pulis had done a decent job when it came to results – he'd stabilised things at the Riverside after the short, shoddy reign of Gary Monk and Boro were a fixture in the play-off places. That was no longer enough, however. This is the Sky Super Sunday Age. Pulis was a chain link fence in Paradise.

'You're not going to go anywhere,' one of the blokes in the Whickham clubhouse said. 'Remember at Ayresome there was always some little old fella at the final whistle stood at the top of the Holgate shaking his fist at the pitch and going, "That's me finished, that is"? Well, that's you now. That's what you've become.'

'Aye,' one of the other men said. 'The Boro have turned you into a granddad.'

It was ten to three and the committeemen got up to

go outside and watch the match. In order to get into the ground without having a long looping walk round the side of the clubhouse, they took a short cut through the kitchen. I followed them past jumbo blocks of orange cheese, catering packs of spongey white baps and jars of salad cream Ali Baba could have hidden in.

There were about a hundred spectators in the ground. A clutch of lads in skinny jeans and pointy monkey-shit brown brogues were hanging round by the Corner Kick Café in a perma-mist of Lynx Africa. A group of players' girlfriends – tanned skin, ironed hair, white D&G handbags and ecru bobble hats with fun fur pom-poms – were clustered at the back of the stand warming their hands on a couple of tiny, fluffy dogs. Over by the dugouts, a duo of straggly standard issue non-League fans, one in cowboy boots and an Indiana Jones hat and the other with sallow, pitted skin who looked like he might have hung around in the background in a 1980s Cinzano advert and sleep in satin, vaped and coughed and occasionally barked an insult at the nearest linesman.

The Glebe was high up above the town and nothing seemed to separate it from the darkness save for a flimsy wire fence. I looked for shelter in the main stand next to an old chap who had the shiny cuddly-toy eyes of Sergio Aguero set in a face so crenelated by age, weather and alcohol he made Raymond Goethals look like Cristiano Ronaldo. At fifteen-minute intervals, he cleared his throat with such thoroughness he must have sucked the dirt out from beneath his toenails.

'Can't even foul proper,' he growled, as a Whickham defender and visiting forward blundered into one another and subsided slowly to the turf like a pair of tired toddlers in an IKEA ball pool.

He soon settled into a nice rhythm, bellowing, 'Get it in the middle for Christ's sake!' every time Whickham crossed the halfway line, and, when a player responded by hoofing the ball into the penalty area, groaning, 'There you go, bloody route one again. Where's our vision?'

He reminded me of the gnarly old bird at Hillheads who yelled, 'Stop interfering and let them get on with the game, man' every time the ref signalled a foul and 'Did you leave your bloody whistle in the dressing room, referee?' whenever he didn't. Sometimes it's not only match officials who need to 'show a bit of consistency'.

Aycliffe's line-up included Vinny Gash, who sounded like he might have been created by Mickey Spillane, but it was the more bucolically named Max Cowburn, a young striker released by Carlisle United in the summer, who opened the scoring for Whickham, smashing a shot past the gigantic James Winter to put the home side in front just before half time.

At the interval I went to get a hot drink at the tea bar. A couple of the Aycliffe fans were standing behind me. One said: 'It's the bloody present list. It gets longer and longer every year. I said you should have seen what my granddad used to get for his Christmas box every year: a pomegranate and a bag of nuts.'

Whickham had just about done enough to justify their lead in the first half, but in the second things quickly went wrong. Former Ashington striker Damien Stevens – who the old bloke to my right had approvingly noted was 'tough, no-nonsense; not one of them fanny-merchants' – launched a challenge as full-blooded as a Quentin Tarantino shoot-out and was immediately shown red. 'It's still a man's game, referee!' the old chap grizzled.

Whickham had previous with red cards. Back in February 2015 they'd been playing another team of Teessiders, Billingham Town. The game became notorious in Northern League circles as one of the few to be abandoned for shortage of players. On that occasion Scott Donaldson of Whickham had been sent off for a professional foul early on. Then with the clock running down and Whickham apparently incensed by an off-the-ball incident, the referee – who had the unlikely name of Peter Osgood – sent off four players in a three-minute flurry of red. A trio of the players – Mark Pattison, Scott Swanston and Craig Poole – were from the home side who now had only eight men left on the field. When their team-mate Ross Peareth limped off in stoppage time they were reduced to seven, leaving Mr Osgood no choice under the Laws of the Game but to call the whole thing off. There was a considerable furore about the matter at the time – well, when I say furore there was a bit of tutting and I believe the word 'shame' may have been mumbled.

There was no repeat of such melodrama this afternoon,

though the red card proved pivotal. Within moments, striker Kurt Matthews had equalised, then in stoppage time Ethan Wood popped up in the six-yard box to grab the winner for the visitors as the home defenders tumbled around like cake-filled infants on a bouncy castle.

11

DUNSTON UTS v SUNDERLAND RCA

Ebac Northern League Division One

Saturday 12 January 2019

Dunston had been having a bit of a post-Christmas wobble. As a Middlesbrough fan I had some sympathy because this was one of our great traditions. Boro always come down with the lights, people across Teesside would say with the sense of satisfaction that only really comes from vindicated pessimism.

In December, UTS had appeared certain to take the Northern League title, but the whitewash by Gateshead, an unexpected defeat in the second round of the FA Vase at Winterton Rangers and a season-ending knee injury to Liam Thear had dented their confidence. Suddenly they were like a man at the top of a high ladder who has just made the mistake of looking down. They'd been struggling to win in the league and had suffered an unexpected home reversal to a mediocre Bishop Auckland.

Sunderland RCA had been one of the better teams in the Northern League for several seasons. They'd begun life back in the 1960s as Ryhope Youth Club. In 1982, they became members of the newly formed Northern League second division, joining such luminaries as Gretna, Peterlee, Northallerton and the reserve sides of Darlington and Hartlepool. They merged with Kennek Roker in 1999 – briefly becoming Kennek Ryhope, which sounds like a 1980s soul singer. RCA had benefited for many years from one of the more unusual sponsorships in North-East football, a deal with Promenade Café that saw them receiving the payment in the form of corned beef pies.

Jimmy and Margaret were away in Spain. So I sat to the left of our normal position next to two men in black NUFC warm-up coats that reached down to their ankles, giving them a priestly air their distinctly un-Latin language quickly dispersed. They'd both been watching *Sunderland Till I Die* on Netflix. 'It's the best fucking laugh I've had in years,' one of them said and guffawed loudly to prove the point.

'Aye, there's always someone worse off than yourselves,' his friend said, 'and it's usually the Mackems.'

I'd been watching *Sunderland Till I Die* too and I understood what they meant. Any documentary about the inner workings of a football club is likely to call to mind William Goldman's famous maxim about Hollywood: 'In this business ... nobody knows anything.' Though in the case of this one I found myself muttering the great screenwriter's adage and appending the words 'and sometimes far, far less than that'.

To an outsider, the financial side of the game is one of the unfathomable mysteries of the universe to rank with whether there is life on other planets, how the Christmas tree lights manage to get in such a tangle all by themselves and why no one at the BBC has yet told Chris Waddle how to pronounce 'penalty'. To the outsider the typical professional football club seems to belong to a man who in one mitt holds a redundancy notice for a minimum-wage part-time ticket office assistant and in the other a briefcase filled with £50 notes destined for the agent of a newly signed midfielder who will display all the mobility of a pillar box while spraying passes around with the accuracy of a carp fisherman laying down ground bait after an eighth can of Tennant's Super. Eventually, he will have to give another briefcase filled with even more cash to the agent to make his client bugger off back into the world of YouTube clips from which he came. Meanwhile, in the parallel universe of non-League, a century-old club will fold over a four-figure debt – which sadly would be the fate of Dunston's FA Cup opponents North Ferriby. As John Cooper Clarke almost said, 'An agent smiles and a football team dies at the back of Beasley Street.'

The wind was blowing from the car park end and Dunston had it at their backs in the first half. The ball sailed around the stratosphere with neither side apparently willing or able to adapt to the conditions. Liam Brooks got sloshed in the face in an aerial challenge and was left prone and yelping in pain. He was led away by the physio, his legs wobbling like they were made of string. Just before half time, Brooks' replacement, Jordan Nellis, played a clever ball into Mark Fitzpatrick in the visitors' box. The striker drilled a shot towards the far post and Scott Heslop bundled it untidily across the line.

In the second period the wind made a determined bid to snatch the sponsor's man of the match award, gathering an RCA corner delivered from the right and swirling it round the defence and into the net off the back post. Dunston rallied and eventually took the lead again, RCA defender Ross Preston deflecting a Fitzpatrick shot into his own net.

The visitors came back strongly but couldn't find an equaliser and when the final whistle sounded the Dunston players punched the air and yelled with relief.

The taxi driver had been watching *Sunderland Till I Die* too. It had made him nostalgic. When I got in the back seat a few days after Dunston's win, he was midway through a peroration which I imagined had been going on some while.

'... Christian Pulisic Dortmund to Chelsea £58 million, Miguel Almiron Atlanta to the Skunks £20 million, Dominic Solanke Liverpool to Bournemouth £19 million, Jonny Otto Atletico Madrid to Wolves £18.5 million ... Meanwhile on Wearside ...' the taxi driver said, 'Grant Leadbitter back on a free, Jimmy Dunne (loan), Kazaiah Sterling (loan) and some fella named Max Power. What kind of name's that? Sounds like a bloody action figure or something out a comic. He'll be changing into his kit in a telephone box, likely. One player we spent on – Will Grigg. From Wigan. Four million. Bank of bloody England club, aren't we?' His voice had the bitter note of somebody whose family had lost a fortune before he was born.

Between 1948 and 1958, Sunderland had indeed spent a phenomenal amount of cash earning themselves that unfortunate title. When football started back after the Second World War, the Rokermen were one of England's grandest clubs. They'd won the league title in 1936 and the FA Cup the following season, played in front of crowds that often exceeded 50,000 and occasionally topped 60,000, and had spent their entire history in the top flight. There seemed little reason to believe that the pre-war success wouldn't continue.

True, manager Johnny Cochrane – the last manager named John to lift an English title, incidentally – had stepped down in 1939 (he'd very briefly take charge of Reading. Lasting just a matter of days, one player recalled that the team's only encounter with the Scot had been when he stuck his head in the dressing room half an hour before kick-off to ask who the opposition were), while the club's greatest-ever player Raich Carter – who'd hit thirty-one goals in the championship season, including a hat-trick against title-holders Arsenal – had left for Derby County.

But club favourite Aberdonian Bill Murray had taken Cochrane's place and with cash rattling in at the turnstiles and County Durham awash with talent, fans were confident. Cochrane had built his team slowly, nurturing young players. This time around the club's directors were determined to move things along faster. Having already spent heavily on England cricket and football international Willie Watson, Shiremoor-born Jackie Robinson and Arthur Hudgell (the latter a £10,000 purchase from Crystal Palace), Sunderland signalled their intent to the football world in February 1948 when they signed Len Shackleton from Newcastle. The £20,050 fee was a British record.

Viewed as a direct replacement for the brilliant Carter, Shackleton, the so-called 'Clown Prince of Soccer', was a player of rare gifts. A ball-juggling genius who laughed at coaches and directors, he might have been a prototype of the style of player who'd either electrify English football in the 1960s and 1970s or signal the death throes of civilisation depending on your point of view. Like George Best, Rodney Marsh and co, Shack had the skills to brighten up even the darkest northern afternoon and yet . . . While these days it is rare to meet any Sunderland fan who doesn't speak of Shack in the sort of awe-struck terms that would make God blush, during his playing days opinion on Wearside was divided. For every fan who cheered Shack's flamboyance there was another who denounced it as self-indulgence. The latter attitude was summarised by another great inside forward of the period, Middlesbrough's Wilf Mannion. Asked about the Sunderland star, Mannion replied, 'Shackleton? He wasn't a footballer, he was a ruddy circus act.'

Though it was Shackleton's fee that caught the headlines, it was not Sunderland's only spending in the quest for goals. Centre-forward Ronnie Turnbull – born in Newbiggin, Northumberland – was brought in from Dundee for £10,000 and Tommy Wright, a stocky Scottish international winger, arrived soon afterwards from Partick Thistle, the fee £8,000.

In January 1949, Sunderland travelled to non-League Yeovil for a fourth-round FA Cup tie. The 2-1 defeat was a shock that rattled teacups 300 miles away. Sunderland's response was immediate. On the Monday following the humiliation in Somerset, the board reached for the cheque book and signed Ivor Broadis, a quick, direct inside-forward from Carlisle United for £18,000. Weirdly, since the 24-year-old Broadis was player-manager of the Cumbrians he had effectively sold himself.

The forward line of Broadis, Shackleton and Turnbull was the most expensively assembled in British football history – a supergroup in an era of soloists. After an eighth-place finish in 1948-49, great things were expected the following season. They came close to being fulfilled. For much of the winter, the title seemed destined for Wearside. Sunderland were easily the division's top scorers and appeared invincible at Roker, where 68,004 turned up for the derby with Newcastle. Then, with four matches remaining, the Wearsiders met the already doomed Manchester City at Roker Park. Bill Murray rested Turnbull and moved Broadis to centre-forward. City won 2-1. It was

Sunderland's only home defeat of the season. They finished third, just one point behind champions Portsmouth with a superior goal average. A draw against City would have brought them the title.

Sunderland's mad spending spree was renewed. In the summer of 1950, they signed Wallsend-born right-back Jack Hedley from Everton for a 'five-figure fee' and Northern Irish winger Billy Bingham from Glentoran (£9,000). And in October of that year the club again smashed the *world* transfer record, paying £30,000 for Trevor Ford of Cardiff City. The Welshman was a bullocking centre-forward whose treatment of opposition goalkeepers was considered rough even for the period (nowadays he'd likely be jailed). Although not huge – he stood 5ft 10 and weighed 12 stone – the former blast-furnaceman made up for lack of stature with sheer ferocity. As Ford himself put it, when he stepped on the field 'I became an animal.'

Ford's home debut for Sunderland against Sheffield Wednesday was a sensation. He banged in a hat-trick that included a characteristic barging of Owls' keeper Dave McIntosh into the back of the net, and at one point smashed into a goalpost with such force he flattened it – to the joy of the Fulwell End.

The Sunderland front three had cost over £68,000. If we take Ford to be the equivalent of current world record purchase, Neymar; Shackleton – a British record two years earlier – to be, for sake of argument, the Romelu Lukaku of his time; and Broadis priced at 90 per cent of Shackleton's cost, we arrive at roughly £340 million. No wonder the taxi driver felt like the pauper child of a grand family.

As many managers have discovered, though, assembling a great side is not simply a question of buying the best players – you have to make them play together. And when it came to Sunderland's forward line that proved a problem. Like a later turbulent centre-forward from South Wales, Giorgio Chinaglia, Ford was a man so full of himself he seemed in danger of bursting. He fell out with his first club Swansea over training methods, and asked to be put on the transfer list by Aston Villa after a dispute with the manager over what position he ought to be played in. At Roker Park, he found himself embroiled in more acrimony, this time with another player – Shackleton.

The pair seemed to have disliked each other on sight. Shackleton went out of his way to make life on the field a misery for the Welsh international. Mocking Ford's lack of finesse and decrying him for his poor positional sense, Shack deliberately played spun passes that arrived at the centre-forward's feet only to jump away again, or that turned like an off break so that the Welshman's swinging boot struck fresh air. This may have amused Shack, and made his many fans chortle, but it did little for the team.

After the near-miss of 1949-50, the 1950-51 season was an anti-climax. Sunderland came twelfth, a finish they repeated in 1951-52.

The 1952-53 season began more brightly and Sunderland were top of the table when they played Scunthorpe in the third round of the Cup. The game was a rough battle in the mud that went to a replay. Ford broke his ankle but typically played on. The Rokerites eventually emerged victorious, but the game seemed to knock the stuffing out of them. They went on a thirteen-match winless run that saw them dumped out of the Cup and tumble down the table. They finished ninth.

That summer Sunderland's by now well-worn cheque book came out again. Over the course of the next nine months they spent another £110,000 on nine new players. The most expensive of them, Ray Daniel, a ball-playing centre-back and Welsh international, was bought from Arsenal for £27,500 – a British record for a defender (so the equivalent of an £80 million Harry Maguire). Along with the cultured Daniel came England winger Billy Elliott (no, not that one) from Burnley for £26,000, and Ted Purdon, a fearless South African forward from Birmingham, for £15,000. Morton's Scottish international goalkeeper Jimmy Cowan was another addition.

The latter proved a Massimo Taibi-style disaster. Capped twenty-five times by his country, Cowan flapped hopelessly in England, played just twenty-eight games for Sunderland in two years, and was swiftly replaced between the sticks by another new signing, Willie Fraser.

Daniel too took time to settle and the team struggled from the off. The campaign began with four defeats in the first five matches and carried on in much the same vein. Sunderland finished eighteenth, conceding eighty-nine goals, a club record. The forward line too, failed to shine. The Shackleton–Ford relationship plunged to new depths and the belligerent Welshman was sold to Cardiff for £30,000.

In 1954-55 Sunderland flashed the cash once again, signing Charlie 'Cannonball' Fleming from East Fife for £20,000 plus the ageing Tommy Wright. Fleming was a striker with a net-busting shot whose goals had almost taken the Fifers to the Scottish title. With the combative Purdon filling the gap left by Ford and Fleming scoring regularly, Sunderland finished fourth and reached the semi-finals of the Cup.

With Newcastle in the other semi-final against lowly York City, a Tyne–Wear derby at Wembley was a genuine prospect, but on a rainswept pitch their old nemesis Manchester City – with Teesside-born Don Revie playing as a deep-lying centre-forward – nudged past them 1-0.

The following season, Sunderland were back in midtable. The 1956-57 campaign began with them signing Revie from City for £23,000 – a buy that brought the cost of Sunderland's forward line – Fleming, Revie and Shackleton – back up to the levels of Ford's day. Alas it proved far less effective. Shackleton was in his mid-thirties and troubled by a persistent ankle problem; Revie suffered from a niggling thigh strain and missed several months. Newcastle hammered their local rivals 6-2 at St James', average attendances dropped by close to 7,000 a game and Sunderland finished the season third from bottom – one place above the relegation slots – with thirty-two points, their lowest for sixty years.

The final nail in Sunderland's coffin came that summer in the shape of an anonymous letter to the FA tipping them off to an illegal payments scam. For five seasons, Sunderland had been using the charges for straw that protected the Roker Park pitch as a means of channelling extra cash to players. The sums were pitifully small by modern standards, but in the days of the maximum wage were enough to see the club hit with a record fine, the chairman and one director banned from football for life, two other directors suspended indefinitely and the rest severely censured. Manager Bill Murray was fined £200 for his part in the affair, and fifteen players were also punished financially, including Trevor Ford who'd been given a brown-paper parcel stuffed with £250 in cash.

Shaken by the affair, Bill Murray resigned his post. Harry Potts's predecessor at Burnley, Alan Brown – born in the same Corbridge maternity hospital as another future Sunderland boss, Steve Bruce – took his place. At the start of the following season, Shackleton retired on medical advice. At the end of it Sunderland went down.

'Aye, Bank of England club,' the taxi driver sighed. 'Mind, when you see some of the bull's knackers we've wasted money on while I've been following them we're maybe better off. Remember that South American? Milton Núñez from Honduras? March 2000, was it? Aye, Reidy signed him. They said he was called "Tyson" 'cause he was built like the heavyweight boxer. Then they brung him out on the pitch before the match. The fella was the size of a bloody pigeon. The kiddy mascot was patting him on the head. I said, "Whoever thought he was built like Mike Tyson must have had his glasses on inside out." Christ-on-a-bike, what a duck egg. Forty-three minutes he played. Cost 1.6 million quid. And I tell you what. Even he was a steal compared to that Jack fucking Rodwell.'

Ah, yes, Jack fucking Rodwell, the shadowy anti-hero of *Sunderland Till I Die*. Just as Alan Brown's disastrous stewardship at Roker Park might lead the uninitiated to think there had once been a football manager named Thatclownalan Brown, so there would be some in the future who would undoubtedly puzzle over what Mr and Mrs Rodwell had been thinking of when they gave their son his distinctive middle name.

Rodwell had been a prodigy at Everton, touted as a future star, a new Wayne Rooney. He'd moved to Manchester City for £12 million and made just sixteen starts in two years at the Etihad. In 2014, he'd joined Sunderland for £10 million and been handed a five-year contract that apparently had no clause in it to lower his wages in the event of relegation. He played just sixty-seven times for Sunderland in four years, including a streak that saw him start thirty-nine games without finishing on the winning side in any of them. During his spell, the club parted company with six managers and were relegated twice. Though none of that was Rodwell's fault, to many supporters he seemed symbolic of all that was wrong with modern football. He played his last game in September 2017, but apparently vowed to honour his contract and was still at the club at the close of the season. He'd finally left – for Blackburn – the previous summer.

'I tell you what,' the taxi driver continued, 'I said it at the time. If the club have got that fucking Rodwell insured, then no worries. Because there's plenty of lads round my way with experience of driving a knackered vehicle over the edge into a quarry and putting in a claim.'

12

DARLINGTON V SOUTHPORT

Vanarama National League North

Saturday 16 February 2019

At the end of January my scarf-burning friend's gloomy predictions had come to pass – Newcastle United had lost their fourth round FA Cup tie at home to Watford 0-2. Since they had been dumped out of the Carabao Cup by Championship side Nottingham Forest before the summer was over, it meant another trophy-less season at St James' Park. It was fifty years since the Fairs Cup victory over Ujpest. The Magpies hadn't won a final you could watch in colour.

On the train back after the Watford defeat – I'd been at Dunston – the two men in front of me growled and grizzled without raising anything that might be rage. Resignation had taken hold.

'Remember when we signed Shearer?' one said. 'Bringing

him back seemed like a signal of summat. But now, even if we brought through anyone decent he'd leave and if he didn't want to leave, we'd sell him anyway.'

It was true what he said about Shearer. Super Al – who'd been a ballboy at St James' Park during Keegan's first coming – was one of the stars who'd been spirited away from the region by Jack Hixon. Hixon, a once-passionate Newcastle fan who'd been disillusioned by the club's internal machinations, was Burnley's chief scout in the region for seventeen years. During that time, he spotted twenty-seven players who went on to play first-team football for the Lancashire club. One of the best of them, Ralph Coates, was officially signed in the house of Kevin Keegan's grandfather. Hixon left Burnley and ended up working for Gateshead-born Lawrie McMenemy at Southampton, which is why Alan Shearer never played at Turf Moor (Burnley's connection with the North East continued for a while, however, thanks to Peter Kirkley, the man responsible for taking Berwick-born Trevor Steven there in the early '80s). When Kevin Keegan brought Shearer back to Newcastle for a British record fee, it seemed like the tide had finally turned, that the North East might become an importer rather than an exporter of talent, that the Bank of England Club had come back in black and white.

Normal service had been resumed when Mike Ashley arrived. The only England international who'd come through the Magpies' youth ranks for decades, Andy Carroll, was sold to Liverpool in 2010 and the drain westward continued elsewhere – Henderson and Pickford, Downing and Johnson all left. The North East might have been producing fewer players than it once had, but it was still struggling to hold onto them. If you wanted to fulfil ambition, you had to go elsewhere, just as Beardsley, Waddle, Gascoigne and all those others had done before.

'I used to think we were a big club. But we're just a small club that's watched by 50,000 people,' the bloke said.

The train strike was suspended and as soon as that was announced it had snowed. After the cabin-fever days of the autumn, I'd been planning a celebratory trip to Tow Law, which involved a train into Newcastle and a bus back out again. But now I was thwarted. In some ways, though, not seeing a game at Tow Law in February was kind of traditional. I'd been a bit disappointed the last time I'd been to Ironworks Road – I'd been able to unzip my fleece and had come away slightly sunburned. When I went in the bank the following Monday, the teller asked if I'd been away skiing.

There are lots of cold football grounds in the North East. Some, such as those at Easington, Horden and Hartlepool, expose themselves to the bracing sea gale, while others are perched on the side of North Pennine hilltops. Here, from October to May, winter mist hovers in the air like resentment at a wedding reception and icy rain pecks and scratches at exposed skin like a carrion bird in a Ted Hughes poem. Over the past two decades, I've shivered in swirling snow at Hall Lane, Willington; been blasted by hail at

Brandon Welfare Ground; and been frozen to my seat at Crook on a day when cups of hot Bovril were passed around as hand-warmers and firemen freed incontinent dogs from lamp-posts.

However, for skin-puckering, nose-numbing, ear-aching, brass-monkey neutering cold, none of these places can compare to Ironworks Road, the windswept, glacial home of Tow Law Town. The Ironworks Road ground was built and then rebuilt by striking pitmen back in the days when Northern League games regularly attracted four-figure crowds and the half- and full-time scores were relayed back to the visitors' home base by carrier pigeons. Tow Law's mines are long gone, as is the foundry that gave the ground its name. The population of the town is now half what it was back in the 1950s. Temperatures remain stubbornly unaffected by climate change.

Tow Law lies a little over 1,000ft above sea level on the eastern fringe of the North Pennines, which probably makes it the highest football ground in England (the fact is disputed by Buxton). From Ironworks Road on a winter afternoon (and there are an awful lot of winter afternoons in Tow Law) you can look westwards into a vast darkness unblemished by any of the spots of light that might denote distant farms or hamlets. A barbaric wind whips out of these barren wastes – the splendidly Dickensian-sounding Waskerley Common.

To avoid the gusts, Tow Law's fans sensibly gather in the shelter provided by a covered enclosure that presents its back to the dun-coloured moors. In this small enclave there is a micro-climate that feels almost sub-tropical in comparison to the more exposed parts of the ground. Even here things can be rough. 'The match was played in a gale force fog,' as Alan Shoulder once said.

As a consequence of its location, cold is a recurring theme in the history of Tow Law Town FC. In 1925, for example, a team from Sir Bobby Robson's home club of Langley Park had to abandon their bus in a snow drift and walk the remaining 3 miles to Ironworks Road. They arrived fifty minutes late, were beaten 6-0 by a Lawyers team who were on their way to a second consecutive Northern League title, and had to report before the management committee to explain their tardiness (the committee, unimpressed by the excuse about the weather, fined them £20). This happened at Easter. Little wonder that Tow Law was one of the first North-East teams to install hot baths.

During the fierce winter of 1962-63, Tow Law was cut off for over a month, all roads blocked by snow drifts, food ferried in on coal trains that occasionally battled up the steep gradient from nearby Crook. By the time the thaw came, the Lawyers faced such a backlog of fixtures they didn't complete the season till the start of June.

The Lawyers reached the FA Vase final in 1998 after a 5-4 aggregate win over Taunton in the semi. Though they lost to Tiverton, they did enter the record books that day – with a population of just 2,200, Tow Law is the smallest town ever to appear in a Wembley final.

Prior to that outing, Tow Law's greatest moment had come in 1967 when they played Mansfield Town in the first round of the FA Cup. The opening match at the Lawyers' Ironworks Road ground was abandoned at half time in a blizzard. In the rematch the Durham boys triumphed 5-1. 'It was like playing at the North Pole,' Mansfield's manager, Tommy Cummings, complained afterwards (that's a man born in Sunderland, incidentally, not some bloke from Rio de Janeiro or Cape Town).

In the second round of the Cup, Tow Law drew 1-1 at home with Shrewsbury in front of 4,000 fans in a howling gale, then, with a home tie against Arsenal awaiting the winner, lost in the replay in the more clement conditions of Shropshire 6-2. 'Shrewsbury,' declared London-born sports hack Frank McGhee in the *Daily Mirror*, 'have saved Arsenal from a fate worse than death – a trip to Tow Law in January.'

That seems cruel to me, not least because Tow Law has some of the friendliest fans, best home-made pies in football and the great Lawyers local-celebrity supporter, Mary Hail – whose surname might be a description of the weather – who even at her advanced age still occasionally bursts out of the clubhouse to berate the match officials whether she's witnessed what they have been up to or not.

The weather cleared up the following week and, on the Saturday lunchtime, I got the train south to Darlington. It was a fine day in County Durham: mild, benign and sunny as Sir Bobby Robson's smile. There was that premature feeling of spring in the air with which February so often cons us before dumping a foot of snow on the flower beds. Darlington's latest home, Blackwell Meadows, is out on the western fringes of the town, on the road that leads to the Yorkshire Dales, across from a swanky country house hotel, surrounded by water meadows where families walk labradoodles and eager tots squeal amid the bobbing snowdrops. While it doesn't have the ramshackle, cattle mart charm of Feethams there's a similar bucolic air about it.

An hour before kick-off, the Southport supporters' coaches were rolling up the driveway and disgorging gaggles of yellow-and-black-clad fans, their cheery coastal Lancashire accents calling to mind a happy world of donkey rides, boarding houses and ukulele tunes.

I'd attended the reverse fixture at Haig Avenue earlier in the season. It was a late summer day, overcast and muggy. The weather had a soporific effect and my abiding memory of the 0-0 draw is of a woman in front of me at the tea bar asking if the rosé wine was chilled. The dullness of the encounter suggested stability. Both sides were in lower half of the table, but neither seemed in much danger, though the diehard fans of both – steeped as they are in bitter struggles – would tell you otherwise, naturally. Fingernails would be bitten till the maths said to stop.

The Feethams site was shared with a cricket field. Blackwell Meadows sees Darlo paired with a rugby club, Darlington RFC. In a strangely symmetrical shift, the town's top union side, Mowden Park of National League

One, now play at another of Darlington's old grounds, the Northern Echo Arena, that 20,000 capacity fever-dream of former Quakers' chairman and convicted felon, George Reynolds.

In Blackwell Meadows' large, modern clubhouse, the trophy cabinet is devoted to the oval-ball code. There are cups for most improved colt and statuettes from various junior competitions at home and abroad. The walls around the bar are decorated with the shields of visiting sides, including one from a club in Belgium that features the image of a wildebeest's head.

National League North is a limbo of former league clubs. Darlington's passage to it was dramatic, a maelstrom of bankruptcies, points deductions and enforced demotions that saw them busted down to the Northern League, ousted from their home town and facing sides with average home crowds of 100.

It had all begun with Reynolds. When he took over the club in 1999, the former-safe-cracker-turned-fitted-kitchen-manufacturing-millionaire stated his intention to first build a stadium and then build a team worthy of it and take Darlo to the Premier League. There was talk of signing Nicky Summerbee and Keegan's future nemesis, Dennis Wise, an aborted mission to secure the services of the fading Paul Gascoigne. Then, on a chilly Tuesday night at Feethams in 2003, with Carlisle United the visitors, Colombian maverick Faustino Asprilla was paraded around the pitch, Reynolds claiming that a man he described 'a close personal friend' was on the verge of signing for the fourth-tier club in a deal that would net him £17,000 a week.

It didn't happen. After days of delay and fevered speculation, Asprilla left the North East for the Middle East. When the gangly striker joined Kevin Keegan's Newcastle from Parma in 1996, the £7.5 million signing arrived in a snowstorm. His departure from Darlington was marked by a blizzard of expletives. As one Feethams' employee bluntly yet eloquently put it, 'Faustino has fucked off.'

It wasn't the first time Reynolds' antics made the headlines. The man with the best scrape-over since Bobby Charlton (though the England number nine never went so far as to fix his in place with hairgrips) kept himself regularly in the news with a series of well-publicised battles, not least with the club's playing staff. He published the team's salaries in a local newspaper to shame them into better performances and had a bitter slanging match with former manager David Hodgson live on local radio. In February 2002, a supporters' club meeting ended acrimoniously when Reynolds' wife Susan stated that 'it isn't unknown for games to be thrown deliberately at this time of year by way of favours.'

Then there was the long-running battle with the *Northern Echo* newspaper and the furious dispute with a Hartlepool-supporting North-East radio presenter, Paul 'Goffy in the Morning' Gough, that saw billboards carrying insinuating references to the DJ's sexual preferences appear outside the new stadium.

For all the Reynolds Arena's gold-plated taps, marble sinks and state-of-the-art lifts, it always felt more *Phoenix Nights* than *Viva Las Vegas*. And it all came to a sudden halt just six months after the club had moved into the new stadium. With 3,500 fans rattling around the vast bowl, their chants and cries disappearing into the void, the costs rapidly mounted. Before the end of the season Darlington went into administration and Reynolds walked away.

Under new chairman George Houghton things stabilised for a while. An unnatural calmness fell. But the stadium continued to drain money and in 2009 the club were back in administration again. They were relegated to the Conference in 2010, won the FA Trophy at Wembley in 2011, then crashed one final time. In 2012, Darlington FC were expelled by the Football Association. A new fan-owned club, Darlington 1883, was formed. They began life again in the Northern League, abandoning the echoing Arena and groundsharing with Bishop Auckland.

Seven years later, still fan-owned, they were finally back in Darlington, had risen four levels up the pyramid and the FA had allowed them to use their original name again. It was a massive achievement brought about by the collective effort of the supporters (it might have been even greater – in 2017 Darlington had reached the National League North play-offs, only to be denied a chance to compete in them because their ground had 280 covered seats rather than the required 500). There was much to be proud of and grateful for. But, in football, memories are short and after eighteen months in National League North there were mutterings among some sections of the support about the need for outside investment, a cash injection to take the club back into the Football League.

'People imagine Roman Abramovich or the Sultan of Brunei,' one of the Darlington FC Supporters' Group said. 'But history shows you are far more likely to end up with Owen Oyston or Francesco Becchetti.' At least the fact that Darlington don't own their own ground – although they have paid for all the improvements to bring it up to FA-approved standards – precludes someone from getting involved simply to burn it down and sell the site to a supermarket.

Darlo attract decent crowds – there were over 1,400 at today's match – but they are totally self-sustaining. Other sides in the National League had sugar daddies – several in the case of Salford City – and three times the budget for wages. Did the fans keep the club as it was and remain in charge of their own destiny, or take a chance on progression and risk another Reynolds debacle?

Darlington now have enough covered seats to satisfy even the FA bureaucrats and I took a position in one of them opposite the clubhouse. There was a surcharge to sit here and, though it was only a couple of quid, like the extra few pennies on a pint in the lounge bar, it encouraged a politer crowd. When someone shouted a comment that included the word 'prat', it drew a rebuke from the man behind him and the brief foray into the language of the saloon and the snooker hall wasn't repeated.

Southport started strongly, the brindle-haired Dion Charles breaking from half way and feeding his fellow top scorer Jack Sampson. 'Don't let him shoot! Don't let him shoot!' the elderly bloke in front of me groaned in a tone that suggested he suspected scorpions lurked in every teapot. Sampson did shoot, but his effort set the tone for the afternoon, sailing high over the bar. Shortly after that, a meaty header from a corner by Darlo's Simon Ainge flew over the bar and splatted into an advertisement for 'The Ironing Man communal laundry'. The thud was the signal for the game to descend into a kind of tepid mediocrity: not bad enough to create laughter or fury, just gradually sucking all enthusiasm from the crowd.

Both sides took it in turns to pass the ball around neatly and then, as if at some signal from the technical area, hoof it into touch so they could regain their shape. After twenty minutes, the drummers in the home and away ends had fallen silent. The chanting had stopped. The first shot on target by either side, if you discount a Southport player almost shinning a corner into his own net during the first half, came in the seventieth minute. The visitors – who squandered the bulk of the clear-cut chances – didn't force Jonny Maddison into a proper save until ten minutes after that. I've done my best to capture it, but frankly even this paragraph makes the game sound far more entertaining than it actually was.

Darlington's Liam Hughes, a mighty defender whose shirt seems far too small for him, coming apart from his shorts in a manner that suggest a comic strip character who's just eaten a piled-high plate of sausage and mash, drew encouraging cheers from the crowd for every beefy clearance. Hughes had been absent for a month of the season with mental health issues and had bravely spoken publicly about them.

Darlington's on-loan left back Sam Muggleton had the sort of massive long throw that would have delighted Tony Pulis, catapulting the ball onto the penalty spot from barely fifteen yards inside the visitors' half. He looked like he would provide Darlington's biggest threat, but a wince-inducing collision with Marcus Wood as half time approached brought his game and his season to a premature end. The Chesterfield defender – who had only been in County Durham for a week – needed ten minutes of treatment for what turned out to be a broken leg and dislocated knee.

There was further work for the Darlington medical staff in the second period when skipper Terry Galbraith, pursuing a hopeful punt into the home box, ran smack into his goalkeeper, Maddison, and was led away suffering from concussion. That aside, the second half trudged wearily on. Subs arrived to cheers but little noticeable effect.

The seconds ticked slowly by. I looked at the clubhouse clock. It showed the time as 7.30. It was clearly fast, though the game definitely felt like it had been going on for over four hours.

Darlington had the better of the closing minutes. 'Keep

the pressure on, Darlo,' a man two rows down shouted, but it was not really pressure, more the occasional light nudge. Some games have 0-0 written all over them, in this case in block capitals with a dayglo marker pen. The final whistle blew to what sounded like a collective sigh of relief.

I got off the bus by a second-hand shop with a sign on the fascia reading 'Let the film your watching help to pay for the next one. Part exchange it. Don't let it gather dust on a shelf' and a window display that looked like the floor of my daughter's bedroom when she was eight. I walked up to the station past a pub with police incident tape across the entrance and a small crowd of e-smokers puffing mushroom clouds of cinnamon-scented vapour into the blue sky. Opposite stood a cluster of flats with partially boarded-up windows and a sign saying the premises were guarded by Spartan Security. I imagined spear-armed men sitting in a transit van wearing nothing but bronze helmets, though not for very long obviously as that would have been weird.

Ahead of me a lone Southport fan in a yellow hat answered his mobile. 'Garbage. Nil-nil. Their 'keeper,' he said before ringing off. It's about all the game merited really, but I've pages and pages to fill.

13

Esh Winning v Easington Colliery

Ebac Northern League Division Two

Saturday 23 February 2019

During international breaks, I tried to persuade various
friends of mine who supported one or other of the North
East's big three to come to a Northern League game with
me. Almost without exception their responses were the
same, a pained look followed by an indulgent smile. 'Yeah,
I know it's probably really great and everything, but it's just
the *standard* of the football, you know? *The standard.*'

I wasn't surprised. These days it appears as if every fan in
the country has been raised on a glorious diet of flowing,
creative football. I understand. I was brought up in an era
when the lack of televised football left fans so starved of the
game they would watch anything – pub teams, foundrymen
playing with a tennis ball on waste ground, bacon sandwiches in their fists and Woodbines in their gobs. When

I was at primary school, we'd sometimes go to a friend's parents' farm and chuck a football into the sheep pen just to see some live action. Today things are different and I am sensitive to the fact that not all fans have had my disadvantages. These days, more and more football supporters are epicureans, Jean Anthelme Brillat-Savarins of what Pelé memorably dubbed 'better than working for a living'. They have become so used to the diet of Heston Blumenthal-style footballing fare, served up at places like St James' Park, the Stadium of Light and the Riverside that they would rather starve than tuck into the game's equivalent of a chip butty; indeed, their refined sporting taste buds rebel at the very thought of it.

I understood, I really did. Because every fan has a right to be pompous and delusional. Luckily, my friend Karl took a different view, despite being a fan of Everton whose stylish brand of football had once led to Goodison Park being called 'the School of Science' (Darlington-born Harry Catterick, Ryton's own Howard Kendall and Bob Dylan-loving Geordie, Jimmy Husband had been part of all that, of course). Karl comes from Dublin and when I asked if he'd like to come to a game, he fair jumped at the chance.

In Durham a mariachi band was playing 'La Cucaracha' and a crowd had gathered around a life-size ice sculpture of Darth Vader. The owner was allowing children and adults to be photographed alongside it, but was getting a bit vexed with a group of little primary school-age urchins who were more intent on melting the dark lord by rubbing their sticky hands all over his cape, while one of their dads – a man in camo-pattern vest with an unlikely tattoo of Britney Spears on his forearm above the legend 'Once is never enough' – hissed 'Liam, I am your father.'

Durham bus station remains one of Britain's architectural wonders, as changeless as Roy Keane's stare. If you really want to know what life was like in the north of England in the 1970s please go and visit. It's like standing inside a chain smoker's lung. It was, however, also a gateway to football wonders – to Crook, Bishop Auckland, Spennymoor, West Auckland, Willington and our destination for the day: Esh Winning.

Esh is a fine place tinged with nostalgia. There are strings of red-brick terraced houses, net curtains, a teenage couple snogging ferociously on the steps of the memorial hall, old men in blue overcoats and flat caps walking wispy-haired mongrels on home-made rope leads. An elderly woman with a headscarf over her hair-rollers who looked like she might be hurrying home to watch *Gunsmoke* with her grandson over a plate of Toast Toppers and some coconut snowballs. Even on a sunny day, there seemed to be the scent of rain on tarmac.

Sadly, the coal-fired fryer at Fields' chippy had been shut down fifteen minutes earlier, so we went to the nearby bakers instead and then walked up the Deerness valley to Waterhouses in the warm sunshine, me munching on an Empire biscuit and Karl on the less politically charged millionaire's shortbread.

At one point, the Deerness valley had over twenty collieries employing close to 7,000 men. Most had closed in the 1950s. The last survivor, Esh Colliery, had lasted till 1968. Back then the landscape had been as scarred as a battlefield. The trees and hedgerows were so dusted in soot that they were, as one local told me, as 'black as a landlord's heart'. But that time had gone. It was now a benign, rolling landscape of woodland and meadows.

The pits had gone all across the North East. The last colliery in County Durham, Wearmouth, had shut in 1993 (the Stadium of Light stands on the site). In Northumberland, the deep, undersea mine at Ellington, a few miles from Ashington, held on till 2005. Now all that remained of them were the old silver bands, the names of the football grounds and the nicknames of the teams. That was true across much of Britain, of course. Every football fan knew that saddles had been made in Walsall, hats in Luton, gloves in Yeovil, silk in Macclesfield and cocktails in Bury (I think that's right, anyway). The ephemera hung on long after the businesses that spawned it had been interred.

The trades that replaced those of the North East's heavy industries didn't seem to have quite the same romantic resonance. Though I guess it's possible that in a century or so visiting fans will glance at a football programme and say, '"The Cold Callers on Behalf of a Conservatory Company Whose Representatives are Currently in Your Area"? Hmmm, I wonder how they came to be known as that?'

The first side from Esh Winning had been Esh Winning

Rangers, who'd won the Northern League title at their first attempt in 1913 (a feat matched only by Teessiders Eston United). They'd performed decently between the wars too, but those were tough days in the Durham coalfields and Esh folded in 1934 due to lack of cash. The current set-up traced its history back to the late 1960s when Waterhouses pit closed down and the locals bought the Welfare Ground from the National Coal Board. Esh Winning Pineapple (named after an exotically christened local pub) played there in the Sunday League before joining the Northern Alliance and then the newly formed Northern League Division Two. They dropped the Pineapple along the way, thus dealing a disappointing blow to future merchandising wizards. They'd had a very brief spell in the top flight but generally bobbed around the lower reaches of Division Two, occasionally escaping demotion because teams in the Northern Alliance or Wearside League didn't have good enough floodlights or enough covered seats to replace them.

Esh Winning's greatest claim to fame was as the starting point to the careers of two of the greatest North-Eastern players of the inter-war years. Or one of them, if you take the word of another, Wilf Mannion. Back in the mid-1990s I'd spent a happy afternoon drinking tea with Wilf. By this time, the great man was well into his seventies. He was good company, but his memory was not entirely reliable and there was a prickly edge to him. He'd had a rough time in the Second World War and a tough time after he'd finished playing. He'd come to feel himself undervalued, forgotten. Other players of his era – Stanley Matthews, Tom Finney, Tommy Lawton – were better remembered, more prosperous, celebrated.

Many older sports people are rude about the current generation of idols. Wilf was no different, but he was equally dismissive of his contemporaries – as if by diminishing them he could make himself seem bigger. When Wilf had begun playing for Middlesbrough, they'd had a famous forward line – all five were internationals. I started off by asking him about that. I said, 'When you first came into the Boro team, you were playing with centre-forward George Camsell.'

Born in Framwellgate Moor, Camsell had played for Esh Winning as a teenage pitman before moving on to Durham City and then to the Boro. He'd played nine times for England, scored in every game, banging the ball in the net an amazing eighteen times.

Wilf's pale eyes sharpened at the mention of the great number nine. 'Aye,' he said. 'And I'll tell you something about Camsell – he was ruddy useless. He couldn't trap a sack of cement.'

I'd been raised by my grandfather to regard Camsell as King Arthur in football boots. I blurted out, 'He scored 345 goals!'

Wilf sneered. 'Oh aye,' he said, shooing away the idea with a wave of his hand, 'he could score goals all right.'

And so it went on. Wilf had little time for any of the players of his era. Matthews was one-dimensional, Lawton a Lancastrian Camsell.

I then asked him about Sunderland's Raich Carter. Wilf sniffed. 'Carter,' he said, then, after a moment of thought, 'aye, Carter was all right.'

From this I concluded that Raich Carter must have been a bloody genius.

Carter was born in the dockside Hendon district of Sunderland in December 1913, the eldest of three children. He had a tough upbringing. His father died when he was young and he was forced to become the family's main breadwinner at the age of fourteen. He won England caps as a schoolboy and played for Esh Winning while working as an apprentice engineer. He made his debut at Roker Park as an amateur when he was eighteen and turned pro a few months later.

Carter played with his shirt collar turned up and his chin held high. There was an air of arrogance about him – like a prototype Eric Cantona. He wasn't a natural ball-player like Mannion, but he was intelligent and creative, a brilliant, incisive passer, a natural in what would now be the number ten position linking midfield with attack, 'giving the strikers the bullets' as Wilf put it.

Even as a youth, Carter had a self-belief that bordered on vanity ('he loved himself' was John Charles's blunt assessment). He was a born leader and was appointed captain of Sunderland when he was just twenty-one – an extraordinary decision at a time when seniority was considered all-important in most walks of life. In 1935-36, he led his side to the league championship, finishing joint top scorer with thirty-one goals including a hat-trick in a 5-4 win over reigning title-holders Arsenal. The following year, Sunderland won the FA Cup, Carter scoring the winning goal in the final. Even his team-mates called him 'the Maestro'.

In December 1945, Carter signed for Derby County (he'd played for the Rams during the war while serving in the RAF at Loughborough). The fee was £6,000, then a British record. When it was put to Carter by reporters that this was a lot of money, his reply was typical: 'Derby are lucky to get me at the price.' Arrogant or not, his record at the Baseball Ground bore out that verdict. He hit thirty-four goals in sixty-three appearances and masterminded Derby's victory in the 1946 FA Cup final.

He left Derby for Boothferry Park, Hull, where he soon became player-manager. By now, age had tinted Carter's once black hair a steely grey. Along with his scheming style of play, this earned him the nickname 'the Silver Fox'. Carter led the Tigers to the third division North title and signed Don Revie from Leicester City before an argument with the club directors led to his resignation. After briefly running a cake shop in Hull, he signed as player-coach with Cork Athletic. Though now turned forty, he was still good enough to play a vital part in his side's winning of the Irish FA Cup.

He returned to England to manage Leeds United. He was at Elland Road for nine years. During that time the club won promotion to the top division but doubts still remain about the Silver Fox's ability as a manager. Certainly neither John Charles nor Jack Charlton was impressed by him, the latter remarking that 'he didn't coach and he didn't employ coaches'. He left Leeds United in 1959, managed Mansfield Town and then Middlesbrough before retiring from the game. He died in 1994.

Carter was hard and self-regarding. He had some sensitivity, though, and an understanding of the world. Once, when he was an old man, a reporter had come to his house to interview him about his career. When he asked about Sunderland, Carter told him of the responsibility he'd felt towards the supporters. They came to see us every week, he said, and those were hard times. He knew how much they'd had to give up to afford the price of admission, knew how much the team winning meant to them. 'We were their only hope,' Carter said. He paused and when the reporter looked up from his notebook he saw, to his surprise, that Raich Carter was crying.

Karl and I had drink in the clubhouse and were joined by my friend Carole, who lived nearby and had popped in to give us both a slice of cake. There were sixty-four spectators in the West Terrace ground, which had the happy homespun look of one of those jumbled collections of holiday chalets you see along riverbanks, or a group of pigeon crees. To make up the covered seating areas to the required numbers, they'd put up some lap-and-shingle sheds on the bank behind the goal with what looked like school chairs in them. 'The executive boxes,' someone said.

Esh's home form was poor; they'd won at West Terrace just once all season and had lost the away fixture at Easington. Colliery came into the game off the back of a draw with Bedlington Terriers. The club from East Durham was founded in 1913. Since joining the Northern League in 1985, the Colliers had been up and down like, as Les Dawson might have said, a bride's nightie. Promoted from Division Two three times and relegated three times, they'd also been relegated out of the Northern League twice and promoted back into it a couple of times.

Their Welfare Park ground was perched on a headland overlooking the North Sea. When you stood on the eastern touchline you hung onto the perimeter fence for fear of being blown into the crashing waves. Welfare Park was beset with floodlight problems, thanks to a generator that seemed about as reliable as a political manifesto, and gale-force coastal winds that occasionally toppled one. All this added a decided level of tension to evening kick-offs and winter Saturday afternoons.

Easington's most famous former player was Owen Williams, who, despite having a name that was as Welsh as Max Boyce singing a song about leeks while sitting on a hillock of lava bread, was actually born in Ryhope. Williams played for Middlesbrough in the 1920s. A scurrying winger, he'd been a regular in the team of 1926-27 that won the second division Championship scoring 122 goals along the way (the useless George Camsell got fifty-nine of them). He was capped twice for England.

In the warm February sunshine, the Colliers got off to a sparkling start, creating several chances in the opening five minutes only to squander them via a series of shinnings, slices and one of those headers that fly off the skull from just behind the ear. Esh were altogether less profligate, a low cross into the box met by the swinging boot of midfielder Glenn Donaldson and smashed into the roof of the net.

The Colliers pulled level just before the quarter-hour mark, through their veteran striker Jack Pounder – who sounded like a midshipman from a Napoleonic naval drama.

Easington might have taken the lead several times after that, but the equaliser seemed to have depleted their store of accuracy and shots whistled high and wide. Once again Esh proved themselves the more clinical – a corner from the left was met by the immense Nicholas Marley, whose mighty shirt-stretching torso carried so many tattoos it was practically a gallery. The former Crook striker's deftly glanced header squirmed under Sam Naylor as if it were coated in soap.

Marley then got his second, collecting the ball with his back to goal on the edge of the Colliers' box, executing a balletic pirouette and then striking a shot straight into the corner of the net. It was the sort of finish football commentators would have described as 'exquisite', but which the bloke behind me summarised more eloquently using a simple 'fucking hell, man'.

Half time arrived. The interval entertainment consisted of one of those pre-school children, shirtless and armed with a stick, running up and down bashing any piece of metal that made a clanging noise before throwing himself belly first into a pile of sand behind one of the dugouts. It wasn't much, but it was definitely preferable to the Sky Strikers.

Twenty minutes of the second half had gone before Karl and I were rewarded with another goal: a simple back pass to keeper Naylor caught a divot and sliced off his boot, presenting Marley with a simple tap-in to complete his hat-trick. Naylor had only signed for Easington from Billingham Town a week or so before. He was another of those Northern League players who'd spent summers playing in Scandinavia, in this case in the top flight for GIF Sundsvall, a club managed by the fragrant-sounding Joel Cedergren and founded by the local Temperance Society. The way things were going this afternoon, he must have wished he'd stayed in the pine forests with a sarsaparilla.

Two minutes later Esh had a fifth. Joe Mole collected a through ball and advanced towards goal. The way things had gone, it was odds-on he was either going to aim a boot at the ball with his right foot, knock it forward with his left, miss it entirely and fall flat on his back, or strike a lightning bolt unerringly into the top corner. Unfortunately for Colls, fate chose the latter option.

Easington pulled one back and a grandstand finish might have followed, but by this stage on a warm afternoon and with a surface that looked like hospital porridge, both sets of players were teetering groggily on the point of collapse and looked in dire need of a sit down and – in some cases – a fag and a pint.

Esh's left-winger who had been effective throughout almost gave up entirely, strolling up and down his touchline and inquiring after the scores in a series of league matches he'd evidently got some kind of accumulator on. The ref allowed things to meander to a conclusion with minimal interference.

Karl and I walked back to the main road and caught the Scarlet Band bus to Durham, dipping up and over hills and valleys, as the sun slowly sank over the open rolling countryside. It was my birthday and I couldn't have had a nicer one.

14

MORPETH TOWN V SPALDING UNITED

Evo-Stik Northern Premier League
Division One – East

Saturday 2 March 2019

Morpeth is the county town of Northumberland. It's a smart place with an immaculate park, a town hall designed by Vanbrugh and roads flanked by curving walls of dressed stone topped with flowerbeds. Even the old county prison was the work of John Dobson and looks like something out of a Harry Potter film. As football venues go, it was certainly quite different from nearby Bedlington and Blyth. It was in the heart of the old Border Reiver country though, and the Northumberland robber clan names – Robson, Milburn, Charlton, Fenwick – had dominated cattle and sheep theft in the region during Tudor times before doing something similar with pages in the local telephone directory.

When they weren't inventing blackmail and perfecting

arson, the Reivers had been keen football players. The Border Ballads, the folk poetry that recorded their bloody deeds, also include the occasional match report. In one, a football match is interrupted by an ambush. One of the players is shot through the head with an arrow and the ballad records: 'He could nae rise, though he assayed/ Best at the thievecraft and the ba'/ He never again shall ride a raid'. Ba' was football. The Reiver who died was called Armstrong, another North-East football name. Morpeth might not look like the kind of industrial hive that produced footballers, but it was here in the blood.

My train had arrived a little early, so I went for a walk through Morpeth's immaculate park where I spotted a white van with a logo on the side that announced it to be the Northumberland County Council 'Rapid Response Cleaning Unit'. I couldn't help thinking these heroic men and women ought to be the subject of a gritty Saturday night action drama in the style of *Line of Duty*. It could star Jimmy Nail as the maverick RRC operative who doesn't do things by the book. 'Damn what it says in regulations. There's a polythene bag over there that represents a suffocation hazard to small birds and I'm not going to stand by and let a chaffinch die just because of a bunch of bureaucrats at County Hall . . .' They could call it *Clenza*. Or not.

Morpeth Town had been formed in 1894. They joined the Northern Alliance in the 1930s. In those days, they played at Storey Park in the town centre. They moved to the athletics ground on the outskirts in 1994, the year before they joined the Northern League. Sadly, this turned out not to have been the venue of the fabled Morpeth Olympics, an annual showdown between professional athletes that had started back in the 1870s and eventually fizzled out in the 1950s. The Morpeth Olympics hundred-yard dash had offered the biggest cash prize in English sprinting and drawn a number of pro footballers who fancied themselves quick, including Jackie Milburn – but that had been held at Grange House Field.

The ground was named Craik Park. Craik sounded like it might be some rare and rangy marsh bird that once nested on the site, but turned out to be the family name of a father and son who'd acted as club secretaries. The club had impressed in the Northern League initially, but then suffered a disastrous run that culminated in them finishing bottom of the second division in 2011 with a meagre fifteen points and a goal difference of minus ninety-seven. By then they were groundsharing with Bedlington and their imminent demise was widely predicted. The Highwaymen, however, came back with all guns blazing (I know, I'm an old pro), finishing fourth the following season and winning promotion the next.

The driving force behind the club was Ken Beattie. Born in Bedlington, Beattie had played over 500 games for Morpeth while building up a global enterprise supplying hoses to the gas and oil industry (despite the closure of massive enterprises such as ICI, the North East still accounted for well over half of the UK's petro-chemical industry).

Nowadays the business was turning over in the region of £40 million annually. He'd become chairman of the club in 1985 and oversaw the rapid development of Craik Park. He'd invested heavily in the playing squad, too. Rumours continually circulated that he was about to pull the plug on his hobby, but there seemed little sign of that.

Craik Park was convenient for the A1, but quite a hike from the town centre, taking me past an old road sign that helpfully announced that Darlington was 46.5 miles away, around a golf course and over a boggy heath. You could hear the announcements and music from the Tannoy but the ground itself was invisible, hidden in woodland like some outlaw encampment. I trudged towards the noise behind a blonde in a quilted jacket who was walking a toffee-coloured setter. It sounded like PA was playing 'Long Hot Summer' by Girls Aloud. Which if true made it possibly the least appropriate song I have heard in a football ground since the bloke at Brunton Park decided that a freezing Wednesday night in February was just the time to give 'Sex on the Beach' a spin.

The visitors, Spalding, were nicknamed 'the Tulips' after the flower fields that surround the Lincolnshire town. They'd started life playing in the Peterborough and District League, which conclusively proved that when the FA said 'Northern' they had a slightly different view of what that meant than most people in the North East.

Spalding had indeed once played in the Southern League, back when that was one of the highest levels of the

non-League game, but they had struggled and been relegated northwards. They came into the match in stuttering
form. Morpeth, by contrast, were on a winning run that
looked increasingly likely to carry them to the title and a
second successive promotion. Their side was packed with
really good non-League players – Ben Sayer, Sean Taylor
and Wayne Phillips – but I was disappointed to find that the
elegant Irish midfielder Keith 'Rasher' Graydon was only
on the bench. Graydon had been instrumental in Morpeth's
recent success, playing outstandingly during the Northern
League title winning season and sparkling at Wembley
when the Highwaymen surprisingly hammered runaway
favourites Hereford in the final of the FA Vase.

'That Graydon at Morpeth, man,' Jimmy had been telling
me the season before. 'Wonderful. When they were here at
Dunston, he just stood there in the centre circle spraying
passes around. The range of them. Ah, fabulous.'

For many older supporters like Jimmy, this non-
movement makes the former Republic of Ireland Under-20
international the *non plus ultra* of footballers. Over the
years, only a handful of players have been described to me
in such respectful terms, among them Alfredo Di Stéfano
and Bobby Charlton. Michel Platini fitted the bill, too. The
Frenchman was a boulevardier, strolling around the field
like Pepé Le Pew after a long lunch. Sometimes he looked
like he was actually whistling. Not everyone was impressed.
During an early game in the 1982 World Cup finals, ITV
panellist Mick Channon criticised Michel Platini for not

getting about the pitch enough. Brian Clough was on hand to rebuke the ex-England striker. In a waspish tone pregnant with meaning he said, 'The good ones, Michael, don't *need* to run about.'

My grandfather – born a few hundred yards across the park from Clough – took a similar attitude when speaking of his boyhood hero, centre-forward George Elliott from South Bank. 'He didn't charge around all over the place like these daft buggers,' he'd say, waving a hand in the general direction of Joe Laidlaw, whose luxurious sideburns – like a couple of sheepskin seat covers – had annoyed him. According to my grandfather, Elliott's abilities included extra-sensory perception. 'George Elliott never had to run about like these modern so-called footballers,' he would say. 'He knew exactly where the ball was going to be and he was there before it arrived. Anticipation, see?' I nodded my head, even though I couldn't quite figure out how, if he didn't run about, Elliott actually got to the place he had so accurately predicted the ball was going to be. Perhaps one of the other players gave him a piggyback.

To my granddad, an apparent lack of effort was the mark of manly superiority. He came from a place and an era where toughness and hard work were a necessity. It was grace that was in short supply. Elliott was a Fred Astaire of footballers. Graydon had the same stylish ease, creating space for himself and others through some magical understanding of the intersection between time and geometry. There was something mystical about it.

Despite all the talent in the two sides, the first half was desperately dull and I walked around the entire perimeter of Craik Park in the vain hope that changing the angle might make it more attractive. The ground had had extensive work done on it over the years and was surrounded by suburban fencing, over which small kids in striped Morpeth football jerseys peeped like children in the *Beano* scrounging an illegal view of a big cup tie. There was a vast stretch of high blue netting behind one goal, presumably to prevent misguided shots disappearing into the woodland and being carried away by badgers. Over by the Donny Carman Stand, a man swaddled in a warming coat like boiler cladding bellowed, 'Is that legal now, referee?' whenever the mood took him, which was frequently.

With nothing to distract me on the pitch, I began reading the player profiles in the programme. Though it was only my second trip to Craik Park, there was a warm familiarity about them. No matter where you were in the North East, a common thread runs through any team below national level. Without exception every squad has at least one of the following:

- A versatile defender who is comfortable across the whole of the backline
- A speedy wideman whose direct style can unnerve defences
- A midfielder who relishes a tackle and is a favourite of the fans

- An experienced, no-nonsense, imposing centre-back who is the lynchpin of the side

There are other descriptions that crop up pretty regularly too: highly rated goalkeepers, midfielders who 'give energy' and have 'an eye for goal', and an overseas player with an unlikely surname who inevitably offers 'something a little different from the bench', but it is the first four that are universal.

The old-fashioned centre-half is the commonest of the lot, almost as inevitable as a cross of St George flag fluttering over the allotments. Every side has one. Generally, he is the sort of walk-tall, chin-thrust-out, firkin-chested block of flesh who looks like he's about to slam through the doors of a Dodge City saloon and whack the men who burned his barn down round the ears with a shovel. Yet there are plenty of times when he isn't. When, in fact, he is quite the opposite of resolute and granite-like. Sometimes, for instance, he is wispy-haired and louche with the studied indifference of a Riviera playboy throwing in the last of his chips. He has elegance and ease. You briefly imagine him hanging out with César Luis Menotti, plotting the defeat of fascism through midfield trickery and an avoidance of barbers. It is a reverie that ends after twenty minutes when he yells a string of expletives at an opponent in a coalfield accent so guttural it comes with bits of his dinner attached.

On other occasions, the rugged centre-back is slender as a giraffe, with a bald patch and lumpy knees and every time the wet ball smacks off his moon-coloured thighs you suck air in through your teeth from sympathy. Yet still the programme proclaims that he is durable as marble and as careless of his bodywork as teenage bandits driving a stolen Nissan. Because in the end it's not really about how he is, it's about how we want him to be. The presence of the no-nonsense centre-back is a comfort to us all.

Luckily for those growing tired of such waffle (yes, me too), things perked up immeasurably in the second period. In the sixty-second minute the Highwaymen's Jack Foalle was wrestled to the ground in the penalty area by a massive Tulip, Rudy Misambo, despite the fact the ball was yards away at the time. Joe Walton was brought on as a sub and his first action was to hammer the spot kick home. 'Penalty specialist,' the bloke behind me said.

A few minutes later, the speedy Foalle received the ball a few yards inside the Spalding half and over by the left touchline. Misambo – who had apparently played for Coventry City – again decided the most sensible way to handle the situation was to grapple. The ref disagreed and sent him off. Things then got even worse for Spalding, as James Cullingworth was shown red for a crunching, thigh-high tackle that looked like something from a mixed martial arts manual. 'They might be Tulips but they're no shrinking violets,' the bloke standing behind me said, possibly to himself. It reminded me of an old wag at St James' Park who used to call out 'David Batty? Nora Batty, more like' at random moments and then cackle to himself as if it was the first time he'd heard it.

In the seventy-fourth minute a Ben Sayer corner was met by centre-half Michael Turner. His header thumped off the cross bar, rebounded out, hit Spalding keeper Michael Duggan on the back of the head and cannoned into the net. It pretty much summed up the visitors' afternoon. Sean Taylor soon slotted home a third.

After the final whistle I exited through what seemed like the back garden of a game keeper's cottage and headed off across the common back into town.

The train south was filled with revellers heading for a night on the Quayside. A young woman in a dress that would have been a hankie in most parts of the world said, 'Well, if he has to move to Middlesbrough, that's not too far away, is it? No, it isn't. No, it's not in the Midlands. Well, I don't know where exactly, but it must be up here some-where. Because there was that lass from Middlesbrough was on *Geordie Shore*, wasn't she? Think about it.'

15

MARSKE UNITED V
CLEETHORPES TOWN

Evo-Stik Northern Premier League
Division One – East

Saturday 9 March 2019

I arrived in Marske a few hours before kick-off after a morning in Saltburn. Saltburn had once been home to the Saltburn Swifts who'd joined the Northern League in 1895 and folded two years later, the only real impact they'd made during this brief stint being a commotion at Stockton that saw one of their players dismissed for a 'pugilistic episode'.

My aunt Mary and her husband had run a grocer's in Saltburn. Back then it was a rather dashing seaside resort that was served by direct trains from London and whose long, sweeping beach had witnessed various knickerbocker-wearing gents – including Malcolm Campbell – making early attempts to set the world land-speed record.

By the 1980s, Saltburn had lost its lustre. The majestic hotels were unwanted and forlorn, the sprung wooden floors of the ballrooms that had once hosted *thés dansants* to the music of big bands were scattered with dust and plaster that had fallen from the bowing ceilings. The town smelled of neglect and mildew. Visitors had once come here for the bracing healthiness of the sea air, but whenever I spent an afternoon there I seemed to immediately go down with a heavy cold.

Thankfully Saltburn had turned itself around since those grim days. The Victorian seafront and the water-balanced cliff lift had been restored and there was a cheery sense of community in the streets around the station. The same sort thing had happened at other seaside resorts along the North-East coast – at Seaham and Amble, and Whitley Bay, where Spanish City had just been renovated and re-opened after years of looming like a derelict Taj Mahal over Long Sands. It was as if people had finally looked up and noticed what was on their doorstep.

My aunt Mary lived in Saltburn, but pretty much all the rest of my family – on both sides – came from, or had lived, in Marske. I hadn't been back since my maternal grandmother had died and so I went on a little journey round once-familiar places.

My gran and granddad had lived in a red-brick semi-detached not far from the headlands overlooking the North Sea. After walks in the howling wind, my granddad and I would sit by the gas fire and prepare for Saturday's football in what was then the traditional manner – by filling in the pools coupon and doing the Spot the Ball competition.

My grandfather and I did these together every week during the season. Spot the Ball was always undertaken after the completion of his pools coupon – an act that was remarkably quick since my granddad did the same numbers in the same lines every week and, in the sort of act that only retired people of the pre-war generation would undertake, had made a cardboard stencil which, when placed over the coupon, allowed him to put his crosses in the correct boxes in a matter of seconds. By my estimation this device saved him at least two minutes every week, which he could then put to more profitable uses such as shouting 'Shut your big mouth, you swollen-headed bugger' at the telly whenever Brian Clough, Jimmy Hill, Malcolm Macdonald or, well, practically anybody else, appeared on the screen.

My grandfather's approach to the pools coupon was mirrored by our methodical efforts to win Spot the Ball. Ignoring the weather notes that were appended to the photo ('Conditions were overcast with a light westerly breeze. The morning showers had abated shortly before kick-off . . .'), we used rulers, set-squares and a draughtsman's pencil to plot the sight lines of the players, and then placed a midgie cloud of crosses on and about the point where they intersected.

It never came to anything. One week, after my granddad had won a small dividend on the football pools, he bought a sheet of quarter-inch graph paper and – in a determined attempt to finally win a prize – used it to place crosses all over the entire Spot the Ball photo, excluding only the players. I can't recall how many crosses were on the picture by the end, but the cost of entering was – to my primary school way of thinking – so massive it made my head spin. We felt certain we must win. And of course . . . we didn't.

We were not alone. Back in the 1970s, close to three million people every week did Spot the Ball. Discussing it with friends over the years, I've discovered that many had made similar diligent and expensive attempts to win a cash bonanza. Some had even purchased a special rubber Spot the Ball stamp which had fifty crosses on it. Others had bought transfer sheets that allowed you to place your marks with mathematical precision. The result, however, was always the same: nothing.

The situation led to a belief among just about every fan I have ever met that Spot the Ball was a rip-off and a fix. Investigations, however, found that the competition was entirely above board and scientifically judged. The only reason none of us ever won is that we didn't guess correctly.

Part of the problem was that entrants weren't trying to put a cross where the ball had actually been, but where a team of experts had decided it was. Whether the experts came to their decision by using mathematical instruments, or simply took the photo down the pub and threw a dart at it we have no way of knowing, though since they were usually retired professional footballers we could probably hazard a guess.

The reason for this strange state of affairs was that

gambling on past events is generally frowned upon, not least because it is fairly easy to cheat. The last I heard of it, the position of the ball was being determined at a weekly meeting between ex-Liverpool winger Ian Callaghan and former Man United centre-half David Sadler. These two names are likely about as familiar to anyone under the age of fifty as the taste of rosehip syrup and the porcine vocal stylings of Pinky and Perky. Or indeed Spot the Ball itself.

I wandered back up the road past an angular cluster of 1960s shops that had once contained a fish and chip shop my granddad refused to patronise because they charged extra for scraps – a heinous crime matched only by that of publicans who demanded money for putting 'a touch' in pints of bitter – and round to a narrow row of terraced ironstone miners' cottages that ran off the high street towards what had once been a Cheshire Foundation Home for the Sick. This was where my great-grandmother had lived, first with her husband, an ironstone miner named Chappie Keeling, and then, when he had died in his thirties from tuberculosis, her six children.

I usually spent match-day mornings here, in a tiny front room packed to bursting with elderly Northern women – at least eight of them my aunts – and the reassuring scent of baking, lavender talc and freshly knitted tea cosies. The house was sealed as tight as an Egyptian tomb, the fire was permanently lit, every chair was covered in soft cushions and fluffy rugs, and every table had a bowl of toffees on it. After dinner my granddad picked me up and we drove to

Ayresome Park and went in the Bob End. The contrast with my great-grandmother's house could not have been more striking. The Bob End was cold, the seats were hard and the air was filled with the stink of frying onions and ale and the roar of the crowd, always teetering between rapture and rage. It was exciting, smelly and scary. Pretty much like manhood, really.

Marske United had formed in 1956 and initially made moderate progress, playing in local leagues around the East Cleveland ironstone belt. They eventually joined the Teesside League, won the championship twice, moved up into the Wearside League and in 1996 did the treble of league title, Sunderland Shipowners' Cup and the Monkwearmouth Cup. They were promoted to the Northern League the following year. They'd won the title for the first time in 2015 playing attacking football with a forward line featuring Sam Garvie, a dark-haired jinky inside-forward who was like a non-League Juninho.

I'd gone to see them play an away fixture at one of their main rivals, North Shields, in the January of that year. It was a Tyneside day so icy it made your joints pop. When I got on the Metro afterwards, my ankle bones ached. I couldn't feel my feet till Byker, which as Ian remarked afterwards sounds like the title of a Lindisfarne song.

The clash with the Robins was supposed to be a tough battle, but Marske destroyed them 4-0 and the home fans had packed away their banners and left long before the final whistle to a sarcastic chant of 'We'll support you till you lose' from the travelling section. Back then, Marske had quite a noisy bunch of fans – variously styled as the Shed Titans and the Chicken Run Collective – who hammered on drums and kept up a noise for ninety minutes. It didn't always go down well with other Northern League fans. At Sam Smith's Park, when the chanting had momentarily stopped, a Benfield fan behind me had bellowed 'Get back in bed with your seals' at them. It remains the weirdest insult I have ever heard at football.

Marske had won the title again in 2018 despite a backlog of fixtures that forced them to play twelve matches in the final twenty-one days of the season. This gruelling schedule was caused by postponements due to bad weather, a run to the semi-final of the FA Vase and the Football Association's resolute refusal to extend the season by more than a week. Ah yes, the FA, whenever I thought of them I came over all Brian Glanville and quoted the Italian poet Giosuè Carducci: 'The farce of the infinitely small, the busy little farce of ponderous clowns.'

Marske's Mount Pleasant ground had once been described as 'a scrapyard' by their own chairman and, despite the club's recent successes and elevation to the Northern Premier League, it still had the look of an unfinished DIY project. The entrance way was a jumble of grey shingle Portakabins, converted shipping containers and oddly angled aluminium fencing. It reminded me a bit of Jarrow Roofing, where a collection of ancient white patio furniture gathered together under a canvas awning had once drawn a warning from a regular: 'You can't sit there. It's Platinum Club members only.'

I bought a ticket and a programme at one of the Portakabins and retired to the clubhouse where a big screen TV was showing Six Nations Rugby. Marske's programme had once been a thing of wonder. Running to eighty pages and featuring a column by Col the Kit Man, it had won national awards. Producing two dozen issues a year had eventually worn down editor Moss Holtby, however, and he'd given up to concentrate on his proper job. The current programme was decent enough, though when I read the editorial comment, 'Where has the season gone? I can't believe we are in February already', I was thrown into a momentary panic, fearing I had stepped through a rift in the time-space continuum outside Marske's Freedom Pre-Owned Furniture shop and gone back a month, possibly to thwart an invasion by Daleks hell-bent on imposing draconian covered standing regulations nationwide. Happily, it turned out that it was just a programme that had been printed for the original fixture on 9 February, which had been postponed.

At ten to three, I walked up the steps into the ground. In the gardens across on the far side of the pitch, over larchlap fencing, bunting fluttered above kids' swings. The local residents had apparently complained about the football – the swearing of the players and fans forcing them to keep their children indoors on match days. Luckily today the weather was so wild and wet – snappy gusts whipping in off the headlands and through the streets with all the intent of a jealous husband chasing a pantless man – no modern child would have ventured out of doors even in the hope of hearing grown-ups yelling 'arse'.

The Mount Pleasant pitch was notoriously boggy and as viscous and lumpy as municipal custard. Combined with the weather, it seemed an afternoon purpose-built to hurt joints, sting thighs and reduce advantages.

Visitors Cleethorpes – the Owls – were pushing for a play-off place and had only lost twice all season. Marske's ambitions were more modest – avoiding relegation back to the Northern League. They looked safe, but the locals, being Teessiders, were never complacent when it came to disaster and muttered darkly of bad runs and results going against them like reverse Mr Micawbers. Pessimism is, after all, our birth right. Optimism is for Little Orphan Annie and Geordies.

The home fans' apprehensions were temporarily allayed when a free kick was hoiked into the visitors' penalty area, swirled around in the wind, wrong-footing the defence before finally and capriciously choosing to land with a dull splat right in front of the right boot of Marske defender Andrew 'Rio' May on the edge of the six-yard box. After a pause to offer thanks for the gift, he poked the ball past Theo Richardson and into the visitors' net.

The bloke behind me was not fooled by this turn of events and his wise observation that 'Sometimes an early lead can be a Trojan horse' had barely registered when the

Owls were level, leading scorer Brody Robertson slashing home a cross from the left.

Marske came back. Richardson made such a hash of a routine clearance it should have come with a fried egg, shanking a hoofed ball straight up into the air. Boomeranged back towards goal by the wind it was volleyed home from fifteen yards by Glen Butterworth.

Five minutes after Butterworth's goal, another apparently innocuous ball into the box somehow slithered under the boot of Owls' defender Oli Donald, squirmed across the muddy surface to Jamie Owens who hammered it in from close range.

Marske striker Owens was a veteran of the Northern League. I'd seen him playing for Newton Aycliffe and Stockton Town as well as for the Seasiders. He was short and chunky, quick over ten yards, with the sort of thumping left-foot shot that in a comic would have left a vapour trail. He always put me in mind of the great German centre-forward Uwe Seeler. In an edition of the *International Football Book* (edited by Tony Stratton-Smith who – trivia alert – also managed Genesis) that I'd been given one Christmas by my auntie Bertha – who ran a fish shop in Marske High Street – I'd read that in his homeland Seeler was nicknamed 'the Hamburg Missile'. This sounded like something you might buy in a brightly lit shop in the Reeperbahn and it had stuck in my mind. As a consequence, I had taken to thinking of Owens as 'the Teesside Torpedo'.

The wind continued to whirl about in the second half, the

ball swerving randomly around above the ground until it had collected enough air miles to get to Jupiter. The heavy surface leached the energy from the players' legs and as they tired the game became so incoherent it ought to have been played to the sound of a toddler hitting a glockenspiel. The Owls had a vague penalty shout waved away and a ballooning cross-shot looped over the advancing Robert Dean, but bounced wide.

And that was about it. The whistle went and everyone in the ground bustled off in search of warmth and shelter.

I walked down the high street to keep warm while I waited for the bus, passing the Duke of Clarence pub, known as the Middle House, where Jack Coulthard had grown up. Coulthard was a buccaneering centre-forward who'd played for South Bank in the 1930s, once hammering ten in a 13-0 demolition of Ferryhill. He'd volunteered for navy service in the Second World War and was serving on HMS *Bramble* when the ship was torpedoed and sank in the freezing North Atlantic. He was thirty-one.

The bus took a route along the coast road, where my granddad had once been blown off his bike by an exploding Luftwaffe bomb and come around a few hours later to see cows standing upright in the field across the road even though the blast and shrapnel had sheared their heads clean off.

On Redcar seafront, just past Pacittos, home of the famed lemon top ice cream, an elderly couple in matching grey anoraks got on and sat in front of me. The man said, 'His car rolls up on Saturday afternoon and it's still there Sunday morning, so it's obviously a nookie night. But he hasn't shown up today.'

Unlike Saltburn, Redcar had not experienced a renaissance. In the 2007 film *Atonement* it had doubled for war-ravaged Dunkirk. 'They must have had to tart it up a bit for the role,' a friend from Stockton remarked drily.

We rolled westward past the floodlights of Redcar Athletic, towards the great hulk of Teesside's last blast furnace, the second largest in Europe. In 2009, the owners – the Indian conglomerate Tata – mothballed most of it, putting 1,700 people out of work. There were protests across the Teesside and steelworkers appealing for government intervention paraded around the pitch at the Riverside. It was a heartfelt gesture by the club, though the fact that Middlesbrough's stadium had been built with steel imported from Germany was not lost on the cynical. The steelworkers had hoped Gordon Brown's government might intervene and take the blast furnace into public ownership. Labour, however, had moved on from that kind of thing, preferring to use public money to prop up impoverished banks. If Redcar had the look of place that had survived bombardment, there was a reason.

In 2011, Tata (who weirdly also owned another of Teesside's big employers, Tetley the tea company) sold Redcar blast furnace to a firm from Thailand. They went bust in 2015. The last 700 workers were made redundant and the coke ovens extinguished. Now there was talk of turning the site into a heritage centre. Redcar blast furnace had opened in 1979. Even events that occurred when I was an adult were now history.

The bus chugged past the giant chemistry set of the Wilton industrial plants – where my gran had worked as a cook in the ICI's directors' dining room – and on into South Bank. Here a high concrete wall flanked the road, either to keep people from getting into the town, or to stop them getting out.

When former Middlesbrough winger Terry Cochrane signed for South Bank in 1992, the Northern League club had problems. Thieves kept breaking into the Normanby Road ground into the ground at night. The Bankers bought a powerful Rottweiler. When training ended for the day, they let him loose and locked the gates. That night thieves broke in again and stole the dog. South Bank, Cochrane concluded, was a pace so tough if a man had two ears they called him a cissy.

Teessiders call South Bank Slaggy Island in honour of the ring of spoil heaps that once cut it off from the outside world. South Bank was the home of the Smith's Dock shipyard, of Bolckow Vaughan and Dorman Long steelworks, clusters of iron foundries, warrens of brickyards, blast furnaces, smelters, rolling mills and fabrication sheds. Through most of the twentieth century, Slaggy Islanders lived their lives under a cloud of bitter-tasting smog. 'We had to catch a bus to see the sun,' my mother who had lived briefly in nearby Grangetown recalled.

Yet there was brutal majesty to the place. The sparks off

arc welders danced in the darkness and at night the sky was tinged dirty orange. When South Bank's most celebrated son, Wilf Mannion, called his hometown 'the enchanted city' he wasn't being sarcastic.

South Bank FC was founded in 1868, the first football club in the North East of England. The Ellis Cup was launched – as the South Bank Amateur Challenge Cup – in 1889, which makes it either the fourth or fifth oldest football competition on the planet (the Northern League – of which South Bank was a founder member – began the same year).

Originally for Under-18 teams, the Ellis Cup soon expanded to include senior sides too, not just from South Bank but from across Teesside and down into the ironstone mining villages of the North York Moors and Cleveland Hills. Over the next century, over a hundred players who'd turn pro played in it, among them some of the most influential figures in the English game.

George Elliott, my grandfather's non-running boyhood hero, played in the Ellis Cup for Redcar Crusaders, signed for South Bank shortly afterwards, then for Middlesbrough. He'd win three caps for England. Aided by two other Ellis Cup Slaggy Islanders, the Carr brothers, Jack and Willie (the latter nicknamed 'Pudden'), Elliott hit thirty-one goals in thirty-two league matches in 1913-14, helping Boro to third place in the English top flight, the club's highest-ever finish.

The father of the great Middlesbrough defender, George Hardwick, worked in the ironstone mines of East Cleveland.

Times were tough. Hardwick's mother picked up old jumpers, pulled the yarn apart and knitted George a red jersey and matching socks to play his football in. He turned out in the Ellis Cup for Saltburn FC (who'd outlasted the Swifts), moved on to South Bank, and signed for Middlesbrough in 1937. A cultured full-back, Hardwick had a matinee idol moustache and the face and physique to match. When he smiled – Kenny Twigg recalled enviously – lady's faces flushed and their legs turned to jelly. My granddad called him 'Gorgeous George' and blew ironic kisses to him from the Chicken Run. Hardwick laughed off the abuse. He captained Middlesbrough and England and lived such a raffish life people muttered excitedly of an affair with a Hollywood 'It Girl' – Veronica Lake or Rita Hayworth, accounts varied. Hardwick cunningly engineered a move to Oldham, worked as a reporter, and made money wherever he went. In the 1970s we'd pass him sometimes in the streets around Ayresome Park, still debonair in a houndstooth sports coat and Clark Gable whiskers, the half-smile on his lips looking like it might turn to a growl if the right woman came along.

The Golden Boy, Wilf Mannion, was born in Napier Street. He was too poor to afford a football. 'We used to get a pig's bladder from the butchers, blow it up,' he'd told me, 'played on pitches of cinders. I tell you what, anyone can control a pig's bladder is a ruddy genius.'

Mannion turned out for South Bank St Peter's from the age of fourteen. In one early match he'd dribbled round a rugged boilermaker who'd told him, 'If you do that to me again, I'll break both your fucking legs.' St Peter's captain intervened, 'You can't do that, he's just a bairn.' 'Well,' the boilermaker replied, 'in that case if he does it again I'll break both your fucking legs instead.'

Despite the menaces, Mannion won the Ellis Cup with South Bank St Peter's when he was sixteen. His side played South Bank East End in the final. East End's stopper got no closer to the blond inside-forward than kicking the ball into his groin. The stopper's name was Harold Shepherdson. Three decades later, as Alf Ramsey's assistant, he'd be leaping off the bench at Wembley when Geoff Hurst scored England's fourth, the manager barking 'Sit down, Harold, I can't see' at him.

Wilf joined Hardwick in a Boro team that included other Slaggy Island alumni. Micky Fenton, also from East End, was the centre-forward, quick, powerful, with a shot that thumped off his boot with a thud like a middleweight hooking the heavy bag. Bobby Stuart, the right-back, won two caps with England in 1936 and was chosen by Wills Tobacco as the Boro player for that year's cigarette card set, alongside Raich Carter, Ted Drake and a youthful, gurning Stanley Matthews.

With George, Wilf, Micky and Bobby, Boro finished seventh in 1937, fifth in 1938 and fourth in 1939. 'If it hadn't been for the war, I know that team would have won the title,' George Hardwick said later. Bloody Hitler.

The influence of the Ellis Cup spread far beyond Teesside. Future Leeds United capo Don Revie played in the competition for Middlesbrough Swifts. Man United boss Matt Busby, a serviceman at Catterick Garrison, helped Portrack Shamrocks defeat Cargo Fleet Home Guard in the 1946 final. Ken Furphy turned out for Stockton West End, turned pro with Everton, achieved great things coaching Watford and ended up in the USA in the 1970s managing New York Cosmos.

By then, the steelyards and shipyards had shut and a different kind of hardship battered South Bank. The population of the town dwindled. Shutters went up over doors and windows, shops closed and derelict streets were bulldozed. Football clung on. Charlie Wyke, the Sunderland centre-forward was schooled here.

After Terry Cochrane quit, South Bank's ground was attacked by vandals, routinely and viciously. Arsonists burned down the clubhouse and torched the main stand. The oldest football club in the region had to play home fixtures 30 miles away at Ferryhill. Soon, unable to fulfil fixtures, the Bankers had been suspended from the Northern League they'd helped start.

A community centre, named Golden Boy Green in honour of Wilf Mannion, had been built where the old ground once stood. In 2009, in what was becoming a tradition, arsonists burned it down. The locals rallied around and rebuilt it.

Nowadays South Bank FC play at Harcourt Road, sharing the pitch with Eston Villa and Middlesbrough Homeless. They're in the Stockton Sunday League. In 2015, they got to the final of the Ellis Cup and won it in a penalty shoot-out against North Ormesby Cons. The Ellis Cup still resides on Slaggy Island. It's on display in the Erimus Social Club.

I still have both ears, so I decided not to get off the bus and a risk a visit.

16

CONSETT V NEWTON AYCLIFFE

Ebac Northern League Division One

Saturday 16 March 2019

It was spring in the Anglo-Scottish Borderlands. The sky was as blue and free from malice as a baby's eyes, dew glittered, lambs frolicked, fruit trees were topped with a foam of creamy blossom, and writers' notebooks burgeoned with frothy verbiage; even the train-spotters heading to Carlisle station for the promise of a steaming Flying Scotsman had discarded their anoraks.

In the Metrocentre, gaggles of tweenie girls brandishing Primark carrier bags strutted about the bus station and-she's-went-and-I've-went-and-she's-wenting until they ran out of breath and their bestie took over.

As the X45 Red Kite bus from Newcastle Eldon Square to Consett bus station via Team Street Gas Works rolled up the hill out of Swalwell and into the leafy Derwent Valley, the scent of celebrity-endorsed perfumes blended with the earthier reek of muckspreading (because there's nothing like the sight of people having picnics in the garden to make a farmer feel like showering pigshit everywhere). I had picked up a copy of the *Cumberland Gazette* that had been left on the train seat opposite. It was filled with the familiar stuff of rural newspapers: drunken affray, shop closures, grinning councillors and prize sheep.

The fourteen-year-old girl in store-ripped jeans sitting in front of me made it hard to concentrate, though. She was talking on her mobile phone. She said, 'I can't. I can't. I can't, can I? I've no money, have I? None. Nowt. Gone. I've spent it all last night on vodka and Fruittellas, man.'

If you'd added the right music it could have been an opera by Mozart.

'I don't know why *she* thinks she's that mint neither,' the girl said as she began to get out of her seat when we passed the signs to Winlaton. 'I seen her the other night, all done up, and she looked like an orange Hillary Clinton.'

She got off in Rowlands Gill and everything went strangely quiet except for the automated stop announcements, a woman's voice that put me in mind of the speaking clock. 'The next stop is ...' she said and there was a pause as if she were a teacher inviting a class of infants to shout out the answer, 'Pity Me!' 'Fatfield!' 'It's on the Tip of My Tongue!' (which is actually a village near Burnopfield in County Durham. Maybe.)

We pulled up the hill past Shotley Bridge cricket club,

where England's Paul Collingwood had started out. 'The next stop is ... The Slonks,' the voice announced. It wasn't an answer you'd have got with an educated guess.

I hopped off at Consett bus station and walked past a supermarket with a large sign reading 'There is no lead on this roof' fixed to the side of it and across the pedestrian bridge over the dual carriageways that circled the town. Consett was high up and the wind seemed to be blowing from all directions at once. Terriers bowled past me like tumbleweeds, owners yelling in their wake.

At Consett's Belle View ground, posters advertised a forthcoming international friendly against Lanzarote. The visitors from the Canary Islands would turn up on a freezing Tuesday night and get thrashed 6-1. Once inside, I bought a cup of tea and walked over to look at the team sheet that was fastened to a wall by the redbrick clubhouse.

Ahead of me I saw a figure I recognised, a bulbous middle-aged man in a beige anorak, swirly, flapping tie and Hank Marvin glasses. I saw him half a dozen times a year, stooped studiously in front of the team sheet board, earnestly scribbling notes on a reporter's pad, occasionally stopping to smooth the remains of a side-parting in his wavy, greying hair. As he bustled past the stands, bulging nylon satchel beating against ankle-grazing slacks, he cheerily waved in acknowledgement at stony-faced codgers who had uttered no greeting. When the match started he gabbled the breathless details of the action into a brick-like mobile at ten-minute intervals. 'The crowd was on its feet in the twenty-seventh minute,' he'd say, his voice ascending to a Tyldesley-esque crescendo-gurgle, though the only person anyone had seen rise from their chair since kick-off was the wife of a senior player when one of her Ugg boots got tangled with her French bulldog's extendable lead.

'He doesn't work for radio or a paper, you know,' someone told me once, nodding in the bloke's direction – he was in mid-flow, speaking into his phone as if addressing a faraway maiden aunt through a megaphone, wresting unexpected melodrama from a goal kick that went straight out for a throw – 'It's not switched on, that mobile of his.'

There was no criticism in the comment, I should add. After all, what is Step 6 football for, if not to offer a safe and soothing haven to the lost, the lonely and the bewildered? There had been times five years back when, were it not for the reassuring sounds of a big-faced man with a voice like a bassoon booming 'Give over, liner, you must be mental,' every five minutes, I'd have slipped the surly bonds of sanity myself.

One spring-like afternoon much like today, the non-reporter sat a few rows in front of me. He went through his usual routine, vivid calls and busy scribbling. Looking over his shoulder, I caught sight of the open page of his notebook, a frenzied diagram of player names drawn up in formation and criss-crossed with directional arrows. It looked like the work of an action painter, or a dithering general. Less surprisingly, perhaps, it looked quite a lot like my own.

I took up a covered seat that offered vague promise of shelter from the wind. Until 2013, Consett had played at the much-loved Belle View. The ground had been built by volunteers in 1950 after the Steelmen's original home, the Vicarage Ground, had been flattened to build an extension to the ironworks. In those days, workers at Consett's giant steel works supported the football club with a deduction taken directly from their pay packets. Back then people had a spirit of community whether they wanted one or not. Still, after sixty years the roofs of the stands had taken on a colander-like quality and the cinder terraces were crumbling like ripe cheese. The club left for this new council-funded facility. It lacked the atmosphere of the old stadium, but at least it kept the rain off.

Consett had been founded in 1899 as Consett Celtic. They'd played in the semi-pro North Eastern League (a record 7,000 turned out to watch a match with Sunderland Reserves) and, when that folded in the '60s, joined the Wearside League, before hopping up to the Northern League in 1970. They'd been in it ever since, but though they were always one of the stronger sides, they had never been champions. The closest they'd come had been in 1976-77 when they'd finished level on points at the top with Spennymoor. In those days the Northern League didn't bother with fancy-dan mathematical stuff like goal averages or differences, and the title was settled with a play-off (the seventh in the league's history). At Hall Lane Willington, with future Premier League official Ken

Redfern of Whitley Bay as ref, Moors swept the Steelmen aside, 3-0.

There had been a near miss more recently, too. In 2009, needing a point to secure the title, Consett had gone two up away at Whitley Bay only for the Seahorses to fight back for a 3-2 win that handed the title to Benfield.

At Belle View it was windy, though I'd seen it worse here. At one game against Dunston, the goals had been bent at almost forty-five degrees, narrowing the target for any team kicking into the gale and making a basketball-style drop shot the best option for those with it at their backs.

Consett had the wind behind them in the first half and Aksel Juul quickly brought a good save out of Adam Pickford. Aged twenty-six he'd been signed from Sunday League side Chilton. Like most current Northern League keepers, Pickford was slim and athletic as an acrobat. That had not always been true. Twenty years ago, many of the North East's non-League keepers had been the sort of roly-poly lads you suspected had been shoved between the sticks as kids because they couldn't run fast enough and never escaped. When these walrus-like custodians dived to save a low shot they fell to earth so slowly the bloke behind you would inevitably yell 'Tiiiiiiiiiimber!' in a fake American accent and, if you were lucky, his mate would sing a chorus of 'The Lumberjack Song'.

Consett continued to attack, moving the ball smartly around. They were helped by the pitch, which was a 3G. For a long while I'd taken the traditional fan's negative attitude to artificial surfaces, but I'd come round to them lately. Not everyone agreed. Every time he saw the rubber crumbs flying up from a player's boot, the bloke beside me who had a face the size of a breeze block and the body to match would suddenly growl, 'Artificial surfaces!' Disdain rolled down his tone like wax down a lit candle.

He told me he'd played for Crook Town and Spennymoor back in the '70s. When he spoke, he wagged a finger in my direction. Not straight on, but with his right arm stuck out at forty-five degrees to his front and his index digit cocked inwards. I got the feeling that if I ever looked at that finger directly the bloke would smack me with a quick left hand, so I just left it out there dancing at the edge of my vision.

He said: 'Plastic pitches? They suck all the romance out of the game. Bloody prophylactics of football, what they are.'

I wasn't surprised by his attitude. A lot of ex-players had an almost mystical fondness for turf. Years back when I told the former Manchester United goalkeeper Alex Stepney that I had seen him play for English League v Scottish League in Middlesbrough, he smiled wistfully, 'I always enjoyed playing at Ayresome Park. It had the finest surface in the country.'

This was a response guaranteed to delight any Boro fan over forty-five years of age. Every visiting team praised our glorious grass. We were proud of it. I spent many happy childhood hours gazing at that pitch (admittedly, there was usually nothing much happening on it to distract me).

At non-league level pitches were often hard to maintain

some looked like they had been entertaining a particularly truculent herd of wildebeest, others were mucky and mushy with a thin sprinkling of green across the top, like pease pudding that had been allowed to lurk at the back of the fridge for several months beyond its sell-by date. For nostalgists keen to be reminded of the days when Malcom 'Supermac' Macdonald churned across mud like a warhorse, a hail of divots flying up behind him and blinding pursuing centre-backs, this may be reason to cheer, but poor surfaces, for all the fun they offer, aren't really good for football. You don't have to be a tactical genius to work out that a short passing game will be ineffective in a ploughed field; that route one is the best way to avoid getting bogged down in the mud. Ugly surfaces tend to encourage ugly football. Purists might not like it, but it seemed to me that at the lower levels of football artificial surfaces are the way forward.

Of course, supporters of Durham City might feel differently. Playing at their New Ferens Park ground on an artificial surface, the Citizens had roared to the Northern League title in 2007-08 with a then record points total of 102 (in 2012-13, Darlington would amass a mountainous 122, scoring 145 goals in the process). They'd done something similar in the Northern Premier League first division and suddenly there was heady talk of league football returning to Durham for the first time since 1928. Unfortunately, the Football Conference then stepped in and informed Durham that they would not be eligible for promotion to the National League North, the next step up the pyramid, because of the artificial pitch. (The National League has since relaxed that policy, but the English Football League still insists on grass. Quite why they take this stance when Fifa and Uefa are happy for international and European competitions to be played on artificial pitches is anybody's guess – apparently what's good enough for the Juventus or Germany is unacceptable for Carlisle or Mansfield.)

With promotion and all the publicity that goes with it blocked, Durham's main sponsors withdrew support. Financially strapped and facing high travel costs, the Citizens were forced to allow their senior players to leave. Soon the team was made up entirely of students and teen-agers. They won just two matches all season (the six points deducted for fielding a player under a false name leaving them on zero) and conceded 168 goals. Though there was sympathy for their plight from opposition fans (the team were given a standing ovation after an 11-0 drubbing at King's Lynn), it didn't help. The downward spiral had continued ever since. Durham City were currently ground-sharing with Willington and bottom of the Northern League second division.

Against the expectation of my snarling companion, the game continued entertainingly. In the sixteenth minute, a headed clearance fell to the excellent Michael Sweet a couple of feet inside the Aycliffe half. He advanced unchal-lenged and planted a dipping shot beyond Pickford for his twenty-fifth goal of the season. He'd scored forty-three the previous one.

After half time, with the wind at their backs, Aycliffe were a completely different proposition and drew level within three minutes of the restart, Ethan Wood lashing in a low shot from the edge of the box. There weren't many chances after that, though the visitors might have snatched a last-minute win, a strike from Wood cannoning off the post in stoppage time.

I walked back to the bus station through the weird, desolate landscape of Consett's fringes. The massive steel and ironworks which had employed around a third of the town's workforce and filled the sky with red dust that gave it a Martian aspect had closed in 1980 as part of Ian MacGregor's machete-wielding march towards a knighthood and been completely demolished soon afterwards. In the forty years since, the massive space it had occupied had only been partially filled – mainly by chain stores and drive-thru fast food outlets. There was an agoraphobia-inducing emptiness that the swishing rows of passing cars exacerbated. Once it was said you needed a gas mask to breathe here, now it felt like you needed a spacesuit.

I sat in the bus station and cheered myself up by thinking about the football. I'd been particularly impressed with Consett's Aksel Juul, a Newcastle-born attacking midfielder who'd played out in the US for Wingate University and Myrtle Beach Mutiny of the NPSL and also tried his luck in Denmark. His Scandinavian name called to mind one of Consett's most notable ex-players, Albert Juliussen. The Blyth-born son of Norwegian immigrants, Juliussen was a marauding frontman for Dundee United who hit ninety-five goals in seventy-three matches, including thirteen in two successive games. He left Tannadice for Portsmouth for a £10,000 fee, but failed to settle at Fratton Park, some newspapers claiming that the warm southern climate didn't agree with him, while others said he was handicapped by severe varicose veins which prevented him taking his socks off even when he jumped in the team bath. He moved to Goodison for £10,000 in 1949, but left for Consett on a free after only a few games – some Everton fans with a taste for the obscure had once named him the worst player ever to don the blue jersey.

17

DUNSTON UTS V GUISBOROUGH TOWN

Ebac Northern League Division One

Tuesday 26 March 2019

My daughter was researching her final year project for fashion college. The collection had to be based on family history and she wanted to use her great-grandfather as one of the inspirations. My grandfather was a snappy dresser. Photos taken in the 1920s show him astride a motorbike wearing Argyll socks, houndstooth check trousers, an immaculately pleated trenchcoat and a raffish beret. Like many tough working-class men of his generation, my granddad wore his clothes with the gangster swagger of James Cagney or George Raft. When my daughter showed the photos to her tutor in London, the tutor smiled and said, 'Wow, wouldn't it be great if men still dressed like that?'

My daughter asked if it was true that my grandfather and

his brothers were always fighting in pubs and dancehalls. There was no denying it. Part of the problem was they all had red hair. Back then it was commonly assumed that people with red hair had uncontrollable tempers. 'If you had red hair,' my mother – a redhead – would say, 'people were always telling you, "You're a hot head, you are. I bet you get angry fast, don't you?"

'When people keep on saying that to you over and over and over,' my mother continued, 'in the end you wind up telling them, "Shut your ruddy mouth, or you'll be waking up on your back with a crowd around you." And then they say, "There you are, see?" I tell you, it drives you bloody mad.'

My daughter has red hair and, having been regularly shouted at in the street as a result, she was empathetic to this point of view.

'One time,' I told her, 'back after the First World War, my granddad and his brother Joe were working putting the sheet-metal roofs on the fabricating sheds down in the Ironmasters District. There was a bloke up there working on the far side from them and he kept shouting stuff – "Fetch a bucket of water, those lads' heads are on fire," and other such witticisms. After a while, Joe says to your great-grandfather that he's had enough of it, so he walks across the roof – these are high buildings, maybe 100, 120ft. He walks over the roof to where this noisy bloke is working. The bloke asks Joe if he can toast some bread by holding it up to his hair. Joe says he can, but only if he lends him a lump hammer first. The bloke goes in his tool bag and hands Joe the lump hammer. Joe looks at the bloke and he looks at the hammer. Then ...' I paused for effect. 'Then he drops it off the edge of the roof – 100, 120ft – watches it fall, turns to the bloke and says, "One more word out of you and you're following it."

'"And our Joe," my granddad would say, "Now, he *was* tough."'

In 1914, Joe had joined the Royal Engineers. He was sixteen. He served on the frontline in France and Belgium for four years, was wounded and gassed and hospitalised with trench foot he'd caught from wearing a pair of leather boots he'd stripped off the body of a dead German pilot. After the war he joined the Merchant Navy and went all over the world. He brought back a ukulele from Hawaii and on Saturday nights after chucking-out time he'd play Al Bowlly tunes and his sister-in-law, my grandmother, fuelled by Theakston's Old Peculier, would do her party piece – tucking her skirt into her knickers and singing 'Swannee River' while turning somersaults across the sitting room floor.

My daughter said she needed to go and see the house where my grandfather and his brothers grew up. I told her I'd come with her. I said, 'We need to go down early. You won't want to be there after sunset.' So we went down to Middlesbrough to look at the terraced house in Essex Street, TS1. We walked from the station, taking a detour down Newton Street. After a pause and regretful sigh at the passing of Jack Hatfield's Sports Shop, I led my daughter down Parliament Road towards the tall angular skeleton of the Newport Bridge, past steel-shuttered houses and clusters of young men with their hoods up and scarves masking their faces.

Just ahead of us, opposite a Chinese chip shop, a haggard woman stood by a lamppost. A ratty-faced man with a jerky string-puppet tread jittered across the street towards her and said, 'Has he been by?'

'Not yet,' the woman said. 'I was here forty-five minutes yesterday.'

'I'm waiting for my man/Got $26 in my hand,' my daughter muttered after we'd walked past them. She'd had her phone out to take photos, but she'd put it away again.

'I'm not sure people round here would want to be on camera,' she said.

Fifty yards further on, a heavily tattooed man riding a tiny bike pulled out of a side street, circled slowly round us twice, dull eyes staring at us from the slit of a black balaclava, then rode back the way he'd come. It was twenty past eleven on Tuesday morning. 'Ah now,' I said to my daughter. 'Another glamorous outing with your dad, eh?'

Ayresome Park is now a housing estate. Back in the 1960s, they'd talked of how television was bringing the football ground into British sitting rooms. Forty years later Wimpey had reversed the situation and plonked British sitting rooms in a football ground. My daughter had been here once before, in 2001, for the unveiling of artist Neville Gabie's Trophy

Room project, a group of sculptures discreetly dotted among the houses to memorialise the past without impinging too much on the present. It quickly became apparent why the council had adopted this tacit approach. One of the guests of honour at the opening was former Boro frontman Bernie 'The Wolfman' Slaven, a dark-haired Scot who'd scored 118 times in 307 matches for the club, despite apparently never running more than three yards per game. Slaven had just wound up his career with a season at Billingham Synthonia where he'd averaged better than a goal a match.

Bernie is an extraordinarily genial and warm-hearted chap. I'd once helped him out with an event for his benefit year and, ever since, whenever he's seen me he's always come over slapped me on the shoulder and said: 'Hey, big man, how's it going?'

Boro-supporting friends who witnessed this were always impressed. 'He called you "Big Man"!' they'd say excitedly. And I'd smile in a faux self-deprecating manner, even though I suspected that the true reason Bernie called me 'Big Man' was because he couldn't quite remember my name. And, frankly, why should he?

Any road, being ever-willing, when the local press photographers asked Bernie to reproduce his characteristic Holgate End goal celebration by jumping on a garden fence, he happily obliged. However, no sooner had he clambered up and turned to the camera with his right arm aloft than the kitchen door of the home owner whose fence he was perched on burst open and a man with a face rapidly turning the colour of an overripe damson stormed out, waving his arms and bellowing: 'Getfuckingdownyou'refucking-trespassingyoufuckingfuckeryoupayforanyfuckingdamage.'

'Hey, mate, it's Bernie Slaven, isn't it?' one of the bystanders called out in an attempt to pacify him. It didn't work.

'Idon'tfuckingcareifit'sfuckingGingerfuckingSpicehecan-fuckingfuckoff,' the man replied.

Bernie got down and made his apologies. The man with the purple face stood in his doorway for the rest of the afternoon scowling. Some people had bought a house on the site of Ayresome Park because they loved Middlesbrough football club. Others had bought one there because they wanted a house.

After the shouting had stopped, there were a few speeches and then some children's events. My daughter got her face painted red-and-white and her mother, who had unparalleled luck in such matters, won the raffle and was presented with a Middlesbrough shirt signed by Alain Bokšić who'd arrived at the Riverside the summer before from Lazio.

'I'm surprised he could summon up the energy,' someone muttered sarcastically.

'I bet he pulled a hamstring lifting the pen,' said another.

The Croatian Bokšić had been one of the last of Boro's round of glamorous and unlikely foreign signings following Juninho, Emerson, Fabrizio Ravanelli, Christian Karembeu and the aged Brazilian Branco, who looked like Uncle Buck from *The High Chaparral* and moved around like he was carrying several extra saddlebags.

Bokšić was a man of supreme talent who was so languid he seemed perpetually on the verge of going into hibernation. Once or twice a game, he'd stir himself and execute a brilliantly disguised dummy, or strike a free kick imperiously into the top corner, before slipping back into torpor. While the former Marseille and Juventus frontman was reputedly pulling in £63,000 a week for putting in the odd performance for Middlesbrough, a friend of mine would accurately predict his availability for matches simply by taking a detour past his house on the way back from work.

While the club issued medical bulletins and talked of late fitness tests, my mate would shake his head. 'No go for Maine Road,' he'd tell me on Tuesday evening. 'Super Al's bins are already out.' Refuse collection day was Friday. You don't put your bins out three days in advance unless you've gone on holiday.

During his time at the Riverside, a story about Bokšić circulated around Teesside. In a classic Armani-suit-and-bovver-boots combination, the ex-Juventus star found himself partnered up front by ex-Leeds and Coventry bruiser Noel Whelan. He was not impressed. And who can blame him? Whelan was a hard worker, a bustler, but he carried all the attacking threat of Tupperware. At one point during his Boro career, he had scored more goals in his own net than he had in the opposition's. Bokšić may have been so slothful he wept when he woke up, but he had standards. According to the story, one Monday, after a particularly inept display by the former Leeds target man, Bokšić went in to see the Boro secretary. 'What does Whelan earn per week?' he demanded. The secretary told him. 'And how long does he have left on his contract?' The secretary told him and the striker stalked out. The next day he returned, waving a cheque.

'This is the money Whelan will earn during the rest of his time here. Give it to him now,' he commanded, 'and tell him to fuck off.'

My daughter and I walked round the site of the Holgate End and up onto a little patch of rough grass near the fence of the damson-faced fence-protector. I was looking for a small bronze sculpture of stud prints that marked the spot from which one of the most famous goals in the history of international football had been scored by Pak Doo-Ik for North Korea against Italy in the 1966 World Cup.

By the time the number seven struck to send the Italians home to a fusillade of rotten fruit, North Korea had already established themselves as Teesside's favourite other team. Indeed, the celebrations of the man from Pyongyang's strike were so vociferous they momentarily fused the Ayresome Park lights. 'They've never cheered Middlesbrough like this for years,' bellowed BBC commentator Frank Bough, who'd worked at ICI Billingham and played a couple of games for Synthonia.

It was an unlikely turn of events all round. With the Korean War still fresh in people's minds, the North Koreans arrived at London Airport and then trundled northwards on British Rail singing their patriotic songs and signing autographs for ladies with beehive hair-dos and bird-wing spectacles. On Teesside they trained at Billingham Synthonia's Central Avenue ground and stayed at the newly opened airport hotel, which belonged to Boro's ambitious and predictably unloved chairman, Charles Amer (the Italians had flown in on the first international flight to land at Teesside Airport, which wouldn't officially open until November, when the ribbon was cut by Princess Margaretha of Sweden, for reasons that remain opaque). Later Amer would entertain the North Koreans at his home Normanby Hall, presenting them all with a gift of a Churchill Crown, though it's unlikely the great Conservative politician was quite the hero in Pyongyang that he was in Britain.

From the outset the crowd at Ayresome Park got behind the North Koreans. 'It remains a riddle to me,' recalled one of the team, Rim Jung Song. 'The people of Middlesbrough supported us all the way through – I still don't know why.'

A friend who watched the games at Ayresome Park offered a plausible explanation: 'They were small, for a start. They were like a team of jockeys.' The size thing (the average height of the team was just 5ft 5) was indeed a factor. In their first game against the Soviet Union, the North Koreans were knocked flying by their much larger opponents who, to use a technical term, kicked the shit out of them. The sight of small men being bullied awakened the sympathy of the Teesside crowd.

After that, North Korea became the home side at Ayresome Park. After the defeat to the Soviets, they rallied from a goal behind to draw with Chile and then caused one of the biggest upsets in World Cup history by beating an Italian side containing Sandro Mazzola, Gianni Rivera and Giacinto Facchetti (sadly, Pino Wilson, the Darlington-born future captain of Lazio, didn't make the squad). Hundreds of fans travelled from Teesside to Liverpool to watch the North Koreans take on Portugal, where they amazingly took a 3-0 lead after twenty-four minutes, only to succumb 5-3 thanks to the brilliance of Eusébio.

In 2002, Pak Doo-Ik – who'd become a gymnastics instructor when his football career ended – and the other six surviving members of the North Korean team returned to Teesside. Feted as heroes, they'd walked out onto the pitch before Boro's home game with Leeds and Pak, decked out in a Boro scarf, had toe-ended the ball into the net in front of the North Stand in recreation of his famous moment. When the ball hit the net he looked up at us with such a modest, beaming smile that thinking about it does my heart good.

After a quick look at the bronze football that marked the old penalty spot, my daughter and I walked back to the Dorman Museum to ask about archive photos of Teessiders in the inter-war years. We were directed to the reference library. 'I'll phone ahead to let them know what you're after,' the cheery woman at the museum reception said.

Outside the museum, I forced another detour to look at the statue of Brian Clough, who'd been born and brought up across on the other side of Albert Park. When I was at primary school in Great Ayton, a friend's dad was the goalkeeper for one of the local village teams. Years later, he'd recall an Ellis Cup tie against nearby Great Broughton – managed in those days by the village post-mistress Nancy Goldsborough – when a shiny-eyed teenage centre-forward banged in a hat-trick and at the final whistle wandered over, patted my friend's dad on the arm, told him, 'One day, when I'm playing for England, you'll brag to your mates about this,' then smiled and introduced himself: 'I'm Brian Clough.'

'If he hadn't been so little, I'd have planted him,' my friend's dad said, telling the story for the thousandth time.

Nowadays, cockiness is seen as a not-entirely-negative trait; some even view it as a prerequisite to success. But back then arrogance was a mortal sin. The slightest sign of confidence was mercilessly crushed. When a mate of mine came back from Scouts in the late '60s and bragged about having just got his badge for knots, his uncles bound him to a chair, told him, 'If you're so clever with knots, untie those' and went down the pub. Nobody liked a bighead. And Clough was, by all accounts, a monstrous egotist right from the start.

Clough signed for Middlesbrough – the team he had supported since boyhood – from Great Broughton in 1955 (the Boro scout who spotted him: George Camsell). Photos show a sharp-featured face beneath a Woody Woodpecker quiff. His skin is so pale it looks as if he has lain under a sun lamp switched to 'suck'. His scoring record for Boro was almost as extraordinary as Camsell's. In his five full seasons at Ayresome Park, his lowest tally was thirty-six. Yet he was never popular with his team-mates. His quest for goals was said to have been so single-minded, he shoved better-placed colleagues out of the way so he could score himself. He allegedly sulked after defeats and criticised others on the field of play; he was accused of being arrogant, scathing and combative. Who'd have thought it?

Clough hit back with accusations of his own – more serious ones. Boro were mired in the old second division and apparently incapable of escape no matter how many times their centre-forward found the net. Clough believed there was something more sinister behind the situation than mere mediocrity. He went public, alleging his team-mates had a habit of betting on themselves to lose, then ensuring they did so by deliberately conceding goals. The accusations led to fisticuffs in the dressing room and, when Clough was made captain, nine players signed a round-robin letter to the directors asking for him to be removed.

The Boro crowd took the majority view (though very few supporters these days doubt Clough's version) and in the next home game barracked the skipper from the kick-off. He responded in typical style – scoring a hat-trick, all with shots from outside the area.

While at Boro, Clough had put in transfer requests every season without fail. He was linked with Everton and Birmingham, but eventually went to Sunderland for £55,000. He liked it much better at Roker Park and hit sixty-three goals in seventy-four appearances, before a collision with Bury goalkeeper Chris Harker smashed his knee. Bob Stokoe, then playing out his career with The Shakers, stood over the injured Clough and accused him of faking. It lead to a venomous feud between the pair that was never settled.

It is hard now to see Clough's playing days as anything but a prologue to his brilliant management career, but in many ways it was his time at Middlesbrough and Sunderland that formed him as a man. He was bright, brash and outspoken before he arrived at Ayresome Park, but his experiences with his hometown club stirred bitterness and frustration into the mix. It was there, too, that he met Peter Taylor, while the injury at Sunderland led to his first prolonged bout of drinking. His instinctive strong sense of right and wrong (evinced by his teams' excellent disciplinary records and his hatred of gamesmanship) was affronted by Boro's habit of frittering away matches for financial gain; the fact that the board turned a blind eye added a mistrust of authority that would be vindicated years later by the behaviour of the board of directors at Derby County.

The thwarted ambition, the back-stabbing and the sense of injustice made him what he sometimes was – particularly during the 'Mike Yarwood' years at Derby, Brighton and Leeds: awkward, confrontational and belligerent.

When I was growing up, Clough wasn't a popular figure round Teesside, but he had mellowed over the years and so had the local attitude to him. The statue had been paid for by public subscription in 2007. Another of English club football's greatest managers had also been born not far away, close by where my grandfather had grown up. As yet, however, there was no public clamour for a statue of Don Revie.

My daughter and I walked off down Linthorpe Road, past the shops selling designer clothes and the pay-day loan firms. In the splendid, wood-panelled Victorian library, a couple of staff sat us down at a table and brought books and files of photos, popping back every quarter of an hour with some new item or idea.

Nearly half the population of Middlesbrough live in areas rated in the 10 per cent most deprived in Britain. One in ten live in areas rated in the bottom 1 per cent. Some 34,000 people live in the postcode TS1 and there are around 900 crimes reported per month. Teesside is one of the UK's crime capitals. You are more likely to be robbed here or have your property burned down than anywhere else in the country. And if that wasn't bad enough, the local police force had just been rated the worst in Britain.

Yet everyone we'd met had treated us with the same courtesy, kindness and brash good humour they'd extended to Pak Doo-Ik and his team-mates. Middlesbrough was, and had always been, a raw and rough-edged town, but the people refused to be bent out of shape by circumstance. Hardship can push you two ways – it can make you parsimonious, mean-spirited and greedy, or generous, careless of the things you have been denied. Life is a game you can't win; the best you can do is battle on and laugh in its face.

We caught the train back to Tynedale. I said goodbye

to my daughter at the Metrocentre, hopped off the train and walked through the darkness towards the floodlights of UTS Park.

Dunston needed a single point to secure the third Northern League title in the club's history. There were still six games to go, but the challenge of nearest rivals Bishop Auckland and Consett had collapsed, though some fans claimed that the late-season run of bad form may have been to avoid compulsory promotion.

Opponents Guisborough had been formed in 1973. They arrived in the Northern League in 1985 and won promotion to the top flight two years later. They'd finished in the top six from 1988 to 1999 but never won the title. The team from the ancient capital of Cleveland had earned themselves a footnote in football history when, in 1988, local Conservative MP Richard Holt used parliamentary privilege to declare in the House of Commons that the club had been 'cheated' out of progress in the FA Cup 'by a biased referee'. The referee in question, Tom Fitzharris, had sent off the Priorymen's skipper Ray Hankin (Wallsend-born star at Burnley, Leeds and, erm, Vancouver Whitecaps) in the first period after a dispute over his armband. Guisborough had subsequently lost their first-round tie with Bury 0-1.

There were over 400 fans in UTS Park and most of them were in a high state of excitement by the time the match kicked off. There was a lot of shrill yelling from over to the left. 'You've heard of the Wags, this is the Mans – Mams and Nans,' Jimmy said.

Dunston took the lead in the fourth minute with what was undoubtedly the strangest goal of the season. Guisborough keeper Jordan Nixon took a free kick from ten yards outside his penalty area, hammering it high towards the edge of the Dunston box. The ball was nodded out to the right edge of the box where Liam Brooks steadied himself, looked up and struck a high volley down the field. The ball travelled eighty yards, Nixon desperately running back towards his own line, glancing anxiously over his shoulder to follow its path. Brooks' towering shot bounced on the edge of the box, looped upwards and over the leaping Nixon, struck the bar and cannoned straight back onto the head of Mark Fitzpatrick, who'd been chasing in the keeper's footsteps. Fitzpatrick headed it straight into the net. It was a goal greeted by applause and excited laughter. The sort you'd remember for decades long after better ones had been lost in the fog.

Guisborough unexpectedly equalised, but in the second half Dunston dominated. Jack Elliott and Fitzpatrick both scored decent goals and the title was theirs.

Jimmy and Margaret gave me a lift to Blaydon bus station. There was twenty minutes before the number 10 arrived, so I bought a pizza and some fizzy pop to have while I waited. I took a bite of pepperoni and a sip of Fanta and thought about Fitzpatrick's bizarre goal and the players dancing on the pitch after the final whistle, arms raised, feet jigging under the floodlights. Cars came in and out of the drive-thru burger bar opposite, a lone can of Red Bull rattled along the pavement by the shopping precinct and from the streets above a drunk bellowed out a chant of 'Newcastle, Newcastle . . .' It wasn't the most romantic place to celebrate a league title win, but it was good enough for me.

18

SUNDERLAND RCA V PENRITH

Ebac Northern League Division One

Saturday 13 April 2019

I took the train to Heworth and changed to the Metro. While I was waiting, I bought some chocolate from the vending machine on the platform. The two models of Selecta snack vending machines used at British stations are the St Tropez and the Santa Fe. Yes, nothing quite says 'shimmering exotic sensuality' like eating a Boost bar as you pass through Brockley Whins.

At Park Lane, I hopped aboard the 61 'Drifter' to Ryhope Hospital and Engine Museum via Spelterworks Road. Passing through Grangetown, I was pleased to see the trend for tattoo parlours with tea rooms was spreading. In Middlesbrough there was one that had an A-board outside offering a range of tattoos 'in 15 minutes' and hot roast beef and gravy in a bun for £2.75. A few months earlier, I'd met someone who owned a small chain of tattoo parlours in South Tyneside. She wasn't a tattooist herself, she said. In that case, I asked, why had she got involved in the business? 'Because it's something people can't get from Amazon,' she said. 'Well, not at the minute, any road. No doubt they're working on a drone.'

RCA's Meadow Park was one of my favourite grounds. There was a cemetery at one end and for a lot of years there'd been a cement mixer in the gents which a Geordie mate of mine said the Wearsiders had mistaken for a hand-drier. In short, the place had character. The supporters were a nice bunch too and I'd watched a brilliant FA Vase tie here when the home side narrowly lost to Bristol Manor Farm in a game one fan billed as Kenickie v Tricky (OK, it was me). The breeze blowing in from the sea at Hendon – where Raich Carter had grown up – that day had been so fierce, by the time the final whistle went I felt like someone had vacuum-packed my face. It was sunnier today, but the wind was still icy, forcing those who'd come prepared into an Alpine bobble-hat-and-sunglasses combination.

RCA would finish the season in fifth. The visitors were marooned at the bottom of the table with twenty-two points. Despite not being in the North East, Penrith had been more or less a permanent fixture in the Northern League since 1948. In the 1950s they'd been managed by former Carlisle United centre-forward Alan Ashman. The Yorkshireman would go on to lead West Bromwich Albion to their victory in the 1968 FA Cup final and then – after a spell in Greece with Olympiacos – returned to Brunton Park and briefly take the Cumbrians to the top spot in English football.

Penrith had played in a lovely old ground in the town centre at Southend Road from 1894 until 2009 when the inevitable happened and it was sold for a supermarket. They now played at Frenchfield, a sports complex a couple of miles out of town on the way to Brough.

Penrith were not the only Cumbrians who'd played in the Northern League. Whitehaven had also been members, despite being closer to Ireland than Durham. But then they'd also been members of the Wearside League. Apparently disheartened by the constant six-hour round trips to games they'd dropped out a few years back and now play in the West Lancashire League. The Cumbrian team that had created the most stir in recent times were Gillford Park. They'd played at the old rugby league ground in the east of Carlisle. In 2011, Gillford Park had secured financial backing from Scottish-born US carwash millionaire Frank Lynch. The Glaswegian Lynch, who'd once been Billy Connolly's manager, poured money into the club, changed the kit to green and white and renamed them Celtic Nation, announcing his intention to build a new ground and reach the National League in five years.

This was not the first time people in Carlisle had heard this sort of stuff. Back in the 1990s, Carlisle United chairman Michael Knighton had promised to bring European football to the Great Border City. If he'd meant league fixtures with Wrexham he'd succeeded, too. As it was, instead of pitting themselves against Milan and Barcelona, Carlisle came within a Jimmy Glass goal of dropping out of the Football League altogether.

Despite this warning from history, Celtic Nation generated rare excitement across northern Cumbria and the club were soon attracting four-figure crowds. They stormed through the Northern League second division, winning promotion in 2012. They celebrated by signing Paul Arnison and Adam Boyd from Hartlepool United. But the Northern League first division proved a tougher proposition. Celtic Nation were up against other well-supported and well-funded sides. Instead of challenging for promotion they finished tenth, over fifty points behind champions Darlington.

The following season, ambitions were renewed. Ex-Carlisle manager Mick Wadsworth was appointed manager and, when he quit, he was replaced in the dugout by the ex-Glasgow Celtic favourite Willie McStay. The proposed charge up the pyramid hit the buffers again, however, as Spennymoor Town pipped Celtic Nation to the title and promotion. Lynch decided he'd seen enough and pulled the plug.

My one visit to Gillford Park had been shortly afterwards to see them play Newcastle Benfield. It was a Wednesday night of teeming Cumbrian rain. It was a long, circuitous forty-five-minute trudge from the station to the ground and by the time I'd completed it I was so wet I suspected

I'd find a trout in my coat pocket. The last eastbound train back left at 9.25 and I was forced to make my way back to the station at half time. The deluge continued. As I passed a pub near the city centre, a drunk burst out through the doors and threw up explosively over my shoes. When I got on the train my mobile buzzed. It was Ian. He gave me the final score. Down 0-2 at the interval, Benfield had staged an improbable fightback in the second half to win 5-4. I had spent two hours on trains, walked for ninety minutes, was freezing, soaked to the skin, stank of someone else's vomit and I had missed seven goals. At that point, it was my life in microcosm.

A few months later, Celtic Nation folded. Reformed as Carlisle City, they would return to the Northern League for the 2019-20 season with more reasonable ambitions.

Penrith too would continue, despite their current difficulties. Though things were going to get worse for them before they got better.

I took up a seat in the main stand and glanced through the programme at the ads for undertakers, architectural salvage and Ian Swansbury, 'voted Sunderland's best small builder 2009'. RCA's squad list included Dimitri Limbo, who joined Impiety Baptiste and Romario Kastrati on the list of intriguingly named Northern League players.

The warm mid-afternoon sun was glinting from the polished granite in the graveyard behind the far goal and Penrith elected to kick into the teeth of the wind and managed to win a couple of corners in the opening exchanges.

It didn't take long for RCA to show their superiority, however, the towering Dominic Moan powering a header into the net.

A few minutes later Nathan O'Neill ran across his marker, Angelos Eleftheriadis, got caught by an arm and went down in a Catherine wheel swirl of limbs. The match official, a short, wombat-shaped man of the sort who might delight the nation by dancing unexpectedly sinuously to Drake in a building society advert, sent off the offender without hesitation, possibly just to avoid having to write his name down. The incident provoked one of those passive arguments that periodically break out between fans following controversy.

'Never a red card, that,' announced one Penrith supporter of the defending side loudly enough to rattle putty from the windows of the groundkeeper's hut. 'Aye. Not in a million years. He was heading away from the goal,' another commented at equal volume, as Eleftheriadis departed towards the empty dressing rooms with a reluctance that suggested they held some sinister childhood memory.

Across on the other side of the committee men's seats that substitute for fencing and a cordon of hi-vis stewards at this level of the game, RCA fans heard what was being said and began their own noisy dialogue with one another. 'A clear scoring opportunity denied, there.'

'Defo. He made the ref's decision easy for him, the defender.'

Like an unhappily married couple addressing each other's faults through a counsellor, no words were exchanged directly, but everyone present knew where they were aimed. The sniping continued intermittently throughout the afternoon until both groups were so entangled in their mutual bitterness you suspected they'd head off to IKEA together after the final whistle and continue to bicker vindictively over offsides and shoulder-to-shoulder challenges amid the home office furniture and the scent of meatballs.

The shouting quieted for the spot kick. Dylan Elliott struck it hard and true.

The game then juddered along with constant stoppages for pointless fouls and goals every fifteen minutes or so for the home side.

It was RCA's last match of the season and the blokes behind me were preparing to face the void. Since the proliferation of satellite channels and internet streaming sites, I've got used to hearing the bloke behind me say, 'Did you watch Stal Kamianske against Vorskla Poltava last night?' and his mate replying, 'Nah, I had the Svenska Cupen on, BK Forward were at home and I have had always had a soft spot for the lads from Orebro.'

This afternoon, the bloke behind me told his mate that he had prepared for the summer by recording the entire MLS season. 'If I limit myself to two games a day, it should see me through,' he said grimly like a man planning for nuclear winter. 'Is it any good, the American stuff?' his friend responded. 'It's football, isn't it?' the bloke behind me answered in a tone shuffling inexorably towards the desperate like an encroaching defensive wall.

In the sixtieth minute RCA got their fourth through Michael Charlton. Luke Page then converted a chance set up for him by O'Neill and in stoppage time Moan added a sixth.

I recalled a match at the old Portland Park, Ashington, in which the Colliers had thrashed Norton and Stockton Ancients. The Teessiders had become disillusioned. Heads went down. As Ashington scored their sixth, the visitors' manager turned to his assistant and said, 'Have you got the petrol money?' It seemed to sum up the futility of it all.

'It might have been different if we'd had eleven men,' a Penrith fan said as we trooped off.

'Way you played you could have had fifteen and we'd still have walloped you,' came the reply. It was hard to argue.

I walked back to the bus stop. The journey back to Park Lane took me past a number of schools with signs outside containing uplifting mission statements. 'Striving for success in a strong community,' said one; 'Bettering lives through achievement,' said another; 'Shattering dreams with maths and sarcasm,' said a third.

Actually, I made one of those up.

At the station, the taxi-driver was nudging towards despair. Sunderland had contrived to lose 4-5 at home with Coventry, throwing their hopes of automatic promotion off course. 'It's still in our own hands, but only just,' he said.

His mobile rang. It was the *Mission: Impossible* theme. 'Aye, fella,' he said. 'No worries. I'm just on a run now, but I'll be there in twenty. See you then.'

'I've got different ring tones for all my regulars,' he said after he'd rung off.

'Why's he got *Mission: Impossible*?' I asked.

The cabbie laughed: 'Cos he's this massive fat lad and I'm never sure he's going to squeeze through the door.'

19

HEATON STANNINGTON V BILLINGHAM TOWN

Ebac Northern League Division Two

Saturday 20 April 2019

The old lady who walked a piebald terrier along the bank of the Tyne had shed her red duffel-coat in favour of a lilac mac, a yearly occurrence which I took as a more reliable natural harbinger of spring than the call of the cuckoo.

In South Gosforth it was hot and sunny. A dozen people were eating al fresco at a table on the pavement outside the Buddhist Centre. The shutters were down on the Northern Education Society and one window had been bricked up. I passed a sandwich bar called Love and Peas and an off-licence with Buckfast in the window. A banner above a social club proclaimed its alliance with CL Drinks Solutions, or at least that's what I assumed it meant – it could have been a description of one of its customers.

Across the street there was a central heating engineers called Aubrey Cornfoot, which sounded like a Native American. I imagined an Arapaho in a 1950s western looking grimly at Lee J. Cobb and saying, 'Combi boiler heap bad medicine.' Later, a Geordie whose surname was Proudfoot told me that whenever he went to the US people assumed he was a Native American.

Heaton Stannington's ground, originally called Newton Park, had once been a quarry. Stan had joined the Northern League in 1939. The Second World War and the fact their pitch had been requisitioned by the military kept them from taking much active part in proceedings until the 1946-47 season. They finished in the bottom slots most seasons and resigned membership in 1952, replaced by Durham City, recently dumped from the Football League. Stan played in the Northern Alliance and Vaux Wearside League and fought off the inevitable application to turn their Newton Road ground into a supermarket in 1983. They rejoined the Northern League in 2013.

In 2012, Stan played the unlikeliest friendly since the 1949 encounter between Bishop Auckland and Nigeria, when they met Gabon at Grounsell Park. The star turn for Gabon was Pierre-Emerick Aubameyang. Five years later, he'd join Arsenal in a deal worth £56 million. Local legend has it that the Gunners' record signing was marked out of the game by Stan centre-back Joe 'Big Red' Wear, though the record shows that he scored twice. Bishops won their encounter 5-2 at Kingsway in front of 13,000 fans. Stan didn't fare quite so well, losing 4-0. The Africans were on Tyneside preparing for the London Olympics. Unlike the Nigerians, they didn't play in bare feet.

Actually, now I think about it, neither of these two games was the unlikeliest match in Northern League history. That honour undoubtedly falls to the February 1984 clash that saw George Best turning out at Appleby Park (North Shields' old stadium) for a side managed by children's TV favourite Supergran.

I arrived at Grounsell Park (it had been renamed in honour of a former club chairman) to see the bloke in front of me buy the last programme. 'Yours for a fiver,' he said, waving it at me as he walked away.

Billingham Town only needed a draw to secure the Northern League second division title. Stan were safe in fourth – an excellent finish for them. They had a clubhouse that won awards from CAMRA for its cask ale and attracted the sort of genial arty crowd that marked them out as the Fulham of North East non-League.

There were 401 in the ground today, including two noisy coachloads from Teesside who had taken up position on the grass bank opposite the clubhouse and during the course of the game could be seen turning gradually redder like some kind of litmus test.

Billy Town had once been Billingham's second club, after the illustrious Billingham Synthonia – four times Northern League champions, and former club of Brian Clough and Frank Bough. But Synners had been relegated to division two in 2015 and vacated their atmospheric but dilapidated Central Avenue ground two years later, taking up residence in Norton under the guidance of chairman/manager and scorer of the greatest own goal in Man City's history, Jamie Pollock. The season before I'd been at a Northern League game and found myself sitting five yards from the belligerent midfielder, or six if you were measuring from the far side of him.

In truth, the young upstarts had been better supported than their famous neighbours for some while. They'd been formed in 1967 and joined the Northern League in 1982. A couple of years later, Town sold a gangly teenage centre-back to Middlesbrough for 'a couple of goal nets and a bag of balls'. Gary Pallister would go on to win four Premier League titles with Manchester United.

The club had moved into their neat and compact Bedford Terrace ground in 1974. Their previous ground had a public footpath running through the middle of it and dog walkers tended to interrupt the flow of matches.

Billingham had once been the home of Imperial Chemical Industries. My grandfather was one of the 30,000 or so Teessiders who worked for ICI back in its great years. Like many of those men and women who laboured for this massive, prestigious company, he was very proud of its achievements, which included – less we forget – the invention of Crimplene (sadly named not, as I had always hoped, after its developer Professor Crimp, but a valley near Harrogate). My granddad was firm in the belief that at some point the white-coated boffins and microscope-wielding eggheads of ICI's laboratories would come up with an alternative fuel to oil, conjuring it – in all likelihood quite literally – from thin air. 'You just wait,' he'd say as we drove past the towering steel minarets and giant intestinal coils of ICI's Wilton plant on our way to Ayresome Park and an afternoon of Victory V lozenges and gruff muttering about the uselessness of Boro boss, Bloody Stan Anderson, 'one day this car will be running on something they're working on in there, mark my words. Maybe a gas made from plankton, or summat.'

It didn't happen, of course. Over time ICI sold off parcels of their Teesside plants until by 2007 – when they were taken over by AKZA – they employed no more than a handful of people in the region. But though they never synthesised a new type of petrol, in the 1960s they did develop something else that would turn out to be a major boost to the local economy – a process to produce fungal biomass for human consumption. Yes, I know, those words fair set your mouth watering, don't they? The upshot of that was Quorn, the meat-alternative made from soil fungus and promoted on TV by, among others, dimple-chinned friend to royalty, Will Carling. The company that made Quorn in factories in Billingham – close by Synthonia's old stadium – and Stokesley (the market town where Julio Arca made his Northern League debut) was now one of Teesside's most successful businesses.

Midway through the 2018-19 season, Quorn would team up with Geordie food ogres Gregg's to produce every Shoreditch hipster's favourite 'down with the proles' lunchtime snack – the vegan sausage roll. It wasn't quite the radical shift in the world's industrial and economic axis my granddad had predicted, but it kept several thousand people in work and that was not something to get hoity-toity about. I had a hope that at some point in the future Billingham Town might become known as the Quornmen, but that didn't seem likely at present.

The home side got off to a lively start, but it was Billy Town who scored first. A corner was swung into the six-yard box where Stan keeper Dan Regan caught it, juggled with it and finally dropped it across the goal line. As the Town players celebrated, Regan sat on his backside with his arms outstretched like Oliver Hardy after a brick has fallen on his head.

It was at this point that I found myself uttering words I thought I'd never hear myself say at a Northern League game: 'I need to find some shade.'

As I tucked myself against the back wall of the clubhouse and breathed in the perfume of a nearby Chinese takeaway, Stan broke out of defence. Under-15 World Cup winner Thibault Charmey (who, had I been able to secure a programme, I feel confident would have been described in its pen portrait section as 'The French Connection') headed the ball on to a Stan attacker. He evaded the attentions of three defenders, all of whom seemed to feel a tackle was an unwarranted intrusion, and struck a low shot into the net.

Without a programme or team sheet it was hard to

know quite who had scored, especially as there were no PA announcements. Although in the latter case that likely wouldn't have helped. In the Northern League, the job of match-day announcer is traditionally commandeered by an elderly bloke with a bitumen-thick accent, bronchial wheeze and turgid catarrh who delivers his messages through a public address system that has been craftily adapted from the sort of crackling wireless set over which a stunned nation learned of the Hindenberg Disaster. As a consequence, the reading of the team sheet sounds like a flu-sick Rowley Birkin QC declaiming a Norse saga, in a gale, while wearing a brown-paper suit. Substitutions and added time are all incomprehensively blurted out to the accompaniment of yapping terriers and the flapping wings of startled pigeons. A goal, meanwhile, provokes the PA to burst into life with a bang, pop and fizz that sends combat veterans ducking for cover and is followed by the illuminating news: 'Hurl hinna firdee-farth mi'hurt hah-scar numble ert a Burpcrup Durban Trarfmah ... mergle.' Norman Collier died in 2013, but the spirit of *The Wheeltappers and Shunters Social Club* is alive and well and immovably ensconced in a box at the back of the covered seating.

With their fans urging them on, Billingham went back in front past the half hour. Striker Craig Hutchinson finished off a move he'd started with a back heel to a team-mate so cheeky it practically did a Frankie Howerd impression.

Hutchinson had hit an incredible fifty-nine goals for Town in the 2016–17 season and had got over forty this time around – including five in a game against the admittedly hopeless Durham City. He'd had a trial with Hartlepool in 2017 without being taken on, but now people were starting to wonder if he might not follow Lewis Wing and Jordan Hugill – who'd left Shildon and Marske to play for Middlesbrough and West Ham – in making the step up to a higher level.

There was a muttering among some that he wasn't big or tough enough to lead the line. The playing style of football had evolved at elite level, but down in the lower divisions – where the teams increasingly made up for shortfalls in pace and skill with sessions in the weight room that made each player a roving defensive wall – a mighty targetman was still pretty much compulsory. 'Robust' was the adjective reporters used to describe these great beasts, or 'uncompromising'. To them, every football pitch was a pub car park at chucking-out time – a battleground. Only the knowledge that the linesman would check before kick-off prevented them from sharpening their studs and concealing a lug-wrench in a sock.

A few seasons back at the FA Cup clash between Easington Colliery and Ashington, I'd stood near a couple of fans from Hartlepool. One of the Poolies reacted to an Ashington forward pulling out of a bruising one-on-one with the keeper by turning to me and saying, 'See that? He's quick, but he's taffy-hearted,' an expression of deepest scorn I'd not heard since my granddad died. 'Time was strikers were hard,' his mate said.

'There was a lad played for Whitley Bay, Billy Wright. Worked in the shipyards at Wallsend. Built like a lime kiln. First corner Bay got, he'd put the opposition keeper straight in the back of the net. Fella'd be half-unconscious failing around in there like a blind pig in a sack.'

Strikers who did not act in this manner were scorned by sections of the crowd. Boro forward Arthur Horsfield – who'd begun his career at Montagu and Fenham Boys Club – was an elegant goal poacher. His lack of combative-ness incensed certain elements in the Holgate End back in the '60s. In one match, he was being berated by a spectator as a useless waste of space, when another stepped in to defend him. 'Leave him alone. He's all right.'

'All right?' the first man said, pointing at the pitch. 'Allfuckingright? Look at him. He's just stood there doing nowt.'

'He's not doing nowt,' Horsfield's defender replied. 'He's lurking.'

Stealth did not meet with the approval of many, however. Boro sold Horsfield to Newcastle United, and the Magpies sold him to Swindon.

The two Poolies would have given Arthur short shrift if he'd ever pitched up at Victoria Park. 'Aye, hard,' the first Poolie said. 'Mick Harford!' He flinched as he said the name. Harford came from Sunderland. He'd played close to 600 League matches, scored nearly 200 goals and his name was a byword for hardness. Just typing it left bruises. If any footballer came along in the North East acting the wiseguy, people would say 'I tell you what, he wouldn't have lasted five seconds with Mick Harford.'

Harford, I should add, had since become a very successful football coach at Luton where his team played a thrilling brand of attacking football totally devoid of welly and thump.

'I played junior football against Mick,' the second Poolie said. 'Even when he was fifteen he was a big bloody lump. You went up with him, he seemed to have twenty elbows. Even when he was flat on the deck, nose to the turf, he could hit you with summat.'

The first Poolie agreed. 'He took no prisoners, Mick. You knew you'd been in game. Come off the field with bruises. Big George Reilly, played at Newcastle? He worked as a bricklayer when he retired. A hod-carrier bit a chunk of his ear off.' He paused and watched as the striker shied out of a 30:70 challenge. 'See that?' he said. 'More guts in a kipper.'

At Grounsell Park both sides wilted in the heat. Hutchinson had the best chance, somehow contriving to miss from six yards, probably because I had been lavishly praising him to the bloke standing next to me. I wandered off to find deeper shade and rehydrate in the clubhouse where Aubameyang's signed Gabon shirt was framed and hung on the wall. The Arsenal striker could cover fifty metres quicker than Usain Bolt and scored every other game, but I wasn't sure how long he'd have lasted with Mick Harford.

20

Newcastle Benfield v West Auckland Town

Mitre Brooks Mileson Memorial League Cup Final

Monday 22 April 2019

The last time I'd been to see Benfield play at Seaham had been on a freezing winter's day. The game was called off ten minutes before kick-off. The match officials' late decision left a small group of middle-aged men listlessly rocking from one foot to the other on the frozen touchline, speculating on what Pascal Chimbonda, then plying his trade at Washington, must make of it all. 'He used to wear gloves at White Hart Lane in April, so God knows what he'll have on if they get a midweek game at Tow Law in February.' Ironworks Road is, as we know, a place of legendary coldness ('The weather was that bad you couldn't see the snow for the fog,' as former Lawyers' chairman John Flynn once summarised) and for a moment the image of the French full-back bobbing down the wing so encased in quilted goose-down he looked like a scale model of the Allianz Arena hovered in the breath-clouded air.

Once I'd been at a February Northern League game that was temporarily halted because the pea had frozen in the ref's whistle midway through the first period. That day at Seaham, the pea had frozen in my whistle too, and it had been a relief to get on the train home.

Today, though it was a bright and sunny midday on a bank holiday and the only sadness I felt was that the early start had stopped me from going to Seaham seafront and buying a giant ice cream. A big crowd had assembled for the game and a special programme had been printed. This was very nice, though it lacked one notable aspect of the regular Seaham Red Star programme – an advert for the New Westlea Club which billed itself as 'The Caesar's Palace of the North East' ('Wednesday 1.30 Domino Handicap (£20 added – 16 players or more) Then afternoon cash bingo.' Take that and party, Frank Sinatra.)

Benfield's season had dribbled to a conclusion. West Auckland came into the game unbeaten in nine matches. They'd been the last Northern League team in that season's FA Vase, losing to eventual winners Chertsey Town in the quarter-final. West had been Northern League champions in 1960 and 1961 and reached the FA Vase final in 2012, losing to Dunston. They were most famous, though, as double winners of the 'first World Cup', the Sir Thomas Lipton Trophy.

Sir Thomas was a Glaswegian tea merchant and grocery store magnate whose main interest was sailing (his yachts entered the Americas Cup five times without winning). The football tournament that bore his name was held in 1909 and 1911. West Auckland seem to have been invited because one of Sir Thomas's most trusted employees was a Northern League referee (other myths are available). Virtually penniless, the team travelled to Italy third class and beat Stuttgart and FC Winterhur to win the first time and Red Star and Juventus the next. After the second victory, they were given the thirty-two-inch solid silver trophy to keep. In 1994, it was stolen from the village social club. It has never been recovered.

The Brooks Mileson Memorial League Cup had also been named in honour of another wealthy benefactor. Brooks Mileson was a self-made millionaire from Sunderland's Pennywell Estate, a place so rough it made South Bank look like Cheltenham. He more or less defined the term eccentric: chain-smoking, scruffy, living on a farm up by Longtown in Cumbria he'd turned into an animal sanctuary. That he loved football was beyond question. Mileson gave thousands of pounds to supporters' trusts at various clubs in England and Scotland, and his generous eleven-year, £500,000 sponsorship of the Northern League (the original £35,000 agreement drawn up on the back of a fag packet) helped preserve it when it was truly struggling.

One year – probably 2005, my memory is hazy – Brooks gave me a lift to the Northern League annual dinner at Ramside Hall, picking me up from my house in his Jaguar and dropping me off on his way home. I spent around four hours with him chatting about his life, how he'd made his money (a whole raft of things from property via insuring rental cars in Northern Ireland to the importation of branded sportswear from the Far East), donkeys, llamas and the Scottish FA (whose arbitrary rules on minimum ticket prices had led him to give free pies to visiting fans at Gretna, the club he then owned). He was engaging company, without a hint of that strain of self-satisfaction that so often comes with success. Brooks had a pony-tail and the dress sense and demeanour of someone who might turn up on *Rock Family Trees* talking about his time playing bass with Dave Edmunds. He despised all the right people. I liked him, and I've not met many in the North East who didn't.

Brooks Mileson had taken over Gretna shortly after they'd been elected to the Scottish League. When I'd first moved back to the North East, they'd been playing in the Northern League. They'd won the title twice and then moved up into the Northern Premier.

They did well in the Scottish League, progressing rapidly upwards. In 2006, Gretna defeated Dundee United to get to the Scottish Cup final. They lost narrowly and unluckily to Heart of Midlothian at Hampden Park in front of an 80,000 crowd. The following season they played in the Uefa Cup. There was to be no glamorous meeting with an Italian, Spanish or French giant, however. Instead, they drew Derry City from the League of Ireland in the qualifying round and were comfortably beaten.

Brooks Mileson told me that playing in the Scottish Premier League against the likes of Glasgow Celtic and Glasgow Rangers was his dream. Sadly, when the opportunity came, it proved to be more of a nightmare. The Scottish Football Association would not let Gretna play their home matches at Raydale Park because it was deemed unfit to host games at so exalted a level. Instead, they had to play 80 miles away at Clyde.

On the field, the step up to the next level proved to be too much for the players and coaches. Gretna were heavily defeated in practically every match they played. Midway through the season, Mileson, never a well man, was taken seriously ill. Without him at the helm, his business empire rapidly began to unravel. Three months later, with players' wages unpaid, Gretna FC were officially declared bankrupt with debts of over £4 million. Reformed by a loyal group of supporters, Gretna took up a place in the first division of the East of Scotland League, the lowest level of organised football in Scotland. They are now back at Raydale Park, playing in front of a few hundred fans. Brooks Mileson died of a heart attack in November 2008.

The game, like most cup finals, was tight and nervy. Benfield might well have settled it with nine minutes to go of the first half. Dennis Knight fed the young and speedy Jake Orrell, who surged forward and smashed a shot beyond keeper Shane Bland, but it struck the underside of the crossbar and bounced down and out. A few moments later, Bland was alert again to save from Alex Francis. Benfield pressed throughout the second half, but Bland, who'd come through the Middlesbrough youth set-up, was inspired.

'He's worth his weight in gold, this keeper,' a bloke behind me said.

'No, he's better than that,' his mate replied. 'He's worth his weight in printer ink.'

There was no way past him. The ref blew full-time with the score 0-0. The game went straight to penalties. Bland saved brilliantly from Reece Noble and Dean Holmes and young West midfielder Ross Colquhoun settled it.

On the walk back to the train, an ageing Benfield fan complained that the once-unmarkable Paul Brayson was now too old and slow, unworthy of a place in the side. 'We need a complete clear-out over the summer,' he said, the voice of a defeated fan.

The rumblings about Rafa Benitez's contract and his future at St James' Park rolled on. The Spaniard had done a decent enough job and he had gone out of his way to engage with supporters, much as he'd done at Liverpool. He'd surprisingly stayed on when the Mags were relegated in 2016, got them straight back up again and managed them to a tenth-place finish in 2017-18. This season too Newcastle were comfortably in mid-table despite limited transfer activity. Still, the belief in Rafa's powers among many Newcastle fans seemed disproportionate. His teams were well organised and pragmatic, a little dull. He seemed like a genial Iberian Sam Allardyce to me, though I tended to keep that view to myself.

I'd been thinking of getting my hair cut, but in light of all the shenanigans over whether Benitez would stay or go I had decided to let it grow for a while. When left to its own devices, my hair twines itself into a feathery silver bouffant, giving me the look of someone who ought to be hosting a daytime TV quiz show. Still, the occasional witty cry of 'Let's play *Mr and Mrs*!' as I pass the smokers standing outside Wetherspoon's was better than the likely alternative.

You see, the barber is a Newcastle season ticket-holder. Like all Geordies, he is keen on talking. The minute I sit down, he whisks the nylon cape around me, pumps the chair lever, fires up his clippers and starts in telling me what – in the prevailing view of his social club – has been going on at the Toon of late. And he doesn't stop snipping and shaving until he's finished. At times of high drama – and these come thick and fast in Newcastle, let's be honest – you need a buffer zone of extra hair to fill the time. Otherwise, you're going to go in and ask for a number three at the back and sides and tidy-up on top and come out looking like Pierluigi Collina.

I had discovered this the hard way the week after the Hall-and-Shepherd-Fake-Sheikh fiasco. There were times during those two-and-a-half hours when I seriously wondered if I was going to keep my ears, I can tell you.

There is another barber in the town. But I abandoned him after a previous incident. The other barber is a Newcastle season ticket-holder too, but he is altogether more febrile and less focused. I was sitting in his chair the day Kevin Keegan signed Alan Shearer. When a passing market trader yelled the extraordinary news through the door, the barber leaped in the air, flung down his comb and rushed out into the street singing that ancient Geordie hymn of praise and deliverance, 'She likes a wheelbarrow, she likes a wheelbarrow.'

In his euphoria, the barber had apparently forgotten that for the past five years he had ridiculed the Blackburn and England striker as 'Billy Bigpockets'. 'You think he's avaricious, then?' I asked him once. 'I wouldn't know about that,' he replied as he squirted water on my head, 'but he's a right greedy bastard.'

I waited for the barber to return from his celebrations, but he never did. The next time I saw him was later that evening on the local news chanting outside St James' Park. I went away with my hair half cut and hanging asymmetrically across my brow. When I got on the bus to go home, the man behind me started whistling 'Don't You Want Me' by the Human League. I have not been back to that barber since.

The peculiar antics of Mike Ashley have kept my hair in squaddie-like shape ever since his arrival in the North East. During that time, the rotund retail maverick has moved from being a seldom-seen recluse to somebody who appears on national TV downing a pint and watching the football wearing the sort of blank yet benign expression adopted by the Queen when attending a break-dancing display by disadvantaged youngsters. In the meanwhile, he has gradually edged away from being widely celebrated as a black-and-white saviour, to the current position in which he seems to have achieved the impossible – making Newcastle fans speak with wistful chuckles of the glorious, happy stewardships of Gordon McKeag and Lord Westwood.

I exaggerate, of course. Though I couldn't help noticing that a few months ago the barber referred to the former chairman known locally as Mr McGreed as 'a total shite-hawk'. I feel the dropping of the words 'and utter fucking' from the middle of that description points to a growing rehabilitation of the egregious solicitor. I doubt, however, that Lord Westwood (aka the Pirate) will ever again stride past the Strawberry without people yelling, 'Where's your parrot, you thieving twat?' at him. And since he has been dead for some considerable time, that's probably just as well.

Such has been Ashley's effect, I have even heard people decry the new owner in comparison with the late Freddy Shepherd. 'At least Freddy was dignified,' one fan told me, an unusual adjective to apply to a man who – among other things – once responded to a reporter asking if he might appoint Sven Goran Eriksson as Newcastle manager with the words 'I'd rather eat my own cock.'

On my last visit to the barber's at the end of February, I was unkempt and in need of a severe trimming, so I asked him what he made of Newcastle's lack of activity in the transfer market. 'Ashley's supposed to have all this money,' I said. 'But he hasn't spent any.'

'Aye, well, we've weighed it up from all angles, haven't

we?' the barber said, his scissors clicking demonically. 'I mean, from what you hear the bloke's been hit by the fall of share values on Wall Street. There's been the House of Fraser business . . .' he continued in this vein until the floor around me was ankle deep in hair, '. . . the general global economic downturn, the collapse of the British high street, which is all mitigating circumstances, obviously. Credit to the fella for making his fortune off his own bat, and maybe we don't see the bigger picture and everything, but at the end of the day the conclusion we've come to is,' he paused for a moment to stare over my head and look me in the eye via the mirror, 'that he's as thick as a Gurkha's foreskin. Is that short enough for you?'

21

HARTLEPOOL UNITED V SALFORD CITY

Vanarama National League

Saturday 27 April 2019

The Professor and I were on the train heading to Hartlepool and we were both childishly excited. The Professor is German and supports Werder Bremen. We had watched a lot of football together in the decade we had known one another. We had been all over the North East and Cumbria and had once flown to the Ruhr to see the Revierderby, Dortmund v Schalke. There were 80,000 supporters in the Dortmund Arena, the Yellow Wall creating a massive din and at half time the Professor had bumped into Franz Beckenbauer and got Der Kaiser's autograph. Yet even this experience did not rank as highly in either of our estimations as a freezing December night we had spent together at the Victoria Park ground five years earlier.

'Haha Hartlepools!' the Professor says whenever he

thinks of it and he shakes his head and grins. 'That was the second-best game I ever saw. It was so fantastic.'

The best game the Professor ever saw was in Mineirao in July 2014: Brazil 1 Germany 7. Since he was also at the final of that World Cup, you may judge how great our night in Hartlepool was. The game was a first round FA Cup tie between Hartlepool and Blyth Spartans. Croft Park was the first place the Professor and I had been to watch a game together – Spartans v Workington – and he was suitably impressed. 'You know,' he said as we drove home afterwards, 'when I moved here, English people were always telling me how they hated footballers play-acting and diving and how English football wasn't like that, the players were really tough. But when I went to watch some Premier League games and I didn't see anything different from Germany, Spain or Italy. Then today, wow! Some of those tackles were so tough, yet nobody complained. You know, I am a medical person and there was one in the first half where I said, "Shit, after that he may never walk again." But within twenty seconds the guy was back on his feet running about like nothing happened.'

He smiled, 'When people talk about English football, this is the football they mean, not the Premiership.'

And so we went down to see Blyth face Hartlepool on a Friday night so cold by the final whistle your legs had gone numb. Spartans came back from one down to win with two spectacular late strikes, a free kick from Stephen Turnbull that wasn't so much a peach as whole tropical fruit salad and a shimmying run and nutmeg finish by Jarrett Rivers. Pools had what looked like a good goal chalked off and hit the bar six minutes into stoppage time. Peter Jeffries in the Spartans' goal alternated between corpulent clumsiness and acrobatic brilliance.

But it wasn't so much the football, as everything else that was so fabulous: the man in front of us in the Mill House Paddock delivering a tirade of foul abuse at a linesman for eighty-nine minutes; the middle-aged women behind us sitting in sleeping bags and drinking prosecco from a thermos flask, saying, 'You can complain all you like about the weather, but at least we don't need a fucking ice bucket'; the half-time pitch invasion by two fearless Poolie lads in day-glo mankinis who were then chased around the pitch by the world's fattest steward, while H'Angus the Monkey mascot waved his inflatable banana at them in admonishment, policemen running everywhere . . .

'Sometime he wakes me up at night with his bloody chuckling,' his wife told me several years later. 'And I say, are you still laughing about that damned football match you went to with Harry?'

And, of course, he is.

The only thing that could have made our evening better was if Hartlepool had chosen the game to revive what was surely the greatest piece of half-time entertainment in the history of what Pelé famously dubbed 'my job' – the by-now infamous DFDS Seaways Deckchair Challenge.

Half-time entertainment at football comes in many

forms. Many of them involve tubby pissed fans. Some TPFs come on in suits and take penalties against a reserve team goalkeeper who invariably looks like John Burridge (possibly because he is), for reasons the PA announcer refuses to divulge. Others, in pairs, take part in a trivia quiz, or, in a troupe, indulge in a humiliating aerobics routine led by a woman in a leotard and Spandex leggings who used to be on breakfast television.

The DFDS Seaways Deckchair Challenge was unique. In it the tubby pissed fan set off from the halfway line, dribbled around a slalom course of deckchairs before scoring into an empty net. Three attempts were allowed and the fastest time counted. Incredibly, one large bloke not only failed to find the net at all, he also succeeded in falling over several times. Invited back for another go the following week, he repeated his abject performance, missing out on a luxury cruise to Norway, but becoming a minor local celebrity.

I had never seen the DFDS Seaways Deckchair Challenge. I knew about it through my friend Ed. We'd met in the maternity hospital. His daughter had been born the day before mine. Ed is a Hartlepool fan and soon we'd started going to watch them play together. The first match we went to was away at Carlisle. Ed said that when he used to visit Brunton Park as an away supporter in the pre-Taylor-Report days and grounds still had security fences, there was an old steward at Brunton Park who used to direct visitors into their pens with a call of 'Come by, come by' as if he were herding sheep. Sadly, this old fellow had gone by the time of our visit, but as we left the Beehive pub we did witness an illuminating exchange between two rival fans. A local likely lad shouted: 'You hang monkeys,' at the Pools supporters.

'You shag sheep,' came the crisp and witty reply from the bloke in front of me.

'Well, you hang monkeys,' the Carlisle fan hit back.

'And you shag sheep.'

'You hang monkeys.'

'Aye well, I'd rather hang a monkey than shag a sheep.'

'Aye, well, I'd rather shag a ... Er, fuck off, you.'

Admittedly, it wasn't exactly Oscar Wilde and James McNeill Whistler, but the recollection has kept me amused during many a dark evening.

In the game that followed, Pools were 0–2 down at half time, but came out for the second period as if possessed by demons and scored three times without reply. It set a precedent and I can honestly say that, though it will be disputed by the notorious moaners of the Mill House Paddock, I have never seen a dull game involving Hartlepool United.

Part of the reason for that was that for an all too brief period in the noughties Pools' attack had been led by one my favourite players, Adam Boyd. A long-haired, perma-tanned seventies throwback, local boy Boyd scored glorious goals and forged glittering memories with his apparently effortless skills, shaking off defenders with a shrug and a shimmy, deceiving keepers with chips, flicks and dinks so delicate they rolled down the goal netting with a sound like ripping chiffon. Off the field, too he provided full value, memorably making the tabloids when he was chased semi-naked across a 'posh housing estate' by the boyfriend of the woman whose bed he'd been warming. When he left for Luton I sighed and ate chocolate.

The train chuntered down the Durham coast past Seaham. I told the Professor about the last time I'd been to Victoria Park. That had been in January 2018. Pools were in the financial mire and needed £140,000 to save themselves from going into liquidation. Back in 1986, they'd loaned Victoria Park to a then-impoverished Middlesbrough and now they were calling on Boro fans to repay the favour by turning up for the home game against Wrexham. Many thousands did so. The game was a sell-out. I sat a few seats along from where the Professor and I had laughed at the pitch invaders, a few rows down from the ones Ed and I had occupied when a Ronnie Moore-inspired Pools had defeated Exeter in the penultimate game of 2014-15 to stave off relegation to the National League. When the PA played the traditional Pools pre-match song 'Two Little Boys' and the crowd sang along, 'Do you think I would leave you dying . . .', I'm sure I wasn't alone in finding I'd got something in my eye.

The game that followed had been a terrible anti-climax. Pools, dithering and inept, lost 2-0. The occasion seemed to have got to the home fans, too. Usually quick and scabrous in their criticism, they watched in an eerie silence until, with fifteen minutes remaining, thirty yards along, a middle-aged woman with bleached blonde hair and a pink puffa jacket stood to her feet. 'Yees are fucking shite. A fucking disgrace to this club, these fucking fans and this fucking town. You should be fucking shot, the fucking lot of yees.' When she sat down, a woman a few seats in front of me rose and called out, 'Eeh Angela, you've been that quiet I thought you weren't here.'

As the Professor and I reminisced about games and players, the train clattered southwards, past the allotments on the eastern fringe of Horden. Above them the streets ran up from the headlands above the sea to the green hill where the colliery once stood, as if that was the only direction the population would ever expect, or need, to travel in. In Horden, 80 per cent of the workforce were once employed in the mining industry. The colliery closed in 1987. Since then the population had dropped by several thousand, and the number of adults claiming benefits stands at 25 per cent above the national average.

The last time I'd been to watch Horden Colliery Welfare they'd been in the Northern League first division. They'd finished as runners-up twice in the 1980s, won the North Eastern League title twice and the Wearside League ten times. In the tea bar, friendly middle-aged women who seemed purpose-built for a role as aunties were frying chips and doling out cups of tea in Princess Diana commemorative mugs. I took mine into the main stand, which is, as it happens, the only stand – a big, old-fashioned barn with a red corrugated roof, a press box and a bit of worn-away graffiti pledging allegiance to the Horden Shed Army. I sat in the Stan Anderson enclosure. Anderson – the only man to captain Sunderland, Newcastle and Middlesbrough – was Horden's most illustrious former player. Colin Bell played for the juniors. Horden also nurtured the young Bob Taylor, an old-school goal poacher who tapped in over 100 for West Brom in the 1990s and was memorably described by writer Matt Nation as combining the face of Dirk Bogarde with thighs that required an HGV licence.

In 2009, the Welfare ground had been revamped using lottery money. The old stand – opened by Spennymoor's celebrity ref George Courtney back in the 1980s – was fitted with indoor toilets and facilities for female match officials. As if to celebrate, Horden won the Northern League second division title in 2009. They were relegated again the following season and in 2013 dropped back into the Wearside League. In 2016, for unspecified reasons the Welfare ground's owners, Horden Parish Council, ordered the football club to vacate. The club protested and the matter went to court. After a five-day hearing in Newcastle, the parish council were given the right to serve an eviction notice and awarded £82,500 in legal costs. Horden Colliery Welfare – founded in 1908 – effectively ceased to exist.

The Professor and I got off the train. There were only about thirty minutes to kick-off, but I told him I knew a short cut that would get us to the Mill House in time to get our tickets and find a seat. As we crossed one of the immense number of roads that seem to separate Hartlepool station from everywhere else in the town, the Professor asked if I was sure this was the right direction. 'Look,' he said, pointing. 'Those fans there are going the other way.' I assured him that I knew exactly what I was doing. It's just along this street and turn right, I said. We walked along the street and turned right. Coming towards us were hundreds of Hartlepool fans. 'I think it must be the other way,' the Professor said. I knew it wasn't, though. And suddenly something humiliating dawned on me: I'd got the kick-off time wrong. It hadn't been the usual three o'clock. It had been earlier.

By now, the Professor had tired of my assurances I knew what I was doing and had stopped one of the Pools fans. 'Which way is Victoria Park?' The bloke gestured back the way he'd come. 'But the game just finished,' he said. I winced.

'Ah, I see,' the Professor said. 'And what was the score?'

I hoped the Pools fan would help me out a little here, say, 'Nils each. Bloody shite. A complete waste of money.'

Instead he flashed a wide grin: 'Won 3-2. Goal in the last minute. Fucking brillo.'

The Professor took this remarkably calmly. 'We can get a beer,' I assured him. 'There's a fantastic real ale pub called the Rat Race. You'll love it.'

But when we got to the Rat Race there was a sign on the door saying it was closed for annual holidays. We went to Wetherspoon's instead, had two pints and got the train home. As we passed through Heworth, the Professor suddenly chuckled. 'When the monkey mascot was waggling his banana at the two naked guys,' he said and shook his head in wonder.

22

SOUTH SHIELDS V
WARRINGTON TOWN

Evo-Stik Northern Premier League
Premier Division Play-Off Final

Saturday 4 May 2019

A section of the Tyne and Wear Metro was once again closed for the replacement of something or other, the failure of this or that, or an invasion of singing gnomes – I had long since ceased to listen. The closure meant getting off at Heworth, getting the replacement bus to Jarrow, getting back on the Metro and going two stops to Bede station.

I waited for the bus replacement. A smell of warm pastry wafted from a nearby Gregg's. Twenty years ago Gregg's had been a small, local firm that slugged it out for lunchtime trade with Peters Cathedral Bakery, Hill's, Cooplands and the like. Then somehow – possibly through existing entirely on a diet of its own bacon slices and custard doughnuts – it

299

ballooned into a mighty behemoth that belly-flopped on all competition and employed over 20,000 people. It was a great North-East success story. Though I felt there was no longer as much orange cheese in the cheese and onion pasties as there had once been. However, when I voiced this opinion, friends tended to roll their eyes and say, 'Aye, and Burton's Wagon Wheels used to be the size of car tyres and there's no longer the same Rococo intricacy to your Curly Wurly ...' before going on to ask if I was hoping Brexit would see the return of Olde English Spangles.

The bus arrived. It was soon so packed that if we'd all breathed in at once the sides would have popped out. The man sitting next to me was in his mid-seventies, wearing a Gateshead scarf. He said he'd been a Heed fan since back when they were a league side. He'd seen the swaggering drunken genius behind Newcastle's last league title, Hughie Gallagher, play at Redheugh Park when the Scot was close to middle age and he was just a kid. Lately, he said, disillusion had set in. Heed's swatting aside of Dunston had been a high point in a season that had subsequently gone downhill faster than John Barnes in a go-kart. The team continued to play fluently, but behind the scenes there was chaos. Owner Dr Ranjan Varghese, a Hong Kong-based businessman, had bought the club the previous year, promising an 'exciting, progressive, long-term vision'. Eight months later, Gateshead had only fifteen senior players, were operating under a transfer embargo and were facing a winding-up order from HM Revenue and Customs over an unpaid tax bill. 'I'm not even sure if we'll exist next season,' the bloke said, shaking his head sadly.

I tried to cheer him up by asking if he'd played football himself. 'Aye, a bit when I was younger,' he said. 'I actually played in the final of the Tyneside Junior Cup. Now, the team that beat us, Fenham and Montagu, had a lad playing for them up front who had a very successful pro career. You'll likely not have heard of him ...'

'Arthur Horsfield,' I said.

The bloke looked amazed. 'Aye,' he said. 'Arthur Horsfield. He was the star of their side. I can't remember how many he scored against us, quite a few, and the same afternoon he signed for Middlesbrough.' (Where, as we already know, he would spend several seasons being savagely ridiculed by the denizens of the Chicken Run as a feckless shirker with all the backbone of an amoeba and moderately less ball skills.)

The bloke had no knowledge of the percolating rage of that infamous section of Ayresome Park; instead he went on to explain that his team that afternoon had contained a mid-fielder who had later played over 200 games for Newcastle United. Now, the laws of football dictate that when this has happened there is only one thing that can be said: 'He was steady enough, but he wasn't the best player in the side, not by a long chalk.'

'And you know what,' the bloke said. 'He was a steady enough, but ...'

I smiled to myself.

'There were three or four lads in that side who were better than him,' the bloke continued. 'But the thing was, when all the rest of us started getting interested in girls and music, he kept on training. He was more dedicated, see.'

Mostly, since the player in question is usually Lee Clark, Stuart Ripley or Gary Owers, it is possible to believe that maybe, just maybe, that might be true – that the only thing that separates the rest of us from top-flight professionals was our inability to concentrate on circuit training during our teenage years. And that if it hadn't been for that blonde who sat in front of us in physics, or listening to Bruce Springsteen with the lights switched off, we'd have had a successful career, won a few international caps and now be an expert summariser on the radio, saying stuff like, 'To be fair, he'll be disappointed with that' or 'At this level you've got to make the keeper work from there' in return for a bunch of readies thick enough to justify a rubber band.

We got off the bus and scurried into Jarrow Metro station. The bloke said that if the worst came to the worst, he wouldn't mind coming to watch South Shields as they and Gateshead had a lot of shared history. That was certainly true. The story of these south Tyneside clubs was so labyrinthine it would make a Byzantine politician's head spin into a knot. When the original South Shields football club folded in 1902, it was replaced by a new club: South Shields Adelaide Athletic, known as 'the Laddies'. They won the North Eastern League title twice in 1914 and 1915. Success stirred the club to even greater ambition and their application to join the Football League was accepted for the 1919-20 season. Their opening League fixture was against Fulham at Craven Cottage and drew a crowd of 20,000.

South Shields, who played at Horsley Hill, remained in the Football League until 1930 when, after finishing seventh in the third division (North), the club upped sticks and moved further west along the Tyne to Redheugh Park, changing their name to . . . Gateshead. Gateshead remained in the Football League until 1960 when their application for re-election was rejected by the League and they were replaced by Peterborough.

While all this was going on, a new club had formed in South Shields. Unimaginatively named South Shields, they joined the North Eastern League and won the title in 1939. In 1974, South Shields relocated to . . . Gateshead and became Gateshead United. They went bust in 1977.

Back in South Shields, a group of die-hard fans who had disapproved of the second move to Gateshead had immediately formed another club, South Shields Mariners (I hope you are paying attention, there will be questions at the end). In 1992, they moved to Filtrona Park, which had been refurbished by the new chairman John Rundle. Rundle ran a double-glazing business, and the windows and doors of the Filtrona Park clubhouse were such a testimony to the power of the company's products that on my first visit there with Ian we didn't hear the kick-off and missed the first few minutes of the match – stuck in a soundless, air-tight bubble.

Alas, South Shields' wanderings were not yet at an end.

Rundle became frustrated, decided to wind the club up and locked the gates of Filtrona Park before a home match, barring players and staff from entering. Fixtures moved to Peterlee, 20 miles to the south. Remarkably, the adversity galvanised the club and they won the Northern League Cup. In 2015, local businessman Geoff Thompson succeeded in buying Filtrona Park from the disgruntled Rundle. He renamed it Mariners Park and the club moved back there for the 2015-16 season, to an outpouring of enthusiasm not seen since Mafeking Night. The signing of Julio Arca had added to the excitement.

Arca, I should say, wasn't the first Argentinean to be involved in the Northern League. Horden had briefly been managed by Buenos Aires-born Gustavo Di Lella, who'd started his North-East football career with Blyth Spartans in the late 1990s. During his time at Hartlepool United, the midfielder had earned a reputation as a bit of a hothead, his collection of cards culminating in an incident after an FA Cup tie at Fulham in which he allegedly thumped opposing defender Simon Morgan in the players' bar after the match. Di Lella had a moustache you could polish brass with and was inevitably serenaded by fans with renditions of 'Why, why, why, Di Lella?'

With Julio in the team, the Mariners were soon playing to four-figure crowds and taking almost as many to away matches. When I had seen them play at Team Northumbria, the tea caravan had run out of chocolate and crisps before kick-off and by half time was out of water.

Under the stewardship of Kevin Keegan's old nemesis Graham Fenton (who had previously worked wonders at North Shields), the Mariners had marched up the league pyramid with three promotions in a row and now found themselves on the verge of entering National League North and a re-acquaintance with old North Eastern League foes Blyth Spartans and Spennymoor. They were now better supported than Gateshead and, given Heeds' current predicament and the past history, there was talk among some of a possible re-merger.

On my first visit to see South Shields, there had been just over a hundred people in the ground. Today there twenty-five times that number. A few hundred had made it over the Pennines from Warrington. The Wire had been formed around the time South Shields had morphed into Gateshead. Their most famous ex-player was England World Cup winner Roger Hunt (is pumpy). They'd been one of the best teams in the Northern Premier League for a few years and lost in the play-offs in 2018.

The game got off to a shaky start. Nerves settling, Shields took charge of the midfield, knocking the ball about quickly and neatly. The breakthrough came when Josh Gillies received the ball from Darren Lough, drove towards the D of the penalty area and curled a powerful shot into the top corner.

In the second period, Carl Finnigan (who'd made twenty-one appearances for Township Rollers of the Botswana Premier League) might have added to Shields' lead, but he shot weakly when free in the box.

With barely an hour gone, Shields' boss Fenton decided to take off attacking midfielder Lee Mason and replace him with the more defensively minded Nathan Lowe. It seemed a little too early to start to defend a 1-0 lead and as Shields dropped back ever further until it seemed only a matter of time before the goalkeeper was playing centre-forward, Warrington took charge.

'It's coming. You can feel it,' the bloke next to me said, rubbing his hands together nervously.

He was right, too. A cross from the left was flicked on at the near post and Dylan Vassallo, who'd created trouble ever since he came on, hammered a shot into the roof of the net from twelve yards. With three minutes left on the clock, a Warrington free kick from the right bounced down in the box. Josh Amis pounced on it, swivelled and shot home.

With so little time to recover the season, Fenton threw on the tall and angular Ben Harmison. The brother of Ashes-winning cricketer Steve, who for a while had been manager of Ashington, Harmison was thrust up front and high balls pumped in his direction. Harmison immediately flattened a defender in an aerial challenge, but that didn't satisfy one of the blokes behind me. 'For such a big lad he doesn't put himself about half enough,' he grumbled.

This is a perennial criticism made of burly footballers – that they are too gentle. Many years ago in the Holgate End, two Boro fans almost came to blows after one of them had loudly voiced a similar criticism of Stuart Boam – a man whose tackling teetered on the edge of manslaughter.

And in the Fulwell End at Roker Park twenty years later, a bloke who seemed determined to prove he was a 'genuine' fan by yelling until he turned puce, offered the view that Thomas Hauser 'should use his physique more', despite the fact the statuesque German striker had spent the previous hour crashing about like a stuntman in a Bourne movie.

Quite how much physicality would actually be needed to satisfy this type of supporter is difficult to assess. I'm sure that even goalkeeper-battering behemoths of yesteryear like Bobby Smith and Trevor Ford had their share of doubters, fans for whom only the cracking of limbs or a custodial sentence would suffice. I imagine some of them would have stood on the deck of the *Pequod* pointing at Moby Dick as he set about Captain Ahab, bellowing, 'Away you great pasty leviathan ponce – show a bit of aggression, for Christ's sake, you've only took one of his bastard legs.'

With Harmison as a focal point, Shields pressed desperately for an equaliser that never came.

The final whistle blew and we trooped out. 'Hope this doesn't signal the start of a collapse,' someone muttered gloomily. Shields had been marching forward for four seasons, apparently unstoppably. Now they needed to regroup. As Darlington had discovered, patience was required – especially among the fans.

Gateshead weren't the only team in the North East going through a pitiful time. The region's northernmost team was facing the ignominy of a first relegation in sixty-eight years. Berwick has a unique character. Its geographical location in an isolated corner of Northumberland, the clannish nature of Border society and the fact that the town has changed hands between England and Scotland thirteen times give it a uniquely mixed-up character. This is perhaps best exemplified by the complex local accent, familiar to many via the TV appearances of ex-England star Trevor Steven – who sold programmes at Shielfield Park as a teenager. Until recently, Steven had been Berwick's most famous football export, but he had been superseded recently by Lucy Bronze, the England full-back who played for Olympique Lyonnais (Steven had turned out for Olympique Marseille) and was widely regarded as one of the greatest talents in the women's game.

Berwick is a singular place and Berwick Rangers are a singular football team. Indeed, the fact that they are an English club that plays in Scotland is probably one of the least remarkable things about them. Ninety per cent of all the players in Rangers' history have come from another country; they play in a stadium that is overlooked by grain silos; one of their all-time-greats is the son of a shepherd; they are not allowed to play in their county cup competition for political reasons; and they won their first-ever football match by a margin of 'one goal and two tries to nil'.

Since that first unusual victory over the Royal Oak back in Victorian times, the Shielfield Park side's history has been the standard plain-cloth of lower-league football the world over.

Aside from the Scottish second division title in 1979, a

campaign masterminded by player-manager Dave Smith and a famous twenty-one-game unbeaten run under boss Jim Jefferies (working as an insurance broker in Coldstream at the time) that earned the club a feature on *Saint and Greavsie*, Berwick's greatest moment was probably the victory over those other, slightly better known, Rangers back in 1967. The player-manager of the Borderers at that time was Jock Wallace. Wallace – who'd end up at Ibrox – had an army background. A Scottish journalist once told me: 'As a young man, Jock was parachuted into the jungle and in many ways he never left it.' Whatever, Wallace was a coach of such ferocious discipline that even his one act of kindness – allowing the players a slug of Scotch to warm them up before matches on cold days – has the bitter whiff of the battlefield about it. During his time as boss of Leicester he'd advertise concrete mixers.

Perhaps Rangers' players might have done better with a shot of the hard stuff before their relegation play-off match with Cove Rangers. As it was, they lost 0-7 on aggregate and dropped down into the Lowland League where one of their opponents would be Gretna.

The play-offs were no kinder to any of the other North-East teams. Middlesbrough lost their Championship semi-final with Aston Villa without registering a shot on target in the second leg, while Spennymoor Town went down on penalties to Chorley in the Vanarama National League North final. Sunderland, meanwhile, were facing a semi-final with Portsmouth.

It had been a decent season for the Black Cats. The chaos of the Netflix season had ended with Ellis Short selling the club to a consortium led by Stewart Donald, a fresh-faced millionaire who'd made his money from insurance and previously owned Eastleigh. Chris Coleman, plausible but ineffective, had gone and been replaced by Jack Ross, a Scot who'd led St Mirren to promotion. As a player, Ross had been under contract at Hartlepool but had left following a dispute, with boss Neale Cooper memorably announcing that he would not return to Victoria Park even if Pools were 'playing in the Champions League'. Ross had made Sunderland hard to beat. They'd only lost five games in the League. Unfortunately, they'd also struggled to win and had drawn nineteen matches.

'I can see it all, I've had a vision,' the taxi-driver said. 'After that defeat in the EFL Cup final off Pompey, we'll make it to Wembley on 26 May and get beat again. Two final defeats in a season. That'll be us.'

'So what?' I said proudly. 'In 1997, Boro lost in two proper cup finals *and* got relegated from the Premiership.'

The taxi driver gurgled appreciatively. 'Aye, fair play, yous lot set a benchmark there.'

23

Newcastle University
v Killingworth

Bay Plastics Northern Football
Alliance Premier Division

Saturday 11 May 2019

'I'm not being funny, but if you've parked a car in the car park go back and check the doors are locked,' the gateman said cheerily as I paid my entrance to Kimberley Park, Prudhoe.

The ground was down the bank from the main road and a large pub that smelled of institutional gravy and rubbery chicken. The estate it was in didn't look that bad. If the gateman was in a panic here, he'd need an oxygen tent if he ever went to North Shields.

Inside the ground, a large number of dogs roamed about the pitch despite the large signs warning that they were forbidden. I thought of a game at Ayresome Park in the

1970s. Striker David Mills – soon to become England's first £500,000 footballer – was going through a bit of a low point in his career. A mongrel ran out on the field midway through the first half and started following him around. After a minute or so of this, a voice from the Chicken Run bellowed, 'Take Mills off and leave the dog on.'

Newcastle University had become a serious force as a non-League football team after the appointment of Neil Baistow as head coach in 2015. The previous season they'd done a League and Cup double and this year had so far been runners-up in the Northern Football Alliance Challenge Cup (beaten by Newcastle Chemfica) and won the George Dobbins League Cup by defeating Cullercoats in the final. They'd finished second in the Northern Football Alliance Premier Division and would start next season in Northern League Division Two.

The original student team in the Northern League came from Northumbria University (the former Newcastle Polytechnic). They had a marvellous pitch, few supporters and fans had to wander through the sports hall to use the toilets. Team Northumbria, under the guidance of Paul Johnson, won three promotions to arrive in the Northern League in 2006. In 2011-12, the students had won the Northern League second division title and the Northern League Cup (beating West Auckland 4-1) and were runners-up in the Ernest Armstrong Cup and Northumberland Senior Cup (losing on penalties to Newcastle United Reserves after a 4-4 draw at St James'

Park). Team Northumbria withdrew from the league in 2018 saying that they were 'rebalancing our sports portfolio to engage more students in a broader programme of participation . . . in line with our wider sport, health and wellbeing programme across the university'. Northern League football had moved on since the days when Langley Park withdrew because they couldn't afford to buy a match ball.

Kimberley Park had previously been the home to Northern League Prudhoe Town. This was good news for the university as it meant they didn't have to spend much money bringing it up to the standards the Football Association demanded for Step 6 clubs. The number of places for covered standing had once been a contentious issue. In the 1990s, Peterlee had tried to squirm their way around it by buying fifty golf umbrellas and handing them out to spectators at the gate. Others were forced into potentially more hazardous operations.

On a moist and mulchy Saturday a few years back I made a trip to County Durham. The welfare park had a football pitch, cricket field and bowling green – the Holy Trinity of coalfield sport. Where the pithead workings might once have been was now a new estate of executive homes, festive lights twinkling in the windows as a host of latter-day Bobs and Thelmas stirred their plum puddings and considered a letter to the council complaining of Saturday afternoons disturbed by floodlights and guttural howls of 'Big five minutes, lads, let's keep our fucking tempo'.

At this level, FA regulations dictate that there must be covered seating for at least a hundred people, even in grounds where the regular attendance is fifty and part of the gents' toilet is taken up by sacks of fertiliser. The welfare ground, however, had seating for only half that number, an infraction that could see relegation. I pointed this out to an elderly man wearing a stab-proof waistcoat of enamel badges who was amusing himself by yelling 'Not with those feet you don't' every time a striker ballooned a volley over the bar.

He shook his head. 'They've got the stands all bought,' he said. 'Two fifty-seaters. They brung the first one round through the estate on a low-loader with a crane. See that double garage behind the goal? They were just going to lift it over that and lower it down. But this woman come out. She says, "What are you doing?" She says, "I've a brand-new Hyundai in that garage, there's no bloody way you're lifting a football stand over the top of it." Adamant, she was. So they brung it round by the cricket club. Couldn't get the crane through the gate. They dropped it by the touchline and tried to shunt it into position with a tractor. Only it got snagged on something and stuck. Which is why, if you look at it . . .'

He pointed across the field to the stand, which on inspection was more parallelogram than rectangle. 'They've still got the second one to install. Reckon what they'll do is wait till the new year, one night when it's pitch black, come back at three in the morning and lift it in, when that woman's asleep. Aye, that's what they'll do.'

The idea sounded like something out of *Only Fools and Horses*. It was hard to believe you'd get all those blokes and heavy equipment through a bijou estate at any time of the night without someone calling the police. Even if you did, hoisting a fifty-seat covered stand over a garage stealthily in the darkness seemed fraught with hazard. I imagined an insurance claim: 'My new Hyundai was parked in the garage when it was struck by a football stand.'

I went over to look at the team sheets pinned to the wall of the clubhouse and then went to the gents which was decorated with a large poster explaining how to give mouth-to-mouth.

The Northern Football Alliance was the eleventh tier of English football (confusingly also known as Step 7). The league had been founded in 1890. While the Northern League was – in theory at least – strictly amateur with no payments made to players of any kind (even for expenses), the Northern Football Alliance was – by the FA's strict definition – professional, because the players received payment. These were likelier much lower than some amateur footballers received, but then as the Italian joke has it: what's the difference between an amateur and a professional? A professional pays tax.

In 1988, the Northern Football Alliance had merged with the Northern Amateur League and the Northern Combination League to create what is still the three-division format of forty-eight clubs. The league contained the reserve teams of Blyth Spartans, Gateshead, Ashington and Hebburn Town as well as Ellington FC who played at Hirst Welfare, the ground where a young Bobby Charlton had mesmerised spectators. Other clubs included Gosforth Bohemians, Winlaton Vulcans and Haltwhistle Jubilee. As well as urban Tyneside the league also encompassed rural Northumberland with teams from Wooler, Rothbury and a side from near Berwick-on-Tweed with the slightly disturbing name Spittal Rovers.

Visitors Killingworth had won the Northern Football Alliance Premier Division title by five points from the University, but the students had amassed a goal difference of +102, scoring 131 times in thirty matches. The star of the team was Niza Chilufya, an engineering student who'd been born in Zambia but raised in Macclesfield. He'd scored nearly a half-century of goals that season in a team brimming with zest and talent.

The only player who'd outscored Chilufya was Killingworth centre-forward Malky Morien. Malky Morien had a past so chequered it was practically tweed. At Killingworth, he was playing at a far lower level than his skills merited. The last time I'd seen him, a few years back, he'd been leading the line for Dunston. He was the Northern League's joint top scorer, having hit three hat-tricks with three different clubs, a clear indication that he was mobile off the pitch as well as on it.

Morien is heavily tattooed and very large. Quite how large is hard to fathom. Back when I was at school, our geography teacher would show us slides of glacial formations always adding as a side note, 'My wife present in the photo for scale.' A lack of a geography teacher's wife makes it hard to judge just how big Malky is, but I have a feeling he may be even larger than Dunston's old skipper Dave Coulson, a strapping centre-back who approached every challenge like a vengeful billy goat.

Morien is a rumbustious performer. I'd seen him score four in the first half against Norton and Stockton Ancients on a UTS Park pitch so heavy it was a wonder none of the players had to be pulled out by a tractor. There was more to him than just muscle and skin-ink, though. He had finesse. Morien appeared to have unusually small feet and he was light on them, tiptoeing across the turf in a manner that suggested, well, Bob Ferris trying to sneak into his home without waking Thelma. He could shuffle the ball past defenders and turn deceptively quickly. When he struck a shot, he rose on the ball of one foot, head thrust forward like Roy of the Rovers about to strike a thunderbolt. He was great to watch.

At Kimberley Park, the university players formed a guard of honour for the champions – who had declined promotion – and Morien trotted nimbly out, last man. It was the only respect the students showed their opponents all afternoon. From kick-off they were yards quicker in thought and movement. The ball whizzed neatly about the turf from player to player. It was all highly impressive and, if I had any idea what it actually meant in a football context, I'd have been tempted to put on a Ruud 'Sexy Football' Gullit accent and say, 'It's, the way they play, very, you know, technical.'

Killingworth looked like men who'd been celebrating all week and were off the pace the entire game. They were barely able to raise even a decent foul and by half time the students were 4-0 up. The second half was pretty much a stroll for both sides, though Killingworth briefly burst into life when a deep free kick found its way to Morien who steadied himself and, perfectly balanced, volleyed first time. The shot flew with such power it should have left a vapour trail, but skimmed the top of the bar and smacked into the fence behind the goal.

With ten minutes remaining, a Killingworth midfielder who'd been substituted with half an hour to go walked past in his stockinged feet, a pint of lager in one hand and a cigarette in the other. And so it was the season ended.

I walked along the southern bank of the rippling Tyne to Wylam to catch the train home. When the train stopped at Prudhoe, two elderly men battled their way onboard, past the scrum of women in white linen palazzo pants and men in dad's-big-night-out shiny shirts who inevitably made up the bulk of the Saturday night westbound crowd on mild summer evenings.

The two men had haversacks and thermos flasks and blundered down the aisle muttering curses, before plonking themselves down opposite me. One had a big red face and the voice to match. The other was smaller, with sharp features, and spoke in the deliberate manner sometime found among people around Tyneside: slowly, and, surely, as, if, consistently, searching, the synapses, for, a word, of precise, exactitude, and then, fully, enjoying, its rich, savour, before, vocally, expelling, it.

The men nodded a greeting to me. We had seen each other before, round and about.

The first time had been at a dark moment in my life and, unbeknown to them, they had brightened it. It was on the train heading towards Carlisle the bleak winter of 2010. 'Did I relay to you,' the deliberate man had said, 'the details of my recent conversation with Peter Beardsley?'

'I didn't know you knew Peter Beardsley,' his companion replied.

The great Beardsley had retired as player in 1999 after a not entirely happy spell at Hartlepool, but memories of his cheeky, jinking brilliance at St James' Park was enough to bring a grin to the face of anyone who had witnessed it. People talked about 'playing the game with a smile on your face', but Beardsley did so almost literally. As a friend once said, 'He looked like a puppy you'd just thrown a ball for.'

'Well, I don't know him, know him,' the first man said. 'But I know him, obviously.'

'Well, clearly, man. Everybody knows Peter,' the second man said. There was a note of envy in his voice. It is always annoying when somebody else has encountered a famous person and you haven't.

There was a short silence, a sort of verbal staring match, until the second man cracked and asked: 'Where was this, then?'

'In Kingston Park Tesco's,' the first man said. 'In the cheese aisle.'

'In the cheese aisle?' his friend repeated.

'Don't sound so surprised. It's not as if he was in the feminine hygene section.'

'So was Peter buying cheese, like?'

'Why else would he be there?'

'What sort of cheese was he buying?'

'I didn't like to peruse his trolley too directly in case he thought I was prying, but I got a glance in it out of the corner of my eye and I suspect it saw a slice of that Wensleydale with cranberries.'

'So what did you say to him?'

'I said, "How, Peter. How are you doing?" And he replied, without the slightest hesitation, "Fine, thanks. How about you?" And I said, "I cannot complain, thank you, Peter." And he said, "That's good. I'll see you then." And off he went. What a lovely feller.' Having finished this anecdote, the smaller man folded his hands across his stomach and grinned broadly.

'You weren't tempted to ask him about the current situation at St James' Park, then?' the other asked.

'I wasn't. And even if I had, I doubt Peter would have commented on it. Being the consummate professional that he is.'

'Aye,' the second man said. 'He'd have kept his own counsel, Peter.'

'Mind, if I were to see him again, I will likely ask him to venture an opinion,' the smaller man said.

'Aye, well,' his friend said. 'You can, can't you. Now you've established a rapport.'

And then they lapsed into silent contemplation of that happy day as the train rattled away from the past and towards the setting sun.

INDEX (PROBABLY)